Immigrants, Baptists, and the Protestant Mind in America

University of Illinois Press   *Urbana Chicago London*

Lawrence B. Davis

Immigrants, Baptists, and the Protestant Mind in America

To my Mother and the memory of my Father

Acknowledgments

In the preparation of this book I have been fortunate to have much wise counsel and able assistance. Professor Milton Berman of the University of Rochester encouraged and aided me in the work in its early stages; later, valuable suggestions were made by John Higham of the University of Michigan, Robert T. Handy of Union Theological Seminary, and David J. O'Brien of the College of the Holy Cross, all of whom read the manuscript. My colleagues at the State University of New York, College at Brockport, John Kutolowski and Walter Boston, Jr., also offered many helpful comments. The research and writing have been partly financed by two grants from the State University of New York Research Foundation.

I owe a special debt of gratitude to Mr. Edward C. Starr, curator of the American Baptist Historical Society in Rochester, New York, where the bulk of the research was done. Mr. Starr's vast knowledge of his collection enabled me to explore its resources much more fully than I could have without his aid. The librarians of the Colgate-Rochester Divinity School Library and Yale Divinity School Library also rendered assistance whenever it was needed. Finally, thanks are due to Mrs. Robert Smith of Brockport, who ably typed the final revision of the manuscript. To all of the above, I should like to offer my profound thanks, which words can never fully express.

L.B.D.
Brockport, New York
January, 1973

Contents

Introduction

One evening in the spring of 1882 an overflow crowd filled the Academy of Music in New York City to celebrate a golden anniversary. As the audience settled back, a distinguished college president from upstate New York began to speak: "Men pass away, but institutions, when they incarnate great moral and religious truths, are as enduring as human society." "Standing as we do on the threshold of the twentieth century," he went on, "it becomes us, like soldiers entering upon a war campaign, to examine our position and resources, to estimate the forces of the enemy, to invigorate our courage and zeal by calmly surveying the issues of the impending conflict, and the terrible consequences of a failure in duty on our part." In concluding his address, President Martin Brewer Anderson of the University of Rochester expressed the hope that the phrase "North America for Christ" would be no longer a formula for the hopes of his listeners but an actually realized ideal.[1]

At the time Anderson spoke, the committed Protestant "soldiers" who listened to his message, in observance of the fiftieth anniversary of the American Baptist Home Mission Society, indeed faced conflict on a variety of battlegrounds. Protestants in general and Baptists in particular, who had early taken up the challenge of evangelizing America, now found themselves on the defensive. In the intellectual arena Darwinism had shaken the

[1] Martin Brewer Anderson, "The Lessons of Fifty Years," in *Baptist Home Missions in North America* (New York, 1883), 259–274.

time-honored theological foundations of the faith, forcing religionists to grapple with the spiritual implications of new scientific information. The Catholic church, ever increasing in membership and influence, was about to launch a major campaign for the extension of parochial education through its own schools. Workingmen, presently becoming a more significant factor in American life, did not seem to accept readily the Protestant message, and attendance at churches in the enlarging urban centers dwindled. As if to compound the difficulties, large numbers of immigrants entered the country, many of whom had a vastly different religious heritage from that of evangelical Protestantism and thus were hostile or at least largely indifferent to the hopes and dreams of such groups as the Baptists. White Protestant Americans with a vision of a homogeneous Christian civilization could not help but view these developments with concern, and the contours of their response to the incoming alien hordes reveal much about the way in which a culture acts to protect and preserve its values when they are threatened. For Northern Baptists, as leading exponents of the evangelical Protestant ideal, the years before and after the turn of the century represent a critical time of adjustment to the problems of the contemporary age.[2]

Long one of the major groups of American Protestantism, Baptists in the period from 1880 to 1925 reflected what may be referred to as the Protestant mind. Their plans for a Christian civilization on the North American continent corresponded to the aspirations of many of their brethren in other denominations. When immigration threatened the prospect of an all-embracing Protestantism, the Baptist reaction bespoke the fears of thousands of Americans. To examine their views of the strangers pouring into the United States is to tell the story of the way in which a native culture meets the challenge of that which is foreign to it. It is a tale of both frustration and hope, illustrating at once the

[2] The most recent "official" history of the Baptists is Robert G. Torbet, *A History of the Baptists* (Philadelphia, 1950). Earlier Baptist histories include Henry Clay Vedder, *The Baptists* (New York, 1902), and Albert H. Newman, *A History of Baptist Churches in the United States* (New York, 1915).

reality of prejudice and the possibility that human attitudes can and do change for the better.

Before considering the full significance of the Baptist position on such social issues as immigration, it is necessary to understand several traditional principles that have affected their organizational development. Like other Protestants, they insist that the Bible is the sole norm for faith and practice in the Christian life; thus the Scriptures rather than church tradition are the source of religious authority. The concept of the priesthood of believers, which holds that clergy and laity are equal before God, is a rather common Protestant assumption that Baptists especially emphasize.

Several Baptist beliefs separate this variation of Protestantism from other Protestants in degree and in substance. For Baptists, baptism is generally performed only upon one who has consciously professed conversion rather than during the period of infancy. The act of baptism is not regarded in any sense as sacramental, or an *ipso facto* bestowal of the grace of God, but purely as a symbol of spiritual regeneration resulting from faith in Christ. The fact that this act of faith arises out of a strictly individual responsibility to God, as they affirm, has led Baptists to stress the principle of religious liberty and the separation of church and state. By this they have meant that the existing government cannot interfere with the religious tenets and practices of individuals or congregations, and that the church has no right to expect any financial support from the state. This was one of the beliefs that caused Baptists to be expelled from Puritan Massachusetts, and it has been the source of a traditional antipathy to the Roman Catholic church. An aversion to ritual has also made Baptists anti-Catholic almost by definition.

But the principle which has perhaps most influenced the development of the Baptists as a distinct denomination is that of the autonomy of the local church and the democracy of cooperation among the churches. In practice, this idea has allowed each Baptist church to decide upon its own form of worship, select its clergymen freely, and define its religious and theological views. The insistence upon local independence, or a congregational polity, has influenced Baptists to refrain from using creedal statements to enforce doctrinal conformity, and to be wary of setting up any central convention that would assume the leadership of all phases of denominational activities.[3]

In America local autonomy has gone hand in hand with the democracy of cooperation, but the former has usually triumphed in the event of conflict between the two. Because some type of general meeting seemed necessary to deal with problems of faith and discipline, Baptist churches voluntarily banded together in regional associations; the first such organization was formed in Philadelphia in 1707.[4] In the years following the American Revolution an expansion of evangelistic activity, coupled with the nationalism that prevailed after the War of 1812, led Protestant churches to form societies organized along national lines.[5] Accordingly, Baptist churches in 1814 sent delegates to Philadelphia to found "The General Missionary Convention of the Baptist Denomination in the United States, for Foreign Missions." The refusal of this group to expand its activities into the area of home missions meant that no centralized polity could develop that might endanger the self-governance of the various churches. The society method, as opposed to a single agency for the direction of all Baptist enterprises, restricted national church organizations to a particular function and forced them to operate independently of one another. Baptist "societies," as it turned out, were financed by both interested persons and individual churches, and they existed as cooperative groups that could not enforce doctrines or forms of worship upon the Baptist congregations scattered throughout the country. In the art of persuasion, however, Baptist nationwide organizations proved influential and often decisive in the nineteenth century.[6]

Following the formation of the General Missionary Convention in 1814, the Baptists set up a general tract society in 1824 to

---

[3] These traditional Baptist principles are fully discussed in Torbet, *History of the Baptists*, 15–34.
[4] *Ibid.*, 229ff.
[5] *Ibid.*, 268ff.
[6] *Ibid.*, 270.

print literature for use in the churches and in mission works; it was known as the American Baptist Publication and Sunday School Society after 1840.[7] But since the General Convention wished to confine its activities to the foreign field, the need arose for coordination of evangelistic efforts in America. Far-sighted individuals in the church saw that the existing state and associational mission societies could not give comprehensive supervision to the conversion of persons in the American West, and because of the perseverance of several influential missionaries the American Baptist Home Mission Society came into being in 1832.[8]

At the outset this agency concerned itself primarily with the evangelization of the frontier. The Home Mission Society not only financed the sending of clergymen to newly settled areas, but after 1850 a Church Edifice Department made loans and grants to assist struggling churches to build meetinghouses. The year 1845 saw the Home Mission Society split apart over the slavery issue, with the resultant formation of the Southern Baptist Convention. The northern branch, still called the American Baptist Home Mission Society, suspended its activities in the South at this time as the churches of North and South went their separate ways.

In 1862, however, the Home Mission Society again began missionary operations in the older southern states, ultimately turning attention to the conversion and education of the freedman as well as to the building of new places of worship. By 1869 one-third of its entire mission force was at work in the South. While the major emphasis still centered on frontier areas, where missionaries also attempted to convert the American Indian, the evangelization of foreign-speaking groups in rural and urban centers gradually gained the attention of Baptists engaged in home mission endeavors. Thus by the time of its fiftieth anniversary, in 1882, the Home Mission Society pressed the cam-

[7] *Ibid.*, 350; Daniel G. Stevens, *The First Hundred Years of the American Baptist Publication Society* (Philadelphia, 1925).

[8] Torbet, *History of the Baptists*, 377ff.; Charles L. White, *A Century of Faith* (Philadelphia, 1932), 38–45; *Baptist Home Missions in North America*, 291–540.

paign to win "North America for Christ" on a number of fronts.[9]

It must be emphasized that because of the nature of Baptist polity, none of the national church organizations operated exclusively in its designated field. Parallel agencies existed at the state, associational, city, and congregational levels, not only in home missions but in Baptist educational efforts,[10] in the support of foreign fields, and in other phases of denominational work. For many years women's missionary societies were common as small voluntary groups, but not until 1877 did Baptist women unite to form two large societies, one based in Chicago and the other in Boston.[11]

In spite of competition for funds, the national Baptist organizations generally enjoyed cordial relations with one another. Often the leaders had been trained together in the same Baptist schools and colleges, if not as contemporaries, at least in similar educational traditions. Gradually the cooperative spirit increased, culminating in the formation of the Northern Baptist Convention in 1907, which was actually a forum of the several societies that had long existed separately. While some Baptists feared that the creation of a central agency would destroy Baptist polity, their apprehensions were ill advised, for even today the Northern Baptist Convention has no power to coerce member churches.

Although Baptists were the last of the major denominations in America to have a single coordinating body, one means of communication in the nineteenth century proved to be a somewhat unifying force. The independent religious weeklies constituted an instrumentality through which Baptists in all walks of life, clergy and laity, could air their views for consideration by men and women throughout the denomination. Baptist correspondents from all parts of the country contested many of the issues of the day in the columns of the Chicago *Standard*, the Boston *Watchman*, the New York *Examiner*, and the Cincinnati

[9] Torbet, *History of the Baptists*, 309, 377–379.
[10] The Baptist Education Society was a latecomer, being formed in 1888.
[11] *Baptist Home Missions in North America*, 514–523.

Journal and Messenger. In spite of the fact that most of these journals changed editors from time to time, patterns in their opinions may be observed. The *Standard* and the *Examiner* often emphasized social and political questions and seemed the most responsive to current trends. The *Watchman,* which merged with the *Examiner* in 1913 to form the *Watchman-Examiner,* remained a bit more cautious toward new directions, but it, too, commented on matters other than the strictly religious. The *Journal and Messenger,* under the same editorship and ownership for more than forty years until its demise in 1920, exhibited a persistent conservatism and hostility to change. Especially anxious to preserve the homogeneity of Protestant America, its editors viewed with constant alarm the influx of large numbers of aliens into the country.

None of these papers bore an "official" stamp in the usual sense of the word. Closest to this concept was the *Baptist Home Mission Monthly,* the promotional magazine of the Home Mission Society, which began publication in 1878 and merged with its foreign counterpart to become *Missions* in 1910. Yet even if the independent journals lacked an imprimatur, they based their appeal on the one essential fact of a Baptist readership. Unlike the Southern Baptist papers, which confined themselves largely to spiritual affairs and theological issues, virtually all Northern Baptist publications showed a lively interest in contemporary problems confronting the nation. While it would be unrealistic to make extravagant claims about the representativeness of the opinions expressed in their columns, it is true that every periodical had to please its readers in a general way in order to sustain itself.

After 1907 Baptists had one major forum where debate could be carried on, and within a few years most of the Baptist weeklies folded. The regional constituencies that they served now became merged, at least on the surface, into the Northern Baptist Convention. Along with the search for order in a denomination long committed to decentralization came changes in theological views, methods of evangelism, and attitudes on social questions.

The response of the Northern Baptists as typical white American Protestants to one of the major issues of the era, immigration in the United States, is our present concern.[12]

Such a case study must focus chiefly on ideas and attitudes, with supplementary attention to evangelistic practices and missionary work among the immigrants themselves. A number of questions emerge at the outset. Were Northern Baptists, in spite of their lack of structural unity in the nineteenth century, in any sense agreed about the nature of the new immigration? Did they concur on the propriety of immigration restriction? If there were disagreements, along what lines, regional or otherwise, did they occur? What changes, if any, took place in the denominational attitude pattern from 1880 to 1925, and why? Was their response a function of their traditional beliefs, or was it shaped more by gradual experience in working with immigrant groups?

A second set of questions has to do with the impact of Baptist discussion and action concerning immigration upon the denomination itself. How successful were Baptists in winning immigrants to their faith? What role did the newcomers play in Baptist activities? Were methods of evangelism changed in an attempt to convert the foreign-born? What type of person assumed leadership in this work?

Finally, where do Baptists fit into the national picture at this time? At what points was their thinking on immigration issues unique in the period under consideration, and when was it just a variant on the views of white Protestant America? Were Baptists caught up in the nativism of the 1890s and, if so, were there limitations to their anti-foreignism? Did they share in the intense feelings against immigrants brought about by American entry into World War I? Where did they stand by the time the

[12] The Southern Baptists have been omitted from this study primarily because their literature is altogether different from that of the Northern Baptists. As indicated, Southern Baptist papers had little or nothing to say about such issues as immigration, confining their content to religious rather than secular matters. Moreover, the polity and theology of the Southern Baptist Convention have undergone a markedly different development from that of the Northern Baptists.

National Origins Act cut off the flow of newcomers? In what respects were they similar to other Protestants, and in what areas did they differ?

While the literature of each Protestant group reveals a great deal, the answers to certain other important questions are either difficult or impossible to obtain. The major issue of the socio-economic composition of the various denominations is not readily clarified by the available evidence. In the case of the Baptists, for example, the assumption has been that the so-called common man has always been most prominent in their ranks. The records of their activities, however, contain little to confirm or deny this supposition. We know that John D. Rockefeller was a Baptist and that he contributed to his church and to various phases of denominational work. But the absence of the names of other millionaires from the Baptist roster does not necessarily prove that here was a "church of the common man," although the dollar amounts given to the Home Mission Society were usually small enough to point in that direction.[13] One can only wish for extensive membership roles listing the occupation of each individual, but the lack of such data places limits on a sociological approach to the problem.[14]

Nevertheless, the implications of a case study of the Baptists have force and meaning. Northern Baptists as a major influence in American Protestantism in the period from 1880 to 1925 attempted to define their unique role in the national life and hammered out a concept of an ideal American civilization. Gradually they modified their *Weltanschauung* in a somewhat reluctant attempt to adjust to the twentieth century. Their reactions to the issues of immigration and to the immigrants themselves con-

[13] See the annual reports of the American Baptist Home Mission Society, 1880–1925, for lists of persons and congregations that contributed to its funds.
[14] Information on the socio-economic background of a given group, much harder to come by in historical research than in contemporary sociological investigations, is best used when confined to a certain locality. For a superb example of this approach, see Stephan Thernstrom, *Poverty and Progress* (Cambridge, Mass., 1964), which adeptly combines sociological and historical methodology in a study of occupational mobility in Newburyport, Mass., from 1850 to 1880 through the use of manuscript census schedules. Unfortunately, no similar data exist for American religious groups in the nineteenth century.

stitute a mirror of very significant developments in the United States as a whole as well as in their own denomination. In many respects a close look at the Baptists at this time opens up an important window upon the panorama of American social and intellectual life in an era when everywhere the old order was passing, giving way to the modern age.

1 /   The Chinese Question

The tide of the Old World's population, whose flow toward our country has been so deep and strong for the last fifty years, is but the ripple of a mountain brook compared with what the next half century will show." So prophesied a respected Baptist layman to a group of denominational leaders in 1882. The American Baptist Home Mission Society, which had asked President Martin Brewer Anderson of the University of Rochester to give the keynote address for its fiftieth anniversary celebration, shortly discovered that one of his major concerns was immigration to the United States. Like others of his time, the Baptist college president was beginning to worry over the challenge that the newcomers posed to America, to Protestant Christianity, and in particular to the Baptists. Anderson affirmed that the great mass of immigrants would become honest and productive citizens, yet he feared an influx of Communists, Nihilists, boycotters, strikers, and "Mormon harems . . . recruited among the ignorant peasants of Scandinavia and Great Britain." It was not enough for Protestants to gather these dangerous elements into the churches, he contended. "They must be trained in the elements of letters and sciences, in trades, in farming, in thrift, in social morality . . . in all that goes to constitute the highest product of civilization—a pure and healthy Christian home." Thus, when he spoke at length upon the "elements of evil" that accompanied the immigrant, the Baptist educator did not intend so much to frighten his listeners as to spur them to enlarge their missionary operations to win "North America for Christ"—more correctly interpreted, to keep the country and its citizens both Protestant and Christian.

But Anderson did not stop with a commentary on the immigrants from Europe. Immediately after a reference to "the most dangerous population" of the Old World, he added that "our Pacific Coast confronts the over-populated deltas of Eastern China." Very much aware of the recent Chinese Exclusion Act, he insisted that "the Chinese will sooner or later force themselves upon our care and attention." In the very next breath the Baptist leader warned again that "we *must not* be unmindful of [the] agencies for evil with which the Old World is poisoning our moral and political life." Anderson's connection of the Chinese with European immigrants and their "attendant evils" indicates that the Chinese question of the early 1880s, contrary to previous assumptions, was directly related to the late nineteenth-century resurgence of anti-foreign phobias. The Baptist discussion of the entire "Chinese problem," moreover, reflects many of the basic arguments that were to become common in the national debate over immigration in the late 1880s and the 1890s.[1]

By the time Anderson spoke, the traditional American policy of open doors for all immigrants was already undergoing a serious test. Ever since colonial times America had welcomed virtually everyone who sought refuge or came to build a home in the new land. Although resentment of foreigners had occurred previously in the United States, especially during the nativist outbreaks against the Irish and Germans in the 1840s and 1850s, until the 1880s such feelings did not result in significant federal legislation to cut off the flow of newcomers.[2] But in 1882 Congress laid the basis for future restriction by passing a law that excluded convicts, lunatics, idiots, and persons likely to become a public charge, in response to a demand by several eastern states that the federal government now assume some responsibility for

[1] Martin Brewer Anderson, "The Lessons of Fifty Years," in *Baptist Home Missions in North America*, 259ff. See also John Higham, *Strangers in the Land* (New Brunswick, N.J., 1955), 167.

[2] The standard general history of immigration restriction policies in the United States is Roy L. Garis, *Immigration Restriction* (New York, 1927).

immigration. The act of 1882 thus gave the Secretary of the Treasury exclusive control over the foreign influx but continued to delegate the actual inspection of incoming aliens to existing state agencies. An immigrant welfare fund, financed by a tax of 50¢ per head, was designed to alleviate the burdens that many indigent immigrants were placing on public and private charity.[3]

Portents of an increasing fear of the stranger appeared in the early 1880s but were not too widespread. Josiah Strong's *Our Country*, a popular work published in 1885, accused the immigrants of crime and immorality, of corrupting municipal government, of swelling the ranks of Catholicism and socialism.[4] While the fiftieth anniversary of the Baptist Home Mission Society did not attract nearly as much attention as Strong's book, the discussions in New York in May, 1882, foreshadowed the attitude pattern that was to follow in the Baptist church and, indeed, in the nation at large.

Martin Brewer Anderson was not the only Baptist leader interested in immigration in 1882. One of the major debates in the national Baptist forum where he spoke was concerned with a very specific group to which Anderson had alluded. Nationwide attention now focused upon the Chinese in California, where alarmed citizens were sending petitions to Congress urging federal legislation to shut out these Oriental laborers. A congressional committee had investigated the Chinese problem in 1876, and in 1882 the Chinese Exclusion Act, which prohibited the coming of Chinese workers for ten years, became law. In order to understand the Baptist position and the lines of division in the denomination over the issues involved, it is first necessary to look briefly at the background of the situation in California.

The Chinese on the Pacific Coast, who had been coming to America since the 1850s, numbered approximately 75,000 in California alone by the year 1880.[5] There they constituted at least three social groups. The merchants, who handled nearly all

3 Higham, *Strangers in the Land*, 44.
4 *Ibid.*, 39.
5 Mary Roberts Coolidge, *Chinese Immigration* (New York, 1909), 501.

the goods used by the Chinese population and who dominated the "companies" to which every Chinaman belonged, were regarded as the natural leaders of their countrymen in America. Most of these men had a high reputation for integrity and business ability. Chinese prostitutes, drawn from the very few women who came to the United States, made up a second class. But the great majority of the Chinese in this country were laborers: industrious, frugal young men who often gambled, sometimes used opium, and did not readily adopt American customs and manners.[6]

By the 1870s the belief prevailed in California that the Chinese were undesirable from the economic, moral, and political points of view. Many persons assumed that Chinese laborers came to America under servile or "coolie" contracts. Californians were convinced that a U.S. statute prohibiting Americans from participating in the coolie trade did little to stop such traffic. Although Chinese businessmen in this country denied that they imported laborers under the coolie system, the fact remained that most of the Chinese who came to the Pacific Coast had their passage paid by others and were bound to make repayment. In any case, Chinese workers could be employed for much less than their American counterparts, which was the real point of contention. The fear of economic competition drove workingmen's groups to demand discriminatory laws and often resulted in crimes of violence against the Chinese.[7]

Allegations against Chinese morals were also frequent. In some instances the foes of the Chinese simply accused them of being dishonest and unreliable, but more often attention focused on opium dens and houses of prostitution. Games of chance seemed to be their chief means of recreation, and the presence of several organized lotteries in San Francisco's Chinatown aroused charges of excessive gambling. It is hardly true that Chinese practices were worse than those of white Californians, but the dissimilarity of their habits alone made Orientals open to much criticism.[8]

[6] Elmer C. Sandmeyer, *The Anti-Chinese Movement in California* (Urbana, Ill., 1939), 12–13.
[7] *Ibid.*, 25–33.
[8] *Ibid.*, 33–35.

From the social and political viewpoint, Chinatown offered much with which to find fault. Filthy houses, illness, and over-crowding were everywhere. Fire hazards arose out of inadequate cooking facilities. But many objected to the Chinese primarily because of their variance from Americans in racial characteristics and their unwillingness to accept American customs and ideals. While some felt these dissimilarities might be removed if the Chinese would wear western clothing and mingle freely with whites, the conviction that Orientals could never assimilate remained widespread. Thus the leaders of anti-Chinese sentiment often saw the situation as a great struggle between eastern and western civilizations.[9]

Initially, Protestants responded to the presence of the Chinese on the Pacific Coast with attempts to convert them. Practically all denominations as well as the Roman Catholic church undertook some special work for the Chinese wherever they were found in considerable numbers in America. The Presbyterians began such efforts in 1853, with the Baptists following in 1854 and the Episcopalians in 1855. Methodist and Congregational missions to the Chinese arose later, in 1868 and 1870 respectively. Ever since these Asians started coming to the United States, Protestant clergymen had been among their staunchest friends and defenders.[10]

The interest of Christians in the spiritual welfare of the Chinese had its roots in the foreign missions maintained in China by the various sects for many years. Convinced of God's providence in sending these newcomers here, an 1882 report of the Baptist Committee on Chinese Missions stated this relationship by proclaiming that "we are not only laboring for the Chinese in America, but through them to strengthen our missionaries in China." [11] For Baptists, the religious aspects of the Chinese question assumed priority over its other implications. As one of the denominational leaders in women's missionary work, Ida Ward,

[9] *Ibid.*, 36–38.
[10] Robert Seager II, "Some Denominational Reactions to the Chinese in California, 1856–1892," *Pacific Historical Review*, XXVIII (1959), 49–66.
[11] Report of the Committee on Chinese Missions, quoted in *Baptist Home Missions in North America*, 97.

put it, the Christian standpoint bade welcome to the Chinese in order to reveal the beneficent effects of the gospel whether or not their coming was advantageous to the federal government. Most of these newcomers were peaceable and law-abiding, she asserted, and because they helped to fill the need for cheap labor in certain industries, it was unfair to "treat them like dogs." [12]

Baptist work among the Chinese in California, never a major part of home mission endeavors, was an outgrowth of the overall effort to expand membership in the West. [13] To see that the Baptist version of a "genuine spiritual Christianity" became known to the immigrants from China, a returned foreign missionary of the Southern Baptist Convention opened a preaching station for them in California in 1854. Failing in 1861, this operation resumed in San Francisco from 1871 to 1879. The latter year saw the appointment of Jesse B. Hartwell to begin an evening school and to organize a Chinese Baptist church. When the American Baptist Home Mission Society took over the project in 1884, the northern group promptly chose Hartwell as their general superintendent of Chinese evangelism on the Pacific Coast. In a few months the Women's Baptist Home Mission Society of Chicago sent a teacher to open a school for Chinese children and to visit among the Oriental women in San Francisco. By 1887 this educational enterprise offered classes in Bible, Chinese classics, and English. [14] Street preaching to large audiences was also a Baptist technique, and soon the cities of Oakland, Fresno, Chico, and Sacramento had Chinese Baptist missions. An official statement indicated that as the result of these efforts, "the Chinese have learned to distinguish between the godless element, from which they have suffered persecution, and the Christian element, which seeks to do them good." [15]

In addition to the work of the national Baptist societies, in-

---

[12] Ida Ward, "The Chinese in California," *Tidings,* III (Aug., 1884), 3–5.

[13] In 1882 Baptists had only 98 churches with 6,375 members in California, where the total population was 864,694 (*Baptist Home Missions in North America,* 555).

[14] 64th Annual Report, American Baptist Home Mission Society (1896), 90–92. Hereafter cited as ABHMS.

[15] 55th Annual Report, ABHMS (1887), 61.

dividual congregations, in keeping with the tradition of autonomy, had shown an interest in the Chinese by setting up schools
that sometimes added secular subjects to the more normal Bible
instruction. As late as 1879 the Home Mission Society advised
that local churches most effectively carried on this type of
activity. Only in the large centers of population, when the
pastor requested aid, should the society act. In less than a decade, however, Baptists justified more extensive financial support
from the national organization on the ground that California
was still a new land whose congregations were too weak to
underwrite the conversion of the Chinese by themselves. An
admission in 1891 that race prejudice among some Christians
on the Pacific Coast constituted a hindrance to winning the
Chinaman helps to account for the change in attitude.[16]

With the assistance of the Home Mission Society and prominent local businessmen, one of the first Chinese preaching stations outside California opened its doors in 1874 in Portland,
Oregon. Again the director was a clergyman who had returned
from China, and once more the pattern of educating the Chinese
as well as Christianizing them became the rule.[17] By 1879 a number of Baptist churches in Portland and Salem sponsored week-
day instruction for children, while other Pacific Coast missions
gave evening classes in English, mathematics, geography, and
Bible for Chinese laborers and artisans.[18] The support of education for the Chinese by businessmen in Portland and Salem,
probably indicating a sympathetic tie between that group and
the Chinese merchants, may also offer a clue to the composition
of Baptist congregations in those cities.[19]

[16] Report of Women's American Baptist Home Mission Society (1891),
quoted in *Baptist Home Mission Monthly*, XIII (Jan., 1891), 19–20.
[17] "Beginnings of Missionary Work among the Chinese in Our Country,"
Tidings, III (July, 1884), 4; *Baptist Home Mission Monthly*, II (Jan., 1880),
15; I (July, 1879), 199–200.
[18] "Our New Chinese Mission House in San Francisco," *Baptist Home
Mission Monthly*, X (Oct., 1888), 262–264.
[19] Unfortunately, the evidence found in Baptist records, both national and
local, yields very few clues about which economic classes predominated in
this denomination, if any generalization of that matter can be made. This
case, together with an occasional mention of commercial advantages in trade
with China, might lead one to believe that considerable numbers of middle-

All of these efforts met with many difficulties. In 1887 Superintendent Hartwell listed several major hindrances to the work he led. Racial prejudice, he noted, resulted in cold and rude behavior on the part of Christians who failed to invite their Oriental neighbors to worship services. Because many of the Chinese in America were untutored, often they knew barely enough English to read the Bible. Their migrant character, both within the United States and in their frequent return to China, made the establishment of Chinese churches on a permanent basis unrealistic. Finally, Hartwell feared that a considerable portion of those who attended the mission schools came ready to resist the teachings of Christianity, with the sole intention of learning English. Even so, the first supervisor of these Baptist activities found hope in the Chinese gratitude for instruction in the American tongue, and his expectation of successful results despite adversity reflected a general spirit of optimism.[20]

In ventures such as these, virtually all Protestants sought not only to convert the Chinese but ultimately to Americanize China.[21] Baptists who hailed the abandonment of that country's policy of commercial isolation and the subsequent migration of Chinese merchants to the United States expected that they would take Christianity and American ideals and ways of life back to their homeland. "When her rich and educated men begin to establish their warehouses and counting rooms on our shores we shall have a grand opportunity to show what the gospel does for society," exclaimed a California correspondent to an eastern Baptist newspaper in 1880. "If we could embrace that opportunity we should send an influence in favor of our religion through these merchants and mandarins greater than that of a

class businessmen belonged to Baptist ranks. Yet the example of I. S. Kalloch (see p. 20) suggests, but does not prove, that his congregation had a predominance of working-class people. Such deductions from the very few hints that the data offer, even if logical, may not be regarded as altogether convincing. The major question of "Who were the Baptists?," in terms of their economic and social position, remains a most difficult one to answer.

[20] Jesse B. Hartwell, "Mission to the Chinese," *Baptist Home Mission Monthly*, IX (May, 1887), 120–121.

[21] Seager, "Some Denominational Reactions to the Chinese in California," 50.

thousand missionaries," he added. This single paragraph reveals a belief in the relation of trade to missionary activity and in the role of Christianity in making America free and prosperous:

China is to be evangelized; and nothing will promote its familiarity with the gospel like a free commercial intercourse with the Christian nations of the earth. When the intelligent and practical men of that land come here and live among us they will be compelled to see that in many respects our civilization is superior to theirs. They will compare the influence of Christ with that of Confucius. They will learn that in spite of the bad men in the land the gospel has made us free and prosperous. They will gradually imitate in China our railroads, our factories, our improved methods of agriculture, our social customs, and thus the way will be prepared for the dissemination of Christianity.[22]

This candid portrayal of middle-class values in the style of the nineteenth century asserted at once American superiority in all things and the causal relationship of the Protestant religion to this pre-eminence. Baptists thus attempted to define their role in the history of the nation: by making the country as Christian as possible through the energetic presentation of their interpretation of the gospel, all foreigners, whether converted or not, would be profoundly influenced.

With this vision before them, many Baptists became alarmed when some of their fellow clergy and the laity involved themselves in political controversies over the Chinese question. It has been argued that most Protestant ministers believed in the value of continued immigration of Chinese labor, standing forward more solidly and positively in defense of the Chinese than any other group in late nineteenth-century America.[23] While this hypothesis may be true for Methodists, Presbyterians, and Episcopalians, divisions among clergymen and laymen over the political issues of Chinese immigration were evident among Baptists and Congregationalists. In the latter denomination one of their

---

[22] "California Letter," *Journal and Messenger*, XLIX (Sept. 8, 1880), 2.
[23] Seager, "Some Denominational Reactions to the Chinese in California," 58, 65–66. Seager's evidence is primarily from Presbyterian, Methodist, and Episcopal sources, virtually omitting Congregationalists and Baptists.

papers could deplore Kearneyism and the denial of basic rights to the Chinese by the California Constitution, while a correspondent in another journal a few months later demanded a new immigration policy because these Orientals were "the most demoralizing competitors labor has yet been compelled to meet." [24]

For Baptists, discord over the various implications of Chinese immigration intensified in the early 1880s. Some of the divisions were between churchmen on the West Coast and those in the Northeast, where Northern Baptists had their greatest strength. But other local differences, indicating an ambivalence of opinion even among California Baptists who lived closest to the problem, separated clergyman from clergyman and layman from layman alike. The entire debate, moreover, ushered in a larger discussion about the issues of immigration as a whole.

Trouble began in 1879 with the election of a prominent Baptist minister, I. S. Kalloch, as mayor of San Francisco on the workingmen's ticket. During the campaign he made very radical speeches against the Chinese, advocating legislation to prohibit their employment by corporations. Under the leadership of Mayor Kalloch, the workingmen turned attention to forced removal of the Chinese quarter. A special committee investigated Chinatown and initiated an extensive program of renovation. But back east the *Baptist Home Mission Monthly*, official organ of the American Baptist Home Mission Society, commented several years later that any clergyman who helped to organize the anti-Chinese party was a black sheep undeserving of the sympathy of the denomination. If any such Baptist lived on the Pacific Coast, the *Monthly* proclaimed, it was he who ought to go and not the Chinese! [25]

As a result of the agitation of men like Kalloch and the better-known sandlotter Dennis Kearney, by 1882 Congress could no

[24] *Independent*, XXXII (Mar. 4, 1880), 17; (Mar. 25, 1880), 17; Carroll D. Wright, "The Chinese and the Chinese Question," *Congregationalist*, LXV (Dec. 15, 1880), 1.
[25] *Baptist Home Mission Monthly*, VIII (Apr., 1886), 82–83. The famous Irish leader of the anti-Chinese movement in California, Dennis Kearney, always ended his speeches with the words "And whatever happens, the Chinese must go." The wording of the *Monthly* article doubtless refers to that expression.

longer ignore the loud clamor of many Californians for the restriction of Chinese immigration. The famous exclusion act,
passed in April of that year, suspended for ten years the entrance
of Chinese laborers into the United States and provided for the
deportation of any violators.[26] The Baptist discussion of this
departure from the traditional open-door policy, and of the anti-
Chinese outbreaks attendant to it, not only shows an east-west
split but reveals other cleavages in the denomination over the
whole Chinese question.

An editorial in the Chicago *Standard* in March, 1882, contained arguments in favor of a general restriction of immigration
and considered the exclusion act a step in the right direction.
The fundamental prosperity of America, asserted the paper,
rested upon the homogeneity of its people. It appeared that the
Chinaman could never assimilate; whether or not this fact justified permanent denial of admission to them, the country now
ought to carefully regulate the foreign influx. "A people not
in some good degree homogeneous is not a people at all," exclaimed the editor. "A congeries of unassimilated, clashing, and
warring elements, is not a nation. The question of the utter dis-
integration of such a population, and its breaking up into mere
antagonisms, is a question of time only." [27]

From this point of view, the time-honored American extension
of a welcome to all was neither statesmanlike nor patriotic. The
literal acceptance of this historic approach, said the *Standard*,
would make America the common sewer of all nations. The
United States had a destiny as a separate and distinct people.
Since those who did not readily assimilate should be kept out,
the exclusion act seemed judicious.[28] In spite of a later condemnation of the legal requirement that all Chinese in this country
register with the government, this periodical remained clearly
pro-restrictionist.[29] Its editors willingly used the widely accepted

26 See Garis, *Immigration Restriction*, 294–296, and Sandmeyer, *Anti-
Chinese Movement in California*, 92–95.
27 Editorial: "National Homogeneity," *Standard*, XXIX (Mar. 16, 1882), 4.
28 *Ibid.*
29 *Standard*, XXIX (Apr. 13, 1882), 4. The *Journal and Messenger* also
favored the restriction of Chinese immigration; see LIV (July 1, 1885), 2, and
LXVII (May 10, 1888), 1.

idea of America's distinct mission to justify the elimination of those who did not fit into the desired "homogeneity."

The *Standard* did, however, print a letter highly critical of the exclusion act from a Baptist in Illinois. The correspondent, A. M. Duboc, especially deplored the provisions of the law that discriminated against the Chinese already here. To him, the new statute violated our treaty obligations with China, an obvious reference to the Burlingame Treaty of 1868, which recognized the advantages of free migration and emigration of the citizens of China and the United States. Recognizing the inconsistency of the compulsory registration provision with the constitutional prohibition on the grounds of race and color, Duboc claimed that the exclusion act would also be a blow to the nation's material prosperity. It brashly asserted that since Americans could not compete with Chinese labor through skill, they would do so by brute force. Most of all, the Baptist correspondent who took issue with his editor feared that the restrictive legislation would give aid and comfort to perpetrators of violence against the Chinese and thus be an indirect blow to the cause of Christian missions both in China and on the Pacific Coast.[30]

This letter had barely had a chance to be read when a rebuttal came forth from a California Baptist who believed that the exclusion act augured well for modern civilization and Christianity. The letter of A. A. Denison of Oakland revealed the resentment of one who lived close to the Chinese problem toward those remote from it who meddled in what was none of their business. If the Baptist admirers of the Mongols could come face to face with them in Chinatown, said the Californian, "it would no doubt dispel some Eastern illusions as to their desirability as a permanent population." [31] The phrase "Eastern illusions" clearly indicates that Denison understood the east-west division in the denomination on this question, which he felt was based on relative proximity to the Chinese.

Even so, the writer from Oakland rested his entire argument

[30] A. M. Duboc, "The Chinese Bill, a Blow at the Cause of Humanity and of Christian Missions," *Standard*, XXIX (Apr. 6, 1882), 1.
[31] Letter of A. A. Denison, in *Standard*, XXIX (May 11, 1882), 2.

not on the repugnance of the Chinese as individuals but on the broader ground of the ultimate results of their competition with American workers. Did the exclusion bill violate existing treaty obligations? Many senators who voted for it must have felt this was not the case; furthermore, the threat of a flood of Chinese coolies excused any disregard of diplomacy. Was the law inconsistent with the spirit of the Constitution? The founding fathers did not say that Indians were to be treated as equals, nor did the writers of the Fifteenth Amendment think it should apply to other races besides the Negro. Was the act a deviation from traditional American policy? Perhaps the time had come for such a change, since the nation no longer contained limitless resources. Denison implied that businessmen and manufacturers in San Francisco would not agree that the new law endangered prosperity.[32]

Two of the major Baptist periodicals in the East reinforced the regional split by coming out strongly against the exclusion act. The Boston *Watchman* pointed to the statute's flagrant opposition to the self-evident truth that all men were created equal with certain inalienable rights, especially that of the pursuit of happiness. The anti-Chinese feeling represented the sheer animus of race prejudice. Mining and fruit-raising industries had a real need for Chinese laborers, who were among the most peaceable and law-abiding people in California. Because western nations had forced China to open commercial relations with Europe and America, ill treatment of Orientals seemed all the more an injustice. The New York *Examiner* printed similar arguments, stating that the policy of exclusion would cultivate hostility in a friendly, wealthy nation that was contributing much to this country through trade. Not peculiar to Baptists, the justification of immigration because of the need for workers and the possibility of endangering commercial relations with China appeared often wherever an anti-Chinese attitude was opposed.[33]

Proximity to the Chinese immigrants did not always determine

[32] *Ibid.*
[33] *Watchman*, LXIII (Mar. 9, 1882), 1; (Apr. 6, 1882), 1; (Apr. 13, 1882), 1; (May 11, 1882), 1; LXVII (Mar. 25, 1886), 4. See also "Our Chinese Fallacies," *Examiner*, LXIII (Mar. 11, 1886), 1.

the divisions of Baptist opinions toward these newcomers. Although many California clergymen had defended the hapless Chinaman for years, notably in the congressional hearings of 1876, other West Coast ministers were equally vehement in their criticism. Rather than indicating a position solidly committed to one side or the other, the words and deeds of the Baptist clergy and laity within and without California show how some churchmen succumbed to the cultural prejudice affecting their generation while others used Christian principles to resist it.[34]

One of the more prominent Baptist champions of the Chinese in California was Oliver W. Gates, pastor of a church in San Diego. Known as "one of the most devout, earnest, and universally beloved of all the Baptist ministers on the Pacific Coast," Gates had arrived in San Diego in 1873 at age forty-three after serving in several pulpits in New York and New England.[35] While many of his California colleagues feared that Chinese immigration, with its economic and racial implications, endangered national homogeneity, this man held a sympathetic regard for these people while living close to them.

According to Gates, the California worker in the throes of the depression of the 1870s had unfairly blamed capital, corporations, and the Chinese for all his woes. Holding the latter especially responsible for his economic distress, the laboring man improperly concluded that relief could be had by waging war against these Orientals. Both ministers and politicians, sensing the feelings of their constituencies, attacked the Chinese. Thus

[34] Sandmeyer, *Anti-Chinese Movement in California,* 81–88; Seager, "Some Denominational Reactions to the Chinese in California," 56. For a discussion of the relationship of Christian principles to the surrounding culture, see H. Richard Niebuhr, *Christ and Culture* (New York, 1951). The word "prejudice" is always a difficult term. I do not mean to imply in the present discussion that all suggestions for the restriction of immigration may be equated with prejudice. There were sound and practical reasons for limiting immigration at the end of the nineteenth century, especially in the need to keep out a truly criminal element. Prejudice appeared, however, when the arguments for restriction contained racial implications and used such emotional phrases as "scum of the world."

[35] William Cathcart, ed., *The Baptist Encyclopedia* (Philadelphia, 1881), 439; *Massachusetts Baptist State Annual* (1891), 90–91.

they accused innocent people of degrading labor, robbing work-ingmen, introducing crime and vice, and engaging in hoodlum-ism. Unjustly persecuted, many Chinese left California for other parts of the country.

Gates passed severe judgment on what was happening in his state. To him, the "claims of Christ" predominated over race prejudice and animosity. Attempts to thwart the divine plan to convert the Chinese by enacting inequitable laws against them would bring perils that no homogeneity of speech, no uniformity of customs, no harmonious type of character could prevent. His statement that Americans encountering Chinese immigrants should not expect them to conform to western dress, tastes, or morals proves that one could be a white Anglo-Saxon Protestant in the 1880s and still endorse what today would be called a sort of cultural pluralism. Indeed, Gates felt it natural that the Chinese would worship their own idols and not be susceptible to Christianity. Some might lie and steal, but most of them could be trusted. Some would bring their vices, but no immigrant group had a monopoly on vice. Some might be dirty in their habits, but so were many Americans. The majority of the Chinese, he was happy to say, did not drink or frequent the saloons; if they did so, they might have had the friendship of more of California's working class.[36]

In setting forth the proper Christian attitude toward these newcomers, Gates admitted that they should be held to a strict obedience to all civil and sanitary laws. He demanded that some-thing be done about the filthy tenements where they were forced to live because their employers had not provided decent housing. Exhorting Christian workers not to anticipate immediate con-versions that would quickly evangelize China, he urged Chris-tians to win the confidence of the Chinese by teaching them English without trying to Americanize them or turn them from their idols instantly. "Do not expect to gain them to your faith by disparaging their false religious knowledge or by berating their bad morals," Gates advised. "Do not put before them creeds

[36] Oliver W. Gates, "The Chinese Dispersion," *Examiner and Chronicle,* LVII (Apr. 8, 1880), 1.

and confessions." The use of the New Testament in language instruction, he felt, would bring the Chinaman "to a knowledge of Jesus" in an understanding way.[37] The San Diego clergyman clearly respected the Chinese and their customs, and an earnest desire to give them his religion did not lead him to advocate evangelism by coercion. Other California Baptists, especially those directly involved in mission endeavors, expressed similar opinions.[38]

When the Home Mission Society convened for its fiftieth anniversary in May, 1882, a major debate on the Chinese problem further revealed denominational differences in California as well as between East and West. Here, in a national forum, Baptists from all parts of the country except the South could confront one another with their ideas. The California representative, Reverend Granville S. Abbott, addressed the convention on "The Christian View of the Chinese Question" in terms that set him far apart from Oliver Gates.[39] Like Gates, Abbott was an easterner by birth and education who had held early pastorates in the Northeast and then gone to California while in his early forties. Arriving in San Francisco in 1878 to accept a call from First Baptist Church, he moved on to the pulpit of one of the largest Baptist congregations in the state at Oakland the following year. From this influential position he spoke to the Home Mission Society in 1882.[40]

During the first two years of his Pacific Coast career Abbott

[37] *Ibid.*

[38] For example, see Jesse B. Hartwell, "Missions to the Chinese in America," *Baptist Home Mission Monthly*, VII (Apr., 1885), 93–94, and James B. Simmons, "The Chinese Question," *ibid.*, II (July, 1880), 132–134. In every case the West Coast clergymen who held views like those of Gates expressed them in the eastern religious papers, not in the *Pacific Baptist*, which was published at Portland, Ore. In the 1880s this paper confined its topics to strictly religious matters, and thus it did not discuss the Chinese question.

[39] Granville S. Abbott, "The Christian View of the Chinese Question," in 50th Annual Report, ABHMS (1882), reprinted in *Baptist Home Missions in North America*, 99–100.

[40] *California General Baptist Annual* (1898), 35; Cathcart, ed., *Baptist Encyclopedia*, 10, 439; *Massachusetts Baptist Annual* (1891), 90. Abbott was pastor of South Boston Church from 1863 to 1873; one of Gates's early pastorates was Hanson Place Church in Brooklyn. Thus both men had had urban parishes as well as churches in smaller towns in New England.

appeared to react to the anti-Chinese sentiment surrounding him in the same way as did his colleague in San Diego. In 1880 he opposed the restriction of Chinese immigration, asking readers of the *Home Mission Monthly*, "Shall our ports be closed to Asiatics and the American nation confess that its founders built unwisely in proclaiming equality and fraternity of welcome to all lands under the stars?"[41] But by 1882 his experience in living in a city having a large Chinese population, coupled with an apparent desire to conform to the wishes of his congregation, had led Granville Abbott to reverse himself and thus argue persuasively for closing the gates to the Chinaman.[42]

The content of Abbott's speech to the Home Mission Society and the replies to it, delineating the east-west split over the Chinese question, have special significance because they reflect some of the basic arguments of the national debate concerning immigration that were to become common in the late 1880s and the 1890s. One interpretation of this period contends that the anti-Chinese movement in the Far West of the 1870s and 1880s did not contribute directly to other anti-foreign phobias.[43] Although this is true in the sense that the exclusion act was not immediately followed by other severely restrictive legislation, and although Abbott himself tried to differentiate between Indo-

[41] Granville S. Abbott, "The Chinese in the United States," *Baptist Home Mission Monthly*, II (Apr., 1880), 59–62.

[42] A story which Abbott told points to the fact that the influence of his congregation was paramount in his change of heart. He said, "A lady who came from Massachusetts to Oakland, came into my office and said: 'Mr. Abbott, isn't it simply awful?' 'What is awful, Mrs. Dudley?' I said. . . . 'Well,' said she, 'a friend of mine came into my office in the machine room (where this lady is a clerk), and said that although she is not dependent upon her work for her living, she still had so much character and personal independence she desired to support herself so far as she could; so she went into a furnishing house where the undergarments of the women and children of San Francisco and Oakland were made by the Chinamen. This young lady said: What will you give me per piece for this tucking? and the man said: I will give you one dollar and fifty cents. Well, said she, if I should work from sunrise to sunset and take but little nooning for six days a week, I could then yet barely earn an honest living. A Chinaman by her side said: I will do that work for twenty-five cents.'" Abbott indicated that he could have recounted other such incidents, thus giving a clue to the composition of his church (*Baptist Home Missions in North America*, 109).

[43] Higham, *Strangers in the Land*, 167.

European and Oriental immigration, many of his ideas were used against European immigrants at a later date. The discussion in the Home Mission Society in 1882, moreover, set Baptists to thinking about the general problems relating to the whole foreign influx.

The Oakland clergyman began his discourse with the familiar notion that America must remain homogeneous in population. The nation could not endure a slave or helot group such as the Chinese, he asserted. *"I believe in desirable immigration,"* he exclaimed, "in that immigration which tends to add vigor and potency and health to our American life; but I do not believe in any force or vigor coming to us, as a Republic, from the scum of the world." And he added emphatically, "I hold that to be an erroneous exegesis of the Word of God, that deduces from the Fatherhood of God the practical amalgamation or assimilation of different race stock." [44]

For Abbott, the Oriental was clearly of such a different "race stock." Because he felt that if the white and yellow races united, the former would lose its identity and the Chinese eye would appear in many succeeding generations, he justified "all proper means and measures . . . [for] any self-preservation that shall be consistent with our prestige as a Christian people." But despite his insistence that America could accept Caucasian or Indo-Germanic blood of its own type without risk of deterioration, Abbott held that as a general principle immigration was undesirable. In an attempt to deny the validity of the doctrine that all men are created equal, he disclosed a firm belief that the "scum of the world" included others besides the Chinese. "The author of the Declaration of Independence would have drawn one long breath before he had formulated its first statement," Abbott exclaimed, "if he had thought that you and I were to accept Nihilism and Socialism and Agrarianism and Romanism and Jesuitism as the equals of us all in the rights and privileges of this grand American Republic." [45] These references to clearly European characteristics in a speech that focused primarily on

[44] Abbott, "The Christian View of the Chinese Question," 99–102.
[45] *Ibid.*

the Chinese in 1882 show that the assumption that Chinese exclusion was a completely separate issue from that of general immigration restriction, and that the anti-Chinese agitation did not contribute to other anti-foreign phobias, needs to be modified.[46] Abbott's use of the word "Indo-Germanic" as synonymous with "desirable immigration" indicated, even in 1882, that the application of racial differentiation between southeastern and northwestern Europeans might not be far off.

The California cleric also revealed an awareness of the competition of Chinese with American laborers. He insisted that the former were coming to the West Coast chiefly to "get possession of the industries there." [47] To those not confronted with the immediacy of the situation, Abbott contended that if the Chinese were as numerous on the East Coast as in California, contesting for jobs and reducing wages to starvation level, easterners who frowned on the anti-Chinese agitation would be more willing to let the workers of his state defend their own interests.[48] Both this common basis of opposition to Orientals and a sensitivity to their different racial characteristics constituted a major preoccupation of church members and clergy, for one of Abbott's eastern supporters claimed that nine-tenths of the Christians on the Pacific Coast held the same views as the Oakland minister.[49]

[46] Higham, *Strangers in the Land*, 167. Higham points out that immigration restrictionists in the late nineteenth century did not argue that Chinese exclusion set a logical precedent for their own proposals. He further states that foreign-born whites led the anti-Chinese crusade while San Francisco's anti-European nativists did not join the campaign against the Oriental, concluding that the issues of Chinese and European immigration were separate from one another. The example of Baptists such as Abbott, who linked the two groups of aliens together in proclaiming them undesirable, qualifies this theory rather than refutes it altogether. The implication that Baptists viewed the matter from a slightly different angle than the groups Higham examined shows the necessity for careful investigation of denominational attitudes toward social questions throughout U.S. history.

For a discussion of the way in which American historians viewed such matters as the superiority of northeastern European peoples at this time, see Edward N. Saveth, *American Historians and European Immigrants, 1875–1925* (New York, 1948), especially chs. 1 and 2, pp. 13–65.

[47] Abbott, "The Christian View of the Chinese Question," 109.

[48] *Ibid.*, 102.

[49] A. K. Potter of Massachusetts, in *Baptist Home Missions in North America*, 110.

Reverend John Quincy Adams Henry of California agreed that most churchmen there favored the restriction of Chinese immigration, adding condescendingly, "I don't believe those who have not been in California are competent in every respect to talk upon this question."[50]

Perhaps in deference to this assumption, Abbott's colleagues chose one who had "been in California" to answer him. Judson B. Thomas, who preceded Abbott in the San Francisco pastorate, had returned east by 1882 to take charge of a church in Brooklyn. Whether or not the estimate of nine-tenths of the Christians on the West Coast supporting Abbott was accurate, the response of the Home Mission Society to Thomas showed that the Baptist denomination as a whole did not feel this way. Applause for his remark that Dr. Abbott had made the best defense possible of the worst cause conceivable cheered him on to a point-by-point rebuttal.

To the argument that nature forbade the intermingling of such separate and distinct races as Caucasian and Mongolian, Thomas replied that both science and the Bible proved the aboriginal unity of mankind. The essential fact that every immigrant belonged to the human race, all of whom had the traditional rights of life, liberty, and the pursuit of happiness, remained paramount in importance above political considerations. Where Abbott contended that God gave the Caucasian and the Mongol each a home, and neither should invade the habitat of the other, Thomas countered that population movements had always been indispensable to civilization, noting that the Pacific Coast seemed to have an "Asiatic" climate. As to the question of national self-preservation and the danger of China overflowing into the United States, he observed that all migrations in history were westward, and that relatively few Chinese had come here when they could do so.[51]

[50] John Quincy Adams Henry, in *Baptist Home Missions in North America*, 114. Henry later became active as a speaker and writer for the American Protective Association, again suggesting that a number of those who took part in the late nineteenth-century nativism were first aroused by the Chinese question.

[51] Judson B. Thomas, reply to Granville S. Abbott, in *Baptist Home Missions in North America*, 104–110.

Abbott had insisted that only European "Indo-Germanic" immigration added homogeneous elements to American civilization. But to his critic, homogeneity had never existed in this country, with its endless diversity of language, religion, political and social culture, rank, and race. The motto of *E pluribus unum* held pre-eminence over any goals of unity of religion or nationality. Thomas dismissed the argument that American workingmen must be protected from cheap competition by asserting that California needed many hands to develop her vast natural resources. Abundant labor would free native citizens for other tasks. Thomas agreed that the introduction of coolies should be prohibited, but he did not accept the contention of Abbott and many Californians that virtually all Chinese laborers in the United States were under the coolie system. Other Baptist clergymen supported Thomas, pointing to the brotherhood of man, the adverse effects of anti-Chinese feelings on missions in China, and the excessive self-interest evident in Abbott's position.[52]

These discussions clearly indicate that although the views of Granville Abbott may have been held by a considerable number of West Coast Baptists, most members of the American Baptist Home Mission Society opposed his anti-Chinese ideas. When the time came to formulate the official statement of the society on the new exclusion act, Thomas and his supporters had decisively won the battle:

We earnestly deprecate such discrimination in our immigration laws as contrary to the fundamental principles of our free government and opposed to the spirit of our Christian religion. We believe that such legislation as has been effected was not demanded by any actual peril to our institutions or our industries . . . it has been brought about by an unchristian race prejudice and the rivalry of political parties ambitious for power, and will be an ineffaceable stain upon our national honor.[53]

---

[52] *Ibid.*, 104–110, 112–114.

[53] Report of the Committee on Chinese Missions, ABHMS (1882), quoted in *Baptist Home Missions in North America*, 96–97. Of the five men who signed this report, three were from the East, one was from California, and one was a Chinese Baptist from Oregon. Already the few immigrants who had been drawn into the denomination, in this case the Chinese, were making their influence felt in the committees of the Home Mission Society.

Conspicuous by its absence from this expression of opinion was any affirmation of the rightness of immigration restriction as a principle. In later years even the most liberal Baptist position on this issue would indicate a belief that some restriction was necessary, but not in 1882. At that time, outside the Pacific Coast, Dr. Abbott's pleas fell for the most part on deaf Baptist ears.

But the whole discussion of Chinese immigration in a Baptist national society did nothing to relieve the tensions among California Baptists. Nor did the passage of the exclusion act end the acts of violence against the Chinese, which had begun in 1871 when a large mob rushed into Chinatown in Los Angeles. In that outbreak the rioters fired into houses, hanged a number of persons, and appropriated all movable property. Similar attacks occurred sporadically throughout the 1870s and 1880s in various West Coast cities.[54]

Many Baptists, including those like Abbott who believed in the restriction of Chinese immigration, vigorously protested this type of activity. William Ashmore, a noted missionary in China, complained that the authorities often neglected to bring the offenders in these outbreaks to justice. Not only were such rampant deeds a cruel wrong, but they might cause China to retaliate against "our missionary interests and our commercial interests of priceless value." Although that far-off nation lacked the power to invade America with armies, they could shift their foreign trade from the United States to Canada, a potential rival since the building of the Canadian Transcontinental Railway. If our officials sat idly by while rioters attacked the Chinese here, warned Ashmore, their government would permit wanton acts directed at merchants and missionaries in Asia.[55] Ashmore's thoughts in tying commercial and religious values together, while not a common theme among Baptists, disclose an awareness of the advantages America enjoyed in its trade with China.[56]

[54] Sandmeyer, *Anti-Chinese Movement in California*, 48ff.
[55] William Ashmore, "A Chinese Peril," *Standard*, XXXIII (May 13, 1886), I.
[56] The connection of commercial and religious values in relation to the Chinese question is one which I expected to find with considerable frequency in the Baptist literature of the period. Such was not the case. In the many

In at least one instance Baptists felt strongly enough to take up arms in defense of the persecuted Chinese. In 1888 gangs organized at Seattle in an attempt to drive the Orientals out. There Baptist laymen joined men from other churches and from the community, armed themselves with rifles, and formed a cordon around the threatened Chinese.[57] This was doubtless more effective than the pronouncements of the Home Mission Society that the anti-Chinese riots were "disgraceful and inhuman outbreak[s] of hatred . . . un-American and unchristian in the extreme." But an 1886 statement "that the American Baptist Home Mission Society utterly reprobates the violent acts of the anti-Chinese agitators, and that it has no sympathy with so-called Christians who even indirectly aid and abet them," implied that not all Baptists were on the same side as the Seattle laymen in the emotional strife.[58] The superintendent of Chinese work on the Pacific Coast, Jesse B. Hartwell, verified this allegation when he expressed regret that "in very many instances, professed Christians have joined the hue and cry against the Chinese, and if they have not taken part in the violent outrages that have been committed, have, by allowing them to go unrebuked, quietly condoned them." [59]

The intensity of anti-Chinese feelings among California Baptists, and the divisions among them, are well illustrated by a church trial that took place in the city of Chico late in the 1880s. There emotions ran so high after a series of riots that a number of Baptist laymen, claiming concern for their church's progress among whites, opposed the admittance of Chinese people into the congregation on a basis of equality. When one of the deacons

articles on the Chinese in the various Baptist periodicals, the idea that the anti-Chinese movement threatened America's commercial relations with China was not mentioned more than four or five times. My conclusion is that this was more of an issue in the nation at large than in Baptist ranks. It is significant, however, that the Baptist who was more aware of commercial advantages in China than any other, William Ashmore, was a foreign missionary in that country and not one who worked only with the Chinese in the United States.

[57] William Ashmore, "In America: The Baptists and the Chinese," *Standard*, XXXV (Jan. 26, 1888), 1.

[58] 54th Annual Report, ABHMS (1886), 68–69.

[59] Letter of Jesse B. Hartwell, in 54th Annual Report, ABHMS (1886), 32–33.

took issue with the pastor's insistence that Orientals be allowed all the privileges of church membership, the lines of battle were drawn.

Supporters of the minister, who evidently controlled the congregation, promptly brought the recalcitrant deacon to account for his extreme anti-Chinese pronouncements. He acknowledged all the charges, begging forgiveness, but as punishment his peers asked him not to exercise his functions as deacon for twelve months. At this he became angry, saying the Baptists were a hard-hearted set and he would never darken their door again.[60] The fact that it was he who left the church and not the Chinese, at a time of intense anti-Chinese prejudice in the community, further reveals that proximity to Orientals did not insure a universally negative response to them. The divisions among Baptists in California itself so damaged the denomination that even Granville Abbott mourned what he had unwittingly helped to bring about.[61]

By the end of the decade, however, the views of Abbott had gained more respect among his fellow Baptists than they were accorded in 1882. This is made clear in comment on the Geary Act of 1892, which extended the original Chinese Exclusion Act for ten years; placed upon the Chinaman the burden of proof of his right to be here; fixed the penalty for unlawful residence at up to a year's imprisonment, followed by deportation; and denied bail to Chinese in *habeas corpus* proceedings. Under this new law all Chinese laborers in the United States had to apply within one year for a certificate of residence, and those failing to do so would be sent back to China.[62]

[60] Jesse B. Hartwell, "The Chinese," *Baptist Home Mission Monthly*, XI (Dec., 1889), 329–330; also XII (Jan., 1890), 14.

[61] Abbott stated that Baptist work among the Chinese in California "has been cut short, as a result of sentiment in our own Baptist denomination, the like of which has been existent in no other." He added that through all the anti-Chinese agitation the Presbyterians, Methodists, and Congregationalists had together spent nearly $10,000 a year, but that the Baptists by comparison had spent very little for the evangelization of the Chinese in the years when emotion was at its height (Abbott, "The Christian View of the Chinese Question," 101).

[62] 27 U.S. Statutes, 25, quoted in Sandmeyer, *Anti-Chinese Movement in California*, 103–104.

While much of the Baptist debate over Chinese exclusion in 1882 centered on the issue of restriction itself,[63] this was not the case in 1892. The Baptist papers nearly unanimously condemned the Geary law, but now they attacked only the provisions that discriminated against the Chinese in America. None of them questioned the propriety of immigration restriction. The *Standard*, one of the few Baptist periodicals to come out in favor of regulatory legislation in 1882, reiterated its position in 1892 but noted that it would not endorse the "hostile portions" of the Geary Act.[64] On the West Coast the *Pacific Baptist*, strangely silent ten years earlier, asserted that it was a mistake to believe that a majority of people in its area sympathized with this "outrage against the Chinese already here," but it hastened to indicate that many Baptists saw the necessity of immigration restriction. The *Examiner* of New York, the *Watchman* of Boston, and the *Christian Enquirer* of Philadelphia disliked the requirement of residence certificates and called for repeal of the new law. But even the Baptist ministers' conferences in various cities that urged Congress to rescind the 1892 statute did not appear to challenge the idea that some limitation of the foreign influx was in order.[65] When the Home Mission Society issued its predictable disapproval of the Geary Act in a resolution characterizing it as "unjust and oppressive," the feature conspicuously absent in 1882 was added in the expression "*Resolved*, we do not advocate unrestricted immigration of the Chinese to this country." [66] A widespread demand remained that any regulation of the flow of aliens to America be carried out on a humane and impartial basis,[67] but ten years of discussion of the immigra-

---

[63] See nn. 27–33 above.

[64] Editorials: "American and Chinese Civilization," *Standard*, XL (June 8, 1893), 4; "China and the Geary Law," *ibid*. (June 29, 1893), 1; "The Chinese Exclusion Bill," *ibid*., XXXIX (May 12, 1892), 4.

[65] "The Chinese Must Go," *Examiner*, LXX (Apr. 14, 1892), 1; *Pacific Baptist*, XVI (June 9, 1892), 1; XVII (May 25, 1893), 1; "Baptists of America against the Anti-Chinese Legislation of 1892," *Baptist Home Mission Monthly*, XV (Mar., 1893), 61.

[66] 61st Annual Report, ABHMS (1893), 11–12.

[67] See Henry L. Morehouse *et al.*, "Conference on Repeal of the Anti-Chinese Legislation of May 5, 1892," *Standard*, XL (Feb. 9, 1893), 2; "Conference on Repeal of the Anti-Chinese Legislation of May 5, 1892," *Baptist Home*

tion question in the nation and in the denomination itself had led to a reconsideration of the criticisms heaped upon the head of Granville Abbott when he argued for Chinese exclusion in 1882.

Abbott's contentions, however distasteful to his colleagues, had a degree of validity in the light of his overall philosophy. Both the Chinese and the immigrants from Europe did pose a threat to the homogeneity of white Protestant America and its cultural and moral value system. For those who dreamed of an ideal Protestant civilization arising on the North American continent, the influx of persons who differed and would not readily convert en masse constituted a hindrance to the realization of this goal. One must be careful not to label every appreciation of this fact as "prejudice" and thus condemn it outright.

Yet the Baptist defenders of the Chinamen, especially on the West Coast where their position was impolitic, deserve praise for their moral courage. Often in the face of adversity, they upheld the principles on which the country was founded, equality before the law and justice for all. Long before the day of attention to "minority rights," these ardent citizens saw the need to treat all dwellers in this land with respect and without discrimination. Self-interest obviously entered into their desire to win the Chinese to the faith, but was not this a relatively humane way of helping a foreigner adjust to a new culture?

No major religious group was as torn asunder over the Chinese question as the Baptists.[68] Those who spoke up in behalf of Orientals used arguments widely expounded by other denominations whom they joined in an attempt to resist a traditional Caucasian aversion to races of a different color. When such Baptists as Granville Abbott justified exclusion, they merely accepted the views of the society around them. Paradoxically, their religious beliefs and vision for America led some Baptists in

Mission Monthly, XV (Mar., 1893), 61–63; Jesse B. Hartwell, "Expulsion of the Chinese," *ibid.*, 64–66.

[68] See n. 61 above. The article by Robert Seager II, showing agreement among Presbyterians, Methodists, and Episcopalians but omitting Baptists from his generalizations, would seem to bear out Abbott's contention that the Chinese question disrupted the Baptists more than other denominations. See "Some Denominational Reactions to the Chinese in California."

the direction of a reaction against the cultural milieu while causing others to acquiesce in its norms and even reinforce them.

In the decade following the 1882 Home Mission Society convention, Baptists, Protestants, and Americans in general began to move away from their previous acceptance of the stranger. The historic concept of the open gate was to be seriously questioned in the years to come. Under the influence of events on the domestic social scene, the debate of 1882 turned into a prolonged discussion among Baptists regarding the relationship of immigration to Divine Providence, the outcome of which prepared the way for a rise in nativism.

America in the 1880s was a society in ferment. The railway strikes of the previous decade, the growth of slums in the cities, the difficulties of the farmer in the rural West and South— all seemed to indicate a widening gulf between rich and poor that raised the specter of social convulsion. Business combinations increased in power and wealth, and when corporations cut wages drastically during a recession between 1883 and 1885, class warfare seemed imminent. At one time in these years unemployment reached over a million, yet tycoons flaunted their affluence in lavish parties and balls in New York City while immigrant coal miners huddled in dirty, poorly heated shanties in Pennsylvania.

Into this brave new world came an ever-increasing number of Europeans. The 1870s saw the arrival of 2,812,191 aliens in America, and in the 1880s the figure nearly doubled, to 5,246,613, an average of more than half a million immigrants a year. The most fortunate of the newcomers got back to the land. The Scandinavians and the Germans usually did not stop at the port of disembarkation but boarded trains to the Upper Mississippi Valley, where they settled on farms in Minnesota, the Dakotas, and Wisconsin. These hardy individuals from northern and western Europe continued to constitute a major tributary to the total stream until well into the 1880s. Then, according to the assumptions of many "scientific" students of immigration who wrote early in the twentieth century, a fundamental change in the character of the influx occurred. Persons of the "old" immigration, ran this thesis, "entered practically every line of activity in nearly every part of the country, mingled freely with . . . native Americans and were thus quickly assimilated." Immigrants from southern and eastern Europe, who began coming in large numbers in 1883, were not of this ilk. The differentiation of the "new" from the "old" immigration, widely held for over fifty years, asserted that the Hungarians, Italians, Russians, Poles, and the Slavic groups had all flocked to the industrial centers of America, where they had "congregated together in sections apart from native Americans and the older immigrants to such an extent that assimilation [had] been slow." Thus the belief that ultimately found its way into the National Origins Act of 1924, with its discriminatory quota system, held that the incoming multitudes from southern and eastern Europe had a higher percentage of males and unskilled laborers, more illiteracy, and a greater tendency to impermanence. Having attempted to prove these facts, the famous Dillingham Commission, authorized by Congress to study the problem in 1907, concluded that the "new" immigration was indeed undesirable.[1]

Scholars no longer accept this traditional view. Recent research has shown that the "old" and "new" groups of arrivals each had too many contrasting attributes to be treated as collective entities. Considered according to each nationality, the differences had to be qualified. Italian and Slavic immigrants were predominantly male, unskilled, illiterate, and transient. But there were larger percentages of men among English immigrants than among Jewish, Bohemian, and Portuguese; Bohemians and Moravians had a higher literacy rate than the Irish and the Germans. Even the shift in geographical origins, which is in general beyond doubt, took place later than 1880 and with less suddenness than a whole generation of contemporaries thought. Not until 1896 did the southern and eastern Europeans coming to America outnumber the "old" immigration, and only after the turn of the century did this disparity become marked.[2]

If this is the reality, what were the origins of the myth? One

[1] Maldwyn Allen Jones, *American Immigration* (Chicago, 1960), 177–182.
[2] *Ibid.*

of the chief critics of the "old" versus "new" thesis has asserted that at root the invidious comparisons concerning southern and eastern Europeans could be traced to the racist beliefs of the late nineteenth and early twentieth centuries. Such ideas, as enunciated by the "scientific school," propounded the notion that the peoples of the Mediterranean region were biologically different from those of northern and western Europe as a result of an inherent inferiority of blood.[3] When closely tied with Anglo-Saxonism, argues a noted student of American nativism, this racial concept helped give rise to the national-origins myth.[4]

Much of the Baptist experience in the 1880s and 1890s confirms this hypothesis but adds to it another dimension. If investigation has shown that a classification of immigrants from southern and eastern Europe according to a preponderance of unskilled workers, or illiterate persons, or a tendency to impermanence is inaccurate, one common factor is not quite as open to challenge. Although the new immigration contained significant numbers of Jews and Eastern Orthodox and even Protestant Christians, a majority of these people were of the Catholic faith. Unlike one another in endless ways, the bonds of the Roman Catholic church nevertheless transcended differences of nationality. How would white Anglo-Saxon Protestant America react to an influx of what was still regarded as an alien creed? Would attempts to convert the stranger prove the viability of Protestant culture? Or would frustration in these efforts give rise to an essentially religious criterion of inferiority, in addition to racial criteria?

A dualism arose out of the experience of former times. The Christian belief in the equality of all men before God, and the confidence of Protestantism in its own ability to convert individuals and mould the nation's culture, justified the American policy of an open door to all until the 1880s. Yet in certain eras, especially the 1840s and 1850s, the fear of Catholicism's power to subvert free public schools, and of its threat to the

[3] Oscar Handlin, *Race and Nationality in American Life* (Boston, 1948), 96ff.
[4] Higham, *Strangers in the Land*, 136–144.

separation of church and state, led to a nativism full of religious prejudice. The dread of radicalism and a belief in Anglo-Saxon superiority often combined with anti-Catholicism to create a general suspicion of the stranger.[5] Until the latter part of the nineteenth century anti-foreign sentiment did not enter into the mainstream of American thought, but in the 1880s a discussion of immigration began that ended only with the virtual closing of the gates after World War I. In this debate Protestant clergymen and laymen played a most prominent role.

Signs of change were beginning to appear in Protestantism in the eighties. For a number of years the churches had presented an almost unanimous front in defense of the status quo. As one interpretation of U.S. social history sums up this attitude, "For a generation slums and depressions, farmer protests and labor parties had been pictured by church theorists as necessary, incidental flaws in the inevitable improvement of society."[6] Then three major events suddenly awakened American religion to a new moral sensitivity: the railroad strike of 1877, the Haymarket riot of 1886, and the strikes and depression of the years 1892–94. Several historians point both to conservative responses to these events and to indications that some religionists were becoming sympathetic to labor.[7] For Baptists, however, the debate over social justice came well after this decade. Their acceptance of

[5] *Ibid.*, 28ff. The best account of nativism before the Civil War is found in Ray A. Billington, *The Protestant Crusade, 1800–1860* (New York, 1938). Statistics on the religion of the immigrants are especially hard to come by, as they were not recorded in the census. One source indicates that Protestant immigrants to the United States from central and eastern European countries, mainly Hungary and Austria, made up less than 5 percent of the total from southern and eastern Europe. Jews comprised 25 percent and Eastern Orthodox persons over 5 percent. The Roman Catholic element made up somewhat less than two-thirds of the new immigration. See Charles H. Anderson, *White Protestant Americans: From National Origins to Religious Group* (Englewood Cliffs, N.J., 1970), p. 11, n. 4. Baptists, however, failed to recognize the religious pluralism of the new immigration until about 1905 and in the meantime dwelt upon its preponderant Catholicism.

[6] Henry F. May, *Protestant Churches and Industrial America* (New York, 1949), 91.

[7] *Ibid.*, 91–112. See also Charles H. Hopkins, *The Rise of the Social Gospel in American Protestantism, 1865–1915* (New Haven, Conn., 1940), and Aaron I. Abell, *The Urban Impact on American Protestantism, 1865–1900* (Cambridge, Mass., 1943).

the existing order was almost universal in the 1880s, and their discussion of immigration reveals an ambivalence partially influenced by such incidents as the Haymarket affair but also shaped by a traditional belief in God's plan to make America the highest civilization in the world.

In the early eighties the Home Mission Society reports and some writers in Baptist journals expressed an assurance that the great influx of peoples came in the providence of God. A strong, naive faith trusted in the power of Protestant American institutions to convert the immigrant, if not literally, at least in the sense of forcing him to adjust to the nation's ideals. But coexistent with this belief, even before the Chicago Haymarket uprising, appeared the three themes of nativism: anti-Catholicism, Anglo-Saxonism, and fear of radicalism. Pessimism tended to predominate in Baptist papers for the entire period, but only after Haymarket did the concept of immigration as a menace seem to become nearly universal. Even then, the idea of mission for America was not destroyed, and Baptists along with other Protestants temporarily eschewed the political solution of immigration restriction in favor of a promotional campaign to win the newcomer.

The existence of two attitudes, then, is the characteristic feature of the decade in which Baptists began to consider immigration as a major issue. One side talked of the many persons who would make good citizens, emphasizing the valuable assets of the foreigner that would enrich American life. In this view a thoroughly Protestant environment had sufficient vitality to improve all those who encountered it. The alternate outlook, which was to triumph by the end of the eighties, regarded most immigrants as undesirables whose customs and beliefs threatened the foundations of society. At that fateful anniversary meeting of the Home Mission Society in 1882, while Granville Abbott and Martin Brewer Anderson warned of the dangers of Chinese immigration, Nihilism, Romanism, and Jesuitism, another Baptist welcomed the delegates with an affirmation of faith in the future. "Send us over your poor and degraded you would trample underfoot," exclaimed Reverend John Peddie of New York City in a gesture to Europe, "and on our wide plains and prairies, under the fostering light of free institutions, of education, and religion, we will make out of them such noble specimens of manhood as never grew on your crammed and narrow soil." Peddie told his fellow Baptists frankly that if America, with all of her God-given advantages, could not assimilate the newcomers, she deserved to perish. "And better to die in the grand attempt," he concluded amidst applause, "than to seek protection behind the barriers of fear and bigotry." [8]

Such optimism was common at this time. God's hand entered into the gathering of men of every nation, affirmed the Home Mission Society in 1881. His purpose for the United States, a country pre-eminent in its privileges of preaching the gospel, envisioned a land where all peoples could hear the story of redemption in their own tongues, through Baptist missionaries. "Does evil pour into our borders at a fearful rate, as the discontented and anarchial elements of the old world add their turbid currents to the infidelity here abounding? When the enemy shall come in a flood, the Spirit of the Lord shall lift up a standard against him." [9]

This attitude manifested itself again at the Home Mission Society's annual meeting in 1885. Once more the society urged Baptists to look at the hopeful side of immigration, which furnished a labor supply for the country's industrial interests, thus adding to material prosperity. To call the newcomers dregs and riff-raff, the criminals and paupers of Europe, constituted libel. Many of them proved their thrift and willingness to work by acquiring property and improving their condition with rapidity. Americans could profit from a number of immigrant characteristics—dislike of divorce and belief in the sanctity of marriage, respect for family ties, and warmth and constancy of domestic affection. Their potential contributions, moreover, included biological reinforcement to replenish the native-born

8 John Peddie, address of welcome to the fiftieth anniversary meeting of the American Baptist Home Mission Society, in *Baptist Home Missions in North America*, 47–48.
9 49th Annual Report, ABHMS (1881), 64–65.

lineage. In social Darwinian phraseology the Home Mission Society proclaimed that "as the barbarians that swept down from the German forests into the Roman Empire infused fresh blood into the decaying Latin race, so these immigrants are bringing to us a brawn that will help save the native American stock from physical deterioration." [10]

If the incoming millions were to have a favorable impact upon their adopted country, so would their new surroundings enrich their lives. When the immigrants cast off the shackles of the old European aristocracy, of a despotic state religion, the argument continued, they would distinguish themselves in all areas under the influence of America's liberal institutions. They adjusted to the new customs, language, dress, and political system with surprising alacrity. An encounter with a religion of simplicity and spirituality, lacking "hateful features," would hasten their acceptance of the American way of life and lessen mutual prejudice. Providence, in sum, had directed immigrants to the United States not only for their own good but ultimately for the welfare of the nation. [11]

Two possible explanations may account for the prevalence of this outlook in the Home Mission Society before 1886. The chief task of that agency, the winning of "North America for Christ," meant that all of its literature would be of a promotional nature. It simply did not make sense to appeal for funds to evangelize the immigrant in one breath and then remark that this was hopeless. In addition, considerable numbers of newly converted Scandinavian and German Baptists were active in the Home Mission Society by the 1880s, and official statements had to exercise care to avoid offending them. [12]

Indeed, many of the arguments that defended foreigners in

[10] 53rd Annual Report, ABHMS (1885), 15–16.
[11] *Ibid.*
[12] The Home Mission Society annual report for 1882 does not give the numbers of immigrants who had entered the denomination at that time. Of the Germans, the report merely urged that greater efforts be made among them and called attention to the encouraging fact that "large numbers of them have been gathered into Baptist churches." It claimed that of a total Scandinavian immigrant population of 450,000, there were between 6,000 and 7,000 Baptists (*Baptist Home Missions in North America*, 118).

Baptist periodicals came from German Baptists. Reverend Julius C. Haselhuhn in 1886 deplored the suspicion with which many Christians viewed the stranger and the lack of concerted efforts to give him the gospel. He lamented the resurgence of old-time nativism, which caused Americans to feel bitter against immigrants when they should show kindness and pity. Haselhuhn especially criticized ministers who blamed all aliens for the sins and crimes of a comparatively small number.[13] William Papenhausen, another German Baptist pastor, admitted that the entrance of a large unchristian population might vitiate the nation's religious principles but agreed with Haselhuhn that few newcomers were criminals or disturbers of the peace. Any potential threat to the republic, he pointed out, underscored the urgency of converting the immigrant, and calling him unpleasant names accomplished nothing. "You will never succeed in making good American citizens of them by calling them 'European refuse,' and a 'sabbath-breaking' and 'beer-guzzling' people," he exclaimed. Only the spirit of the gospel could reach the alien heart: "Let a foreigner become a citizen of the kingdom of Christ, and he . . . will love this country and its institutions more than any other, because [they are] more Christian than any other." [14]

Aside from the writings of foreign-speaking Baptists, most of the optimistic pronouncements on immigration in Baptist journals appeared in the first half of the decade. In answer to those who emphasized the dangers, an 1881 author listed hopeful signs. To the argument that immigrants might form political combinations, he countered that their very diversity of nationalities, different in religion, intelligence, character, and sympathies, would tend to prevent such action on a large scale. He expressed confidence in the impact on the foreigner of American public schools, libraries, newspapers, and free discussions. Most aliens, enchanted by political, civil, and social life in the United States, quickly came into sympathy with it. Discovering opportunities

[13] Julius C. Haselhuhn, "Our Foreign Population," *Journal and Messenger*, LV (Nov. 17, 1886), 1.
[14] William Papenhausen, "What to Do with the Foreigner," *Watchman*, LXX (Feb. 14, 1889), 3.

unknown in the Old World, their hopes awakened and their ambitions rose. Another writer pointed out that because most immigrants came to the New World to own their own homes and enjoy equality with other men, these motives had Americanized them before they set foot on our shores.[15]

Persons who judged the foreign element by a few tumbledown shanties or by the saloons of large cities, claimed an 1884 editorial in the Chicago *Standard*, were as mistaken as if they characterized a typical Yankee by looking at a tramp in New England. Even to the casual observer, ample evidence confirmed that the gifts of the Old World to the New were to be prized for their ultimate role in the life of the nation. Did not the newcomers show an ability to command prosperity? Did not many of them undertake public duties efficiently? These additions to America's population clearly fitted into the providential plan to make this country the fountain of all good influence in a world brought more closely together by the migration of peoples.[16]

Closely connected with the optimistic view of immigration as a part of Divine Providence were ideas of Anglo-Saxon superiority. Long existent in the national tradition, Anglo-Saxonism did not merge with nativism until the end of the nineteenth century.[17] Baptists in the 1880s interpreted prevalent racial ideas in two ways, as did others.[18] The older approach emphasized the

[15] "Immigration—Does It Imperil Our Republic?" *Watchman*, LXII (Jan. 6, 1881), 1. See also J. C. Grimmell, "The Problem of Americanizing the Foreign Population," *Baptist Home Mission Monthly*, V (Apr., 1883), 73–76. There was an almost universal belief among Baptists that if the immigrant were converted, the rest of the Americanization process would take place automatically. This undoubtedly reflects their conviction that the individual had primary responsibility for his own fate, which he could work out under the guidance of a true and spiritual religion. Because of this faith that Americanization would be a logical outcome of conversion, there were no programs to Americanize the immigrant at this time.

[16] Editorial: "American Nationality," *Standard*, XXXII (Oct. 16, 1884), 1.

[17] Higham, *Strangers in the Land*, 132–134.

[18] *Ibid.*, 133–137. For a discussion of the impact of racial ideas upon the views held by American historians about immigrants at this time, see Saveth, *American Historians and European Immigrants*. In some respects the American Protestant clergy accepted, simplified, and disseminated among their congregations ideas of race held by intellectuals. But the present study of the Baptists indicates that their reaction to race ideas differed from that of other intellectuals in several ways. (1) The conception of Divine Providence was

vitality of American culture and the strength that immigrant strains would add to the Anglo-Saxon race. The opposite attitude regarded the incoming tide as a debasing influence that would destroy God's intentions for a Protestant, ethnically homogeneous America. These two variants of racism, often vaguely delineated, operated somewhat independently of events on the social scene. Because of this the interpretations of the Anglo-Saxon theme constituted an intellectual bridge between the optimists, who centered their attention on the positive attributes of immigrants, and the pessimists, who began to fear the stranger as they read of daily happenings in the nation.[19]

Samuel Graves, a Baptist leader in Michigan and one-time theology professor at Kalamazoo College, set forth his version of the traditional, confident Anglo-Saxonism in 1882. Millions of Europeans considered the United States bountiful in land and liberty, he stated. God had foreordained the location and composition of this nation to make it the supreme commercial and political power of the world. Most Americans were Anglo-Saxon in origin and thus derived from a lineage noted for intelligence, independence, and self-assertion—a race that had given Europe its rulers for the last thousand years and led the earth in all substantial progress. The very immigration that some felt

emphasized by religious men in connection with the future of the Anglo-Saxon race in the United States. (2) The anti-Semitism that found its way into many contemporary race theories was altogether absent from Baptist writing. (3) The Baptist belief in a melting pot, although they did not use this term, was contingent not upon the existence of the frontier but upon the sufficiency of their interpretation of the gospel as the refining element in the production of the master race. (4) The historians studied by Saveth viewed immigration from afar, while many home mission workers gained first-hand acquaintance with the immigrant. This latter fact ultimately mitigated Baptist views of Anglo-Saxon superiority and tended to draw limitations around the nativism that engulfed religious leaders in the 1890s.

[19] Most of the articles attempting to interpret Anglo-Saxon superiority to Baptists did not include references to current events. The theorists of Divine Providence dealt in generalities, not specifics. Quite apart from this type of thought were clergymen who cited immigrant contributions to prove that the situation was hopeful, and those who offered facts and figures, plus specific situations—city slums, labor strikes, parochial schools, etc.—to show that American institutions were in imminent danger. Whatever their theories, all Baptists at this time used their arguments to spur the denomination to missionary activity, not to urge restriction of immigration.

might endanger Anglo-Saxon culture in America, said Graves, would actually enrich the population with the blood of all other peoples. In the great tradition of the social Darwinists, Graves confidently expected that the mixture of races, with the Anglo-Saxon dominant, would create a finer and higher manhood, "the blossom of all the ages, if the strength and beauty of the Christian faith be brought to it." On the North American continent God had placed the Anglo-Saxons on trial, to determine the fitness of the white man to control the world at this point in history. The outcome of this testing depended not on enterprise, learning, statesmanship, nor even on a growing command of natural resources, but upon the ability of this segment of humanity to act in concert with God's purposes. Failure on its part in this respect would result in a divine choice of other races to rule the globe.[20]

In 1887, the year after the Haymarket riot, another Baptist proclaimed his faith in the all-encompassing destiny of Anglo-Saxon America. Dwight Spencer, a prominent businessman in New York who gave up his vocation to become a missionary on the Utah frontier, wrote of the impending reunification of the Aryan race in the New World. Quoting the biblical prediction of Genesis that the three sons of Japheth (the white race) should have supremacy over all others, Spencer pointed out that these aboriginal figures had pushed westward to build European and then American civilization. Because the "master race" to be built up in North America would derive from the various descendants of Japheth, Spencer allowed for the infusion of peoples other than Anglo-Saxon into the United States. He did not differentiate among Caucasians: here Teuton and Celt, Scandinavian and Slav, were living side by side, forgetting their old animosities. From the different branches of the family of Japheth, God was fulfilling his prophecy in the crowning accomplishment of forming a race intellectually and physically superior to any in history.

[20] Samuel Graves, "Our Nation and Its Perils," *Standard*, XXIX (June 8, 1882), 3. It is significant that Graves still held this outlook after the Haymarket riot of May, 1886; see Graves, "Which Race?" *ibid.*, XXXIV (Dec., 1892), 375–380.

Spencer compared the astonishing progress of America with a Europe stagnating under archaic state conventionalities and an Asia that had slept for thirty centuries. Here was a land destined to be the Christian model for all humanity. She was to prove this by righteousness, the outstanding characteristic of the master race that was developing out of the gathering of nations. Hence Baptists and other Protestants now faced an urgent situation. The words of Spencer as missionary expressed the opinion of a whole generation: "Evangelize America and the world is evangelized; let the light in America become darkness and the world sinks into the gloom of night." [21]

The fact that Spencer wrote in 1887 and Graves in 1882 and 1886, and that their views expressed similar confidence, brings into question the assumption that the labor strife of the middle eighties acted as a universal catalyst upon Protestant thought of the time.[22] Social and industrial unrest in which immigrants were involved undoubtedly exerted a profound influence upon many persons. Yet the other variant of Anglo-Saxonism, which saw immigration as a threat to the building up of a perfect civilization, is also visible at both the beginning and the end of the decade, and was not always related to the total contemporary scene by its advocates. In 1880 Adoniram J. Sage, clergyman and college professor, noted that the nature of peoples thrown together at a nation's beginning determined its future destiny. If only the English founding groups had occupied the continent, he claimed, America's development would have been unsurpassed in history. A commingling of races, however, was now in full swing. For some time the United States had received hetero-geneous immigration without showing any change, but at this moment the influx threatened the purity of the Anglo-Saxon element. Unwilling, in 1880, to suggest restricting the flow of aliens, Sage contented himself with the belief that the "superior

---

[21] Dwight Spencer, "America in Prophecy," *Baptist Home Mission Monthly*, IX (Sept., 1887), 234–237. For very similar views expressed by other Baptists, see P. S. Henson, "The Valley of Decision," *ibid.*, VIII (Sept., 1886), 207–214, and H. W. Tilden, "Marks of Providential Design in the Discovery of America," *ibid.*, XIV (Dec., 1892), 375–380.

[22] May, *Protestant Churches and Industrial America*, 91.

[Anglo-Saxon] race will rule" and the affirmation that the religion of Christ and the Bible could bring unity out of the confusion resulting from the mixing of ethnic groups.[23]

Nine years later Hubert C. Woods, midwestern superintendent of missions for the Home Mission Society, saw God's design for America endangered by the flood of strangers rather than fulfilled by it. Woods, like Graves, Spencer, and Sage, felt that since the Anglo-Saxon peoples had made known the two great ideas of civil liberty and spiritual Christianity, God had charged them with responsibility for the world's welfare. Those who spoke English already ruled one-third of the earth's surface and one-fourth of its population. At some not too distant day their language would be the universal one. Convinced that Divine Providence had ordained this country to be the great evangelizing nation of the earth and that a struggle to achieve this end was shaping up on his native soil, Woods graphically set forth his vision:

In the gathering of all nations and races upon our shores, do we not witness the providential preparation for a second Pentecost that shall usher in the millennial glory? All these facts lead us to the conclusion that under God and by his appointment *"America holds the future."* But whether we recall the past, or review the present, or forecast the future we are profoundly impressed with the conviction that the strength and stability, the greatness and glory, aye, the very existence of this Republic depends upon the thoroughness of its evangelization. . . . We of this generation and nation occupy the Gibraltar of the ages which commands the world's future.[24]

---

[23] Adoniram J. Sage, "Christ and Our National Future," *Baptist Home Mission Monthly*, II (Oct., 1880), 188–190. Sage was a very prominent Baptist. He was professor of Latin at the University of Rochester and of homiletics at the Baptist Union Theological Seminary of Chicago. At the time he wrote this article, he was pastor of First Baptist Church in Hartford, Conn., and he served as president of the Connecticut Baptist State Convention. His last years were spent in Ohio, where he was highly regarded; from 1888 until his death in 1902 he was a director of the Union Central Life Insurance Company (*Connecticut Baptist Annual* [1902], 44; Cathcart, ed., *Baptist Encyclopedia*, 1021).

[24] Hubert C. Woods, "Home Missions: The Hope of the Country, the Opportunity and Obligation of the Church," *Standard*, XXXVII (Nov. 28, 1889), 2.

But immigration could destroy this prospect of the glory to come. The founders of America, said Woods, could not possibly have foreseen the volume of immigrants that would one day come to her shores when they had enacted laws which welcomed those of all lands. The Baptist missionary sounded an ominous note that found its way into federal policy many years later in the National Origins Act. In recent years, he stated, the character of persons arriving had degenerated; many from Russia, Hungary, Italy, and Bohemia not only had ways vastly different from Americans, but their illiteracy had made them unfit for learning. Worst of all, these "most turbulent and dangerous of our people" were incompatible with the Anglo-Saxon race and thus threatened its mission and destiny in the United States.[25]

Many Baptists who began to worry over immigration in the 1880s expressed no thoughts of Anglo-Saxon superiority but, rather, concerned themselves with what they regarded as practical dangers. Early in the decade articles appearing in Baptist papers pointed to the evils of the Catholicism and radicalism that came in with the newcomers. Clergymen, writing to promote home mission activities, foresaw dire consequences if Baptists did not succeed in evangelizing the incoming hordes. Under the pressure of events in the nation, what began as a campaign to win the immigrant ended in a shock wave of fear and near hysteria. Yet throughout the commotion both Baptists who criticized the stranger and those who praised him as a valuable addition offered a nonpolitical solution to the immigration problem. Faith in the ability of Protestantism to convert and assimilate remained fairly constant in the eighties: bring the foreigner into the church, and Americanization would automatically follow. Not until the next decade did Baptists turn to restriction.

In 1880 George C. Lorimer, pastor of Boston's Tremont Temple from 1870 to 1879 and then minister of First Baptist Church in Chicago, argued that immigration had helped to hinder the progress of a truly vital Christianity in American history. The flow of peoples had brought many advantages to national life, but in some ways it had retarded the growth of

[25] *Ibid.*

spirituality. Many immigrants lacked religious principles or blindly clung to superstition, he claimed, thus making the work of the churches more difficult. Even so, Lorimer hastened to add that legal enactment to hinder the migration process would be inconsistent with the spirit of freedom.[26] In like manner Philip S. Moxom, who preached at Cleveland's First Baptist Church, in 1883 characterized the infidelity and Catholicism of foreigners as constituting "Our National Problem." But Moxom, like Lorimer, challenged Protestants to Christianize and educate these millions, concluding that "it would be neither right nor conducive to our highest interests, to prohibit immigration even if we could." [27] In other denominations various spokesmen throughout the 1880s rejected demands for restriction while calling upon their constituencies to support mission work among the newcomers as the solvent that would preserve the nation.[28]

The religion of many of the immigrants, "Romanism" as Protestants called it, received criticism for a myriad of reasons. Philip Moxom, always a foe of parochial schools, voiced a common Protestant conviction in his accusation that Roman Catholics desired to destroy the public education system. This despotic and cruel faith, he cried, stood "positively and steadfastly opposed to the best institutions of free popular government." Because Catholics owed supreme allegiance to the pope rather than to the laws of their country, he reasoned, Romanism subverted all true patriotism. "It puts itself in unyielding antagonism to the culture and progress of the age," he warned, "and resolutely perpetuates in its principles and spirit the moral and intellectual despotism of medieval times." [29]

[26] George C. Lorimer, "Religion in America; Its Progress and Prospects," *Standard*, XXVII (Feb. 5, 1880), 2.

[27] Philip S. Moxom, "Our National Problem," *Watchman*, LXIV (Dec. 6, 1883), 2.

[28] For a Presbyterian view, see P. A. Schwarz, "Should Immigration Be Restricted?" *Church at Home and Abroad*, II (Aug., 1887), 135-136; "Immigration Our Power and Peril," *ibid.*, 132-134; "Our Immigrant Population," *ibid.*, IV (Aug., 1888), 133-134. The position of a Congregationalist is given by M. W. Montgomery, "Immigration," *Congregationalist*, LXXIV (Mar. 21, 1889), 97.

[29] Moxom, "Our National Problem." For a thorough discussion of the historical roots of anti-Catholicism in the United States, see Billington, *The Protestant Crusade.*

While Moxom fretted in Cleveland, Professor Eri B. Hulbert of the Baptist Union Theological Seminary in Chicago wrote in the same vein. To him, America stood in imminent danger from the "foe of free thought, free schools, free inquiry, and free religion." The church that hated human advancement and modern civilization would bend all efforts to conquer the United States. "Already her prophets predict that men are now living who will see Romanism the state religion," he cautioned, "[and] the victory over Protestantism made complete." Hulbert spoke for many others when he stated that "her gains in wealth and numbers are indeed alarming." [30] Across the land Baptists began to attribute this increased power of Catholicism to the immigrant. A West Virginia group worried that "Infidels, Catholics, Formalists and all classes of Gospel-haters are coming. . . . Most of our Catholicism is imported." [31] Where once America had been separated from the papacy and paganism of Europe, now Romanism and idolatry, inseparable in the eyes of Baptists, found no barriers to dispersion.[32] Yet legal obstacles were not the answer; the preaching of the gospel alone would save the nation from the terrible penalties of unchristian and un-American agencies. The conversion of the immigrant to Protestantism would assure the proper outcome of the conflict in North America between the powers of darkness and the children of light.[33]

Baptists deplored many qualities of the newcomers besides their religion. Like other Protestants, they especially condemned Germans for their customary lack of respect for the sabbath. The Sunday parades, the bands, the beer drinking—all seemed to Europeanize and destroy the sanctity of that special day.[34]

[30] Eri B. Hulbert, "Our Peril and Our Defense," *Standard*, XXXIV (June 23, 1887), 2.

[31] Report of the Committee on Home Missions, West Virginia Baptist Convention, quoted in *Baptist Home Mission Monthly*, IV (Nov., 1882), 303. See also 48th Annual Report, ABHMS (1880), 24.

[32] Franklin Johnson, "Home Missions for the World's Sake," *Baptist Home Mission Monthly*, VII (Jan., 1885), 185–186.

[33] "Enormous Immigration," *Baptist Home Mission Monthly*, IX (Oct., 1887), 255–256. See also "Our Foreign Population," *ibid.*, VII (Nov., 1885), 283–284, and Dwight Spencer, "Startling Facts and Figures," *ibid.*, IV (Jan., 1882), 10–12.

[34] "Who Are the Foreigners?" *Journal and Messenger*, XLIX (July 21, 1880), 1; Marsena Stone, "Our Foreign Population," *ibid.*, LV (Oct. 20, 1886), 1.

Another moral question revolved around the issue of temperance. Religionists held foreigners responsible for the "saloon curse" and for the sale of beer and wine. One writer noted that out of 865 liquor license applications processed within a given time in Philadelphia, 669 (roughly 77 percent) of the applicants were naturalized citizens. Persons of German origin, moreover, largely controlled the great brewing interests. "But for the adverse foreign influence on the part of the makers, venders and drinkers of intoxicating beverages," lamented this commentator, "the temperance reform in this country would easily and speedily become victorious." [35]

Prominent spokesmen of the Baptist denomination joined other Americans in the common fear that the growing political power of the immigrant might well destroy municipal government. Daniel C. Potter, for many years pastor of the influential Sixth Street Baptist Church in New York City, warned his parishioners that the buying and selling of immigrant votes would corrupt elections, legislatures, and courts of justice. Whenever a given ethnic group banded together in a large city, he advised, its members became involved in public affairs under the banner of their nationality. The Manhattan clergyman shared a widespread feeling that universal suffrage subjected America to a terrific strain because it allowed the "larger immoral class" of foreigners to play a major role in politics.[36]

One objection to immigration prevalent in other quarters seldom appeared in the Baptist press. Only once in the eighties did the *Standard* call attention to the threat posed to the economy by a vast flood of laborers. In 1882 the editor of that periodical pointed to a decline in the previous need for workers in mining and railroad building. If this trend continued, an unchecked influx could become a serious economic problem. Other Baptist writers, however, evidently did not share the fear, and their

[35] *Journal and Messenger*, LVII (Apr. 19, 1888), 3. See also Stone, "Our Foreign Population"; "Who Are the Foreigners?"; and the 51st Annual Report, ABHMS (1883), 13–15.

[36] Daniel C. Potter, "What to Do with the Foreigner," *Examiner*, LXVI (Jan. 17, 1889), 1. See also A. K. Potter, "The Duty of the Hour for American Baptists," *Baptist Home Mission Monthly*, II (July, 1880), Supplement.

failure to mention this issue may indicate the lack of a solid working-class constituency among members of the denomination.[37]

The whole question of the laboring man and the church had much to do with the Baptist reaction to foreign radicalism in the 1880s. Even before Haymarket a number of Protestants became concerned over the alienation of the worker from organized religion, while others quailed in terror at the prospect of the spread of socialism and communism by immigrant agitators. In part because Baptists were slow to adopt the ideas of social Christianity, the emotion of fear gradually triumphed over feelings of sympathy among them.[38] As early as 1881 Reverend Willard W. Boyd of St. Louis charged that most rebels against the laws of property had received training in Communist and socialist tactics in Europe. These ideologies had roots in the mob principle, Boyd argued, and they grew in America largely because immigrants had imported them. What little fruit such doctrines had borne, he said, clearly warned Americans of the dangers that threatened them from the foreign element.[39]

The habit of blaming newly arrived aliens for domestic social problems appeared more than once among Baptists. Two years after Boyd spoke out, Daniel C. Potter portrayed the typical socialist as a malcontent incapable of earning a living, who

[37] Editorial: "Immigration and Political Economy," *Standard,* XXIX (Aug. 24, 1882), 7.
[38] As a rule, Baptists were slow to adopt the social gospel, and not as many Baptist clergymen gave attention to the workingman in the 1880s as did ministers of other denominations. Two individuals cited in this chapter who did discuss problems of labor and capital at length were George C. Lorimer, *Studies in Social Life* (Chicago, 1886), and Philip S. Moxom, *The Industrial Revolution* (Boston, 1886). T. Edwin Brown, an early Baptist social gospeler, wrote *Studies in Modern Socialism and Labor Problems,* also in 1886. Henry F. May characterizes Brown as the first important Baptist to set forth theories of social Christianity, but he does not appear in the denominational debate over immigration in the eighties, either in the Home Mission Society or in the Baptist press. Walter Rauschenbusch's well-known group, the Brotherhood of the Kingdom, did not organize until 1892, and many years elapsed before his own denomination accepted the ideas that made him a national figure. See May, *Protestant Churches and Industrial America,* 178, n. 25, 179–180, 190–191.
[39] Willard W. Boyd, "The Foreign Element in the West," *Examiner and Chronicle,* LVIII (June 22, 1881), 2.

had always been under restraint and poverty in his native land. Quite often a political refugee, the radical agitator had left debts and crimes behind him. He wanted to use the freedom of the United States to change the whole structure of society. Of some 30,000 socialists in New York City, Potter claimed that most were Germans. He flayed them for railing against such prominent men as Jay Gould and Cornelius Vanderbilt, asserting that only foreigners approved of such rantings. "If immigration were stopped," Potter concluded, "there would be small chance for any culmination to this mischief." But the New York clergyman realized that the flood would not abate, and he proposed that the churches press hard the truth of the gospel. Such a message would make genuine Americans of all who came here, and thus adequately counter radical teachings.[40]

The year after the New York *Examiner* published Potter's article, that paper printed an editorial indicating that not all Baptists agreed that socialism was merely a product of immigration. In a candid phrase the *Examiner* stated that Christianity would confess its incompetence or indifference if it refused to consider social questions, leaving them to infidel philosophers and economists. Conceding that many socialist theories were indeed "wild and wicked," animated more by hatred for the rich than pity for the poor, the writer added that workers in this country had well-founded grievances under the present social organization with its great monopolies and tenant farms. Therefore, the bitter temper and outlandish fallacies of social reformers, however extreme and repulsive, must not alienate Christians from the struggle of the laboring man to improve his condition. Labor's just complaints and demands should elicit prompt and cordial sympathy from men who professed the Christian religion, which had traditionally cared for the poor and oppressed. Much of the unrest and striving of the lower classes derived support from Christ's teachings, the editorial concluded. The Christian church distinctly opposed all exclusive

---

[40] Daniel C. Potter, "The Socialists and Socialism of New York City," *Examiner*, LIX (Feb. 8, 1883), 1.

privileges based upon the idea that some human beings were inherently better than others.[41]

The pastor of a large Baptist congregation in Cleveland, George T. Dowling, showed accord with these opinions in the face of an urban riot in 1885. Although he condemned communism for inciting violence under the pretended cry of liberty and equality, Dowling recognized the existence of inequities in the wage system and consequently did not regard the Cleveland outbreak as strictly the outgrowth of an imported doctrine. He pronounced immoral the situation that forced workingmen to choose between the terms of employers and starvation. Although wages had risen in the United States, the arrangement of society violated standards of justice. Dowling suggested the cooperative company, which would distribute stock shares to workers as part of their pay, as a solution to the conflict of interests between labor and capital. Because he did not view the problem as simply a foreign one, the Cleveland minister repudiated immigration restriction on the ground that the United States had no right or power to cut off the flow of newcomers into the country.[42]

But events of nationwide import shortly dissipated the views of Dowling and those like him among Baptists. In May, 1886, Chicago police killed one workman and wounded others while restoring order during a strike at the McCormick Harvester plant. Anarchists and various radicals called for a mass meeting in Haymarket Square, where a policeman died after someone threw a bomb. By the time the ensuing melee had subsided, more than a hundred persons lay dead or injured. Seven of the eight anarchists put on trial for murder were convicted and sentenced to death, even though no evidence connected them with the bombing.[43]

Baptists joined in the hysteria that swept the country, which presently tended to equate fear of radicalism with fear of the

---

[41] Editorial: "The Socialism of Today," *Examiner*, LXI (May 8, 1884), 1.

[42] George T. Dowling, "Capital and Labor," *Standard*, XXXII (July 30, 1885), 2.

[43] The standard monograph on the Haymarket riot is Henry David, *The History of the Haymarket Affair* (New York, 1936).

immigrant. At its annual meeting in the same month as the Haymarket riot, the Home Mission Society dropped the optimistic statements of previous years in favor of an ominous warning that socialist and anarchist ideas brought by foreigners might swamp American institutions. The belief of Willard Boyd and Daniel Potter that radicalism originated abroad came alive; George Dowling's analysis of an unjust economic system was now submerged under angry feelings. Events in Chicago had convinced officials of the Baptist denomination that immigrant leaders hostile to Christian civilization had whipped up the foreign populace to fever heat. Where once churchmen had pointed to the gospel's recognition of the rights of the poor and toiling, they now emphasized the duties of the citizen. Dowling had used the Christian doctrine of the equality of capitalists and laborers to call attention to the needs of the latter and the obligation of the former. In the light of Haymarket, the Home Mission Society set forth the dilemma of employers and the responsibilities of those who worked for them. Even so, its official statement in 1886 suggested that only the conversion of the foreigner would strike at the roots of anarchy and industrial warfare. More drastic measures would not do; the answer lay in the more successful promotion of home mission work among immigrants.[44]

The Baptist press, following the general pattern set by other religious and secular newspapers, did not content itself with such moderation. In Chicago the *Standard* praised the conduct of city law officers in the prompt arrest of the Communist plotters who planted the bomb. The happenings in Haymarket Square, it asserted, showed that certain American ideas and institutions were being tested by agitators of the most violent sort who abused the right of free speech. The cause appeared obvious. Oppression in Europe might have brought about socialistic extremism there, but only inherently bad blood could lead individuals to purport such notions in the United States. Chicago officials had undoubtedly erred in permitting socialist processions and meetings on Sundays, and now violence had reared its ugly head. Therefore, the *Standard* demanded swift justice for the

[44] 54th Annual Report, ABHMS (1886), 29–31.

rioters, so they could not make a mockery of the judicial system.[45]

After the trial of the anarchists, the *Standard* rejoiced that the offenders had been shown that this country had no place for them. The convictions proved that their teachings had too serious implications to be regarded as silly outcries. Red and black flags, the doctrine that law was a tyrant and property the result of robbery of the poor, the equation of existing social institutions with oppression—all now seemed a real menace. No longer could these loudmouthed proclaimers of treason, anarchy, and murder be shielded by the argument that their oratory represented "mere sound and fury, signifying nothing." The organ of Chicago Baptists suggested that henceforth malicious and incendiary language, spoken or written, ought to be made a crime against the well-being of society.[46]

Constant references to the events of May, 1886, in Baptist papers for some time revealed the profound effect of the Chicago uprising. In 1887 Professor Eri B. Hulbert of that city warned of the perils of socialism in emotional terms: "Its moderate form tends to its extreme form. In its extreme form it believes in the grossest materialism. It is shockingly blasphemous, being thoroughly atheistic. It aims at the crushing of private property, all authority, the state, the family, the church. It prefers bullets to ballots, and bombs to either. It riots in violence, incendiarism, assassination, revolution and anarchy. It is organized, is arming and drilling, is increasing with alarming rapidity." [47] Influenced by this spirit, Baptists strongly disapproved of efforts to secure pardon for the condemned. Such a reprieve, commented the *Journal and Messenger* of Cincinnati, would cost the lives of many innocent people in the future and make the slaughter of the Chicago policemen the beginning instead of the end of anarchism in the United States. "These criminals are all foreigners, and

45 Editorial: "Communism in the West," *Standard*, XXXIII (May 13, 1886), 4. For the reaction of other denominations, see Lewis F. Wheelock, "Urban Protestant Reactions to the Haymarket Affair, 1886–1893" (Unpublished Ph.D. dissertation, University of Iowa, 1956), 196–236.
46 Editorial: "The Anarchist Trial," *Standard*, XXXIII (Aug. 26, 1886), 4.
47 Hulbert, "Our Peril and Our Defense," 2.

there are hundreds of their kind in Europe waiting for the result," exclaimed the editor. "If the convicted men are pardoned, America will be the paradise of the Anarchist. If executed, the word will go back that America is a no more hopeful field than Europe." The hanging of these unfortunates for their first assault on society was deemed necessary to avoid further attacks. The *Journal and Messenger* made no attempt to ascertain if the men in question were actually responsible for the bomb-throwing at Haymarket. Prevention as well as punishment required the taking of their lives; such was the extent of the hysteria.[48]

While segments of several other denominations showed restraint despite the ferocity of the religious press,[49] among Baptists the rising tide of emotion seemed to engulf all in its path. The Women's Baptist Home Mission Society of Chicago, usually sympathetic to the immigrant, now criticized citizens who grew sentimental as the execution of the agitators drew near. Those who had compassion for these wretches, said the normally docile Baptist ladies, had forgotten the scores of law officers injured by their bombs. The anarchist lovers failed to realize that all the world watched and respected America for the "guilty" verdict handed down in Chicago. As a rebuke to those who favored pardon for the accused, the Baptist women of that city offered a quotation from Count von Bismarck: "The blubbering sentimentality of the nineteenth century, which beholds a martyr in every fanatical rebel, and in every hireling a barricade fighter would, in the end, occasion more bloodshed than a stern and resolute justice practiced from the beginning." [50]

As a result of the Haymarket affair, one Baptist paper recognized that some restriction of immigration might be desirable.

[48] Editorial: *Journal and Messenger*, LVI (Sept. 22, 1887), 1.

[49] Wheelock, "Urban Protestant Reactions to the Haymarket Affair," 237–312. Wheelock shows how some individual clergymen distributed blame for the Haymarket uprising on the general community, not just labor, and a few discerned that the condemned were victims of legal injustice. He stresses the importance of separating the views of the religious press from official denominational statements and individual sermons. But among Baptists an intense reaction against the anarchists pervades the various home mission societies as well as the religious papers.

[50] Statement of Women's Baptist Home Mission Society, quoted in *Baptist Home Mission Monthly*, IX (Dec., 1887), 320–321.

Pointing to the discovery of a conspiracy to kill two of the judges involved in the trial of the radicals, the *Examiner* urged the taking of protective measures against dynamiters and their fiendish plots. The time had clearly come for the United States to shut out such worthless creatures, who arrived daily in large numbers. The *Examiner* lauded a proposed bill to have the federal inspectors at major ports return anarchists and dangerous persons to the country of origin, with imprisonment the penalty for a second attempt to reach American shores.[51]

Several years later, when Governor John P. Altgeld of Illinois pardoned the three alleged inciters of the Haymarket riot who were yet in prison, Baptist spokesmen united with other Protestants in widespread condemnation of his action. If the foreign criminals carried out their promise to remain aloof from radical associations and gave up the idea of turning the world upside down, then executive clemency would have no evil effect. But in broader perspective, said the *Standard,* such an act might encourage anarchist movements in America and elsewhere and thus weaken, if not destroy, the moral effect of the original punishment of the Chicago offenders. The Boston *Watchman* claimed that Altgeld exemplified the worst tendencies in political life, hostility to law and domestic institutions. Because the beliefs of the Illinois governor closely paralleled those of communism, charged this paper, he was living proof that certain immigrants had remained unassimilated and continued to resist American ideas. Two Chicago sermons by Baptist ministers reinforced the judgment that the religious press made of Altgeld's pardon.[52]

After Haymarket most of the optimistic pronouncements on immigration disappeared from Baptist periodicals. The only Baptists who continued to look upward were those who had worked out theories of God's providential design for America as contingent upon the gathering of nations here, or immigrant

[51] Editorial: "Anarchism and Immigration," *Examiner,* LXXII (Aug. 9, 1894), 1. See also "Anarchy Lifts Its Head," *ibid.,* LXV (July 26, 1888), 1.

[52] "The Pardon of the Anarchists" (editorial), *Standard,* XL (July 6, 1893), 4; "The Present Peril" (editorial), *Watchman,* LXXVII (July 9, 1896), 7; Wheelock, "Urban Protestant Reactions to the Haymarket Affair," 246–247.

pastors who defended their countrymen to native Americans. Confident Anglo-Saxonism, which envisaged a master race arising out of the cosmopolitan melting pot, gave way to fear that the new components of the mixture would ruin the end result. Baptist clergymen who showed too great a degree of sympathy for the alien and the workingman either went about their business quietly or left the denomination. George Dowling, for one, became an Episcopal priest in 1895. Philip Moxom, at once skeptical of the foreigner and a friend of the laboring man, cast in his lot with the Congregationalists.

The belief that Divine Providence had sent millions of newcomers to the shores of North America, though shaken by the Haymarket riot, remained in scattered corners of Protestant thought through the end of the decade, along with occasional attestations of faith in spiritual solutions to the immigration problem.[53] Events in Chicago in 1886, however, accentuated tendencies to question this approach already present among Baptists before the fateful bomb-throwing. The "dregs of society" theory, which viewed foreign radicals and Catholics alike as a menace to American life, had been well enunciated since the beginning of the 1880s; its roots were deep in the nation's history. The challenge to this idea, which rested on confidence in the ability of American culture and religion to remake all who came here, fell mortally wounded with the dead in Haymarket Square. Whether denominational spokesmen regarded the immigrant as friend or foe, most of them in the eighties offered their interpretation of the gospel as an answer so adequate that restriction was not necessary. But now, under the influence of their own opposition to Catholicism and socialism, they began to rethink even that most basic premise of the Protestant tradition.

[53] See P. A. Schwarz, "Should Immigration Be Restricted?" *Church at Home and Abroad*, II (Aug., 1887), 135–136; "Our Immigrant Population," *ibid.*, IV (Aug., 1888), 133–134; and George F. McAfee, "Perils of Immigration," *ibid.*, XV (Mar., 1894), 221–223. The latter article came at a relatively late date for acceptance of the providential view.

$\mathbf{A}$s the nineteenth century drew to a close, the United States seemed to be entering upon a state of crisis. Many Americans accepted Frederick Jackson Turner's assertion that the year 1890 saw the passing of the western frontier, thus ending a whole cycle of American history. Although only 40 percent of the population of the United States lived in towns of over 4,000 in 1900, the national trend toward urbanization had begun. In an age of big business that witnessed the concentration of wealth in fewer and fewer hands, large numbers of people considered themselves among the dispossessed. The immigrant flood into the cities, especially in the East, continued without abatement, swelling the ranks of the unemployed. Both the urban workers and the farmers of the West and South were caught in what appeared to be a squeeze between corporations and the boom-and-bust cycle. Strikes, economic depression, and farm revolt added up to what one historian has described as "the psychic crisis of the 1890s."[1] For a variety of reasons, neither city laborer nor tiller of the soil could unite effectively enough to drive the business class from the seat of federal power. The defeat of William Jennings Bryan in the election of 1896 caused many of his followers to lose hope that their myriad needs would ever be met, and despair gripped large segments of the nation's population.

[1] Richard Hofstadter, "Manifest Destiny and the Philippines," in Daniel Aaron, *America in Crisis* (New York, 1952), 173–200.

Frustration in the 1890s was not confined to groups with economic grievances. The Protestant churches gradually began to grasp the full significance of the rise of the city, the alienation of workingmen from religion, and the problems of the day. Baptists had sponsored an unofficial annual forum, "The Baptist Congress for the Discussion of Current Questions," beginning in 1882. Social issues were often included in the program of the congress, which provided a sounding board for men destined to become the leaders of social Christianity—Walter Rauschenbusch, Leighton Williams, Samuel Zane Batten, Charles R. Henderson, and Philip S. Moxom.[2] With awareness, however, sometimes came fear; with enthusiasm for the Christianization of society came a hatred of anything that would prevent this goal. Corporations that stood in the way of a decent life for the individual brought down the curses of some clergymen, while others fiercely defended respect for law and insisted upon homage to the status quo. Immigrants whose religion was anathema to virtually all Protestants at this time had to be converted to the dominant American faith, or the vision of the most spiritual civilization would never come to fruition. Failure in efforts to win the stranger would for a season lead to aggressive demands to shut him out. The changing mind of the Baptists in this era, with all its inner tensions, is one significant ray from the Protestant prism.

The conflicts of Baptist thought determined their response to immigration in the 1890s. Reverend Edward Brooks expressed a dichotomy in the Anglo-Saxon dream when he spoke of the role of different races in the "wonderful development" of the United States as "the first and foremost . . . seat of enterprise for the world's conversion and the lifting of the nations up to God" and in the next breath stated that the chief enemy of this mission came from the hundreds of "degraded foreigners" now arriving.[3] One Baptist journal could condemn the action of management in the Homestead strike of 1892 in the most vocifer-

[2] Hopkins, *Rise of the Social Gospel in American Protestantism*, 112.
[3] Edward H. Brooks, "An Outlook upon the Nation," *Standard*, XLI (Aug. 2, 1894), 2.

ous terms, claiming that "if capital is justified in hiring men
. . . to force the measures of capital, then labor is justified in
resort to armed force."[4] Another could uphold a sheriff in
Pennsylvania who fired upon a group of striking Hungarian coal
miners on the basis that "he was the representative of the law,
confronted by an infuriated mob of half-civilized foreigners bent
on violating the law." The latter editor himself revealed an inner
conflict that was characteristic of his denomination: he sympathized with those cruelly wronged and oppressed, like the miners
in question, but insisted that the interests of society required that
the "majesty of the law be upheld."[5] Clergymen who had qualms
of social conscience began, timidly at first, to suggest legislation
as a possible solution to the nation's problems. A Baptist who
spent much of his life in the mining towns of Pennsylvania attempted to balance the denominational emphasis on the responsibility of an individual for his own fate with the newer demands
for social action to relieve distress. "Let [the minister] look with
clear moral insight into . . . the eternal moral questions of capital and labor, and all others," advised Reverend John S. Wrightnour in 1896. The modern clergyman, he felt, ought not to stay
"in the scented seclusion of his church on a quiet street" but
should make his voice heard in the marketplaces. He should see
that "right laws" were made, but since legislation never changed
the hearts of men, the man of God should not enter into political
combinations but should preach the gospel along with practical
efforts to alleviate human suffering.[6]

Immigration related to all of these tensions. Hostile foreigners
endangered Anglo-Saxon Protestant civilization. The babel of
strange tongues pervaded every violent labor dispute. The immigrant seemed at the center of urban problems, which needed the
attention of the church. Many Americans, perceiving the change
in the origins of immigration, began to share a growing conviction that the natives of northern and western European countries

[4] *Pacific Baptist*, XVI (July 14, 1892), 1; XVIII (Apr. 19, 1894), 1.
[5] *Examiner*, LXXV (Sept. 16, 1897), 1. See also *Journal and Messenger*,
LXVI (Aug. 26, 1897), 1.
[6] John S. Wrightnour, "The Relation of the Pastor to the Social Problems
of the Day," *Standard*, XLIII (Feb. 1, 1896), 4.

were inherently better than those who now arrived from southern and eastern Europe. Influenced in part by the "scientific" race thinkers who propounded biological theories of inferiority,[7] Baptists gradually enunciated a distinct standard upon which to judge the worth of the various nationalities. All agreed that as a child of God, every immigrant deserved a presentation of the pure gospel. But what if he should refuse to convert to the truth of evangelical Protestantism? Did not such a rejection of spiritual Christianity indicate some basic deficiency of character? Clearly the time had come for a full consideration of immigration and related issues by the denomination.

A universal starting point for Protestants in any discussion of the foreign influx centered upon the widespread hatred of Catholicism. As the eighties merged into the nineties, disdain for the Church of Rome filled the hearts of "liberal" and "conservative" alike, of the minority group of social gospelers and the majority of Baptists who preached an individual gospel. This rather common feature of the American tradition once again united with anti-foreignism to form an insistent nativism, and the fear of Romanism helped lead Baptists to advocate shutting out those newcomers who revealed a fundamental inadequacy by clinging to the faith of their fathers. The prevalent habit of attributing "that which is great and good in our nation and its institutions to the spirit and enterprise of Protestantism" [8] made the arrival of large numbers of Catholics all the more alarming. Apprehension of the power of Rome now became overwhelming, and as Protestantism began to doubt its own viability, governmental barriers seemed the only solution.[9]

It was not always thus. For the many Protestant denunciations of Catholicism in the eighties, there were answers designed to

---

[7] For a brief discussion of the major thinkers in this school, see Higham, *Strangers in the Land*, 149–157.

[8] "Romanists and Foreigners," *Church at Home and Abroad*, XVII (Aug., 1895), 112.

[9] For examples of the attitude toward Catholicism in other denominations, see M. M. G. Dana, "Our Immigrants," *Congregationalist*, LXV (June 30, 1880), 1; "Romanists and Foreigners," *Church at Home and Abroad*, XIV (Aug., 1893), 118–120; "Romanists and Foreigners," *ibid.*, XVI (Aug., 1894), 132–134; and "Romanists and Foreigners," *ibid.*, XVII (Aug., 1895), 112–114.

allay misgivings. Romanism could not retain its ancient character and so dominate the nation in the free atmosphere of America, the anti-immigrant *Journal and Messenger* assured its readers in 1881. Catholic children who grew up in the midst of a pre-eminent, progressive, liberty-loving Protestant culture could not fail to imbibe at least some of its religious and political ideals.[10] Contacts with Protestantism made American Catholics superior to their brethren in other countries by elevating their intelligence and piety, agreed Reverend Norman Fox in 1885. The Roman Catholic creed contained all the "fundamentals of salvation," he admitted, and a confrontation with Protestant civilization would make easier the removal of "error" with which that creed was "smothered." [11] A Presbyterian colleague added his belief that Romanism could not endure a healthy voyage across the ocean because of the ability of the North American environment to reduce its effectiveness.[12] Encouraged by such expressions of confidence, the *Examiner* as late as 1889 boasted that Catholicism would never fulfill its goal of becoming the state church in this country. The second and third generations of its immigrants would probably desert their religion, and attempts to unite church and state by law would meet a solid opposition of all non-Catholic citizens. In short, the fear of Rome was "an imaginary danger." [13]

In the mid-eighties, however, the Catholic church took a step that again brought down the wrath of the usual critics upon its head. Pointing to the domination of public school boards by Protestants and apprehension about the faith of youngsters who attended, the Third Plenary Council of Bishops in 1884 made attendance at parochial institutions virtually mandatory for Catholics. The church thus determined to supervise the education of its native and immigrant children alike; the generation for which Protestants had such hopes was to be removed from a

10 "Protestantism and Popery," *Journal and Messenger,* L (Sept. 28, 1881), 3.
11 Norman Fox, "Our Romanist Neighbors," *Baptist Home Mission Monthly,* VII (Nov., 1885), 278–279.
12 Charles S. Pomeroy, "Is Romanism Overwhelming Us?" *Church at Home and Abroad,* II (July, 1887), 28–31.
13 Editorial: "An Imaginary Danger," *Examiner,* LXVI (Mar. 21, 1889), 4.

traditional American institution, the common school.[14] In the face of such a threat to the future of the nation, Baptists and others readied themselves for the frontal assault on the "Scarlet Beast of the Apocalypse." When the first lines of attack failed, they called upon the federal government to keep out the unwanted, adapting theories that posited the racial inferiority of southern and eastern Europeans to their own desires to retain the dominance of Protestant culture and ideals in the United States.

Daniel C. Eddy, pastor of First Baptist Church of Brooklyn and a former Know-Nothing representative to the Massachusetts legislature in 1854, bridged the gap between the old nativism and the new in a speech to the Baptist Home Mission Society in 1889. In the wake of an extended discussion on Romanism by the Baptist Congress, he described the two rival flags that waved over the continent: one inscribed "North America for Christ," the other "North America for Rome." Before the European powers had recognized the United States, he explained, the Vatican had plotted to convert all Protestants here—to turn descendants of the Puritans into defenders of the papacy. But the plan miscarried; Bible-educated Christians saw and escaped the trap. Refusing to give up its ambitions, now the church sent huge numbers of the faithful of Europe to gain control of the land of the free. To Eddy, immigration thus fostered Rome's subversive designs:

The hope of the Catholic Church to overthrow our common-school system and substitute the parochial system is based on immigration! The expectation of Rome to subjugate our liberties and control our government is founded on immigration! The determination of the church of Rome to capture our great cities, those centres of life and power, rests on immigration! The plans of the Vatican, the efforts of the propaganda to make this a Roman Catholic country, are inspired by the immensity of immigration! Our dangers as a free people, dangers against which the wisest men of the world have warned us, spring from immigration.[15]

[14] John Tracy Ellis, *American Catholicism* (Chicago, 1955), 102.
[15] Daniel C. Eddy, "Immigration," *Baptist Home Mission Monthly*, XI (Sept., 1889), 247–252.

Although Eddy's papal plot was reminiscent of mid-century nativism and foreshadowed its resurgence in the 1890s, his solution to the problem clearly belonged to the Baptist attitude of the 1880s. Only the gospel could save America from Rome. The influx was bound to continue. Because the day for legislation had passed fifty years before and such a remedy would not convert the Catholic, Eddy rejected immigration restriction. He agreed to the modification of naturalization laws in order to make intelligence a factor in the qualification for citizenship and to restrict the leadership of the nation to the native-born, and he endorsed the exclusion of paupers and criminals. But beyond this he would not go: to send back the stranger would be un-American. To bar the oppressed of any land was inconsistent with national traditions: "Tramps and vagabonds may be beaten back by the policeman's club, but immigration must continue without regard to race, nationality, or religion." In spite of his intense anti-foreign and anti-Catholic feelings, Eddy had not yet found the answer in a law singling out the Catholic elements of southern and eastern Europe for discriminatory treatment. It remained for other Baptists to seek such a solution a few years hence.[16]

Throughout the 1890s many Baptist leaders followed a Protestant pattern of thought similar to that of Daniel Eddy's description of the nature and purposes of the Catholic church. Thomas Jefferson Morgan, editor of the *Baptist Home Mission Monthly*, in 1894 expressed his belief that Catholicism and Americanism were incompatible. Former Commissioner of Indian Affairs and an active member of the American Protective Association, Morgan showed how traditional freedoms—of speech, of the press, of the ballot—were at war with the Roman hierarchy and its centralized power, rigid organization, and de-

[16] *Ibid.* A year earlier William M. Haigh, superintendent of home missions for the Mississippi Division, had voiced similar apprehensions. After making all wise allowances, he noted, incoming foreigners were for the most part out of sympathy with the religion and religious ideas that were fundamental in American life. "Romanism," he asked, "what is it but largely a question concerning the foreign population?" Like Eddy, he rejected immigration restriction except for that of criminals and paupers as neither possible nor politic, holding that "only the Gospel is the ultimate answer" (William M. Haigh, "Our Present Peril," *Baptist Home Mission Monthly*, X [Feb., 1888], 28–31).

mands for obedience to authority over conscience. As proof of the antagonism of the papacy to the American republic, Morgan accused Romanism of taking millions of dollars from the nation's treasury to propagate itself. The church had put forth candidates for all possible offices, formed secret coalitions, promoted bossism to perpetuate and extend its political influence, and manipulated primaries and state and national conventions. It had attempted to defame the public schools in order to get government support for parochial institutions. But now a number of patriotic organizations, among them the American Protective Association, were at last combating this menace. Morgan praised this "renaissance of patriotism" and urged anti-Catholic groups to unite in a single agency "for the protection of our common schools; resistance to the encroachments of foreigners; the restriction of immigration; the reform of our naturalization laws; the purification of politics; the prohibition of sectarian appropriations; and the absolute separation of Church and State." [17] Before he finished his indictment, Morgan held Catholicism responsible for the social unrest of the 1890s, pointing to the Catholic saloon keepers and a priest who had supported the Pullman strikers as evidence of a causal relationship between Romanism and domestic violence.[18]

Dwight Spencer, the formulator of the theory of America's divine mission, agreed with Eddy and Morgan that the current influx of immigration was part of a papal conspiracy to subjugate the United States. The man who in 1887 had so clearly discerned the beneficial effects of the infusion of many nationalities into the Anglo-Saxon race had by 1895 serious second thoughts, based exclusively on a fear of Rome. Looking at the cities, Spencer loathed the foreign sabbath, with its early mass followed by drunken revelry, and was horrified that an "army of foreign priests parade the streets with rosaries and crosses, with

[17] Thomas J. Morgan, "Renaissance of Patriotism," *Baptist Home Mission Monthly*, XVI (June, 1894), 185–187. Morgan's mention of "sectarian appropriations" clearly referred to the Indian Department's use of federal funds for Catholic mission schools.

[18] Thomas J. Morgan, "Romanism and Rioting," *Baptist Home Mission Monthly*, XVI (Aug., 1894), 316–317. For a similar view fourteen years earlier, see C. H. Kimball, "Western Work," *Standard*, XXVII (Feb. 12, 1880), 2. See also the *Pacific Baptist*, XVI (Dec. 1, 1892), 1.

unblushing insolence in the faces of plain American worship-
pers." He, too, was apprehensive of political as well as moral
implications: "Servile tools of this Romish priesthood plant
their saloons upon every street corner, and locate their beer
gardens under the very shadows of Protestant houses of worship, and use the enormous profits to fill the treasury of this
foreign church. Millions of dollars of taxes paid by Protestants
have been seized by the greedy army of office holders, and
used to make converts to the church of Rome." [19] Like Morgan,
Spencer lauded the increase of patriotism and greater concern
for evangelism by which Protestants were responding to this
situation. Faced with these two forces, the "foreign octopus"
might not be able to fasten itself upon the United States any
longer. While Spencer did not mention immigration restriction,
as did Morgan, the picture he painted surely suggested it.[20]

Nowhere were Baptist anti-Catholic and nativist sentiments
so pronounced as in connection with their work with the French
Canadians of New England. Although this operation never
constituted a major part of the Home Mission Society's activities in terms of monetary expense, the frustration encountered
in attempts to convert these people precipitated much of the
gloom that pervaded the organization in the 1890s. French
Canadian opposition to Protestant ideas also hastened Baptist
acceptance of the notion that certain white ethnic groups were
basically inferior to others. Thousands of the inhabitants of
Quebec migrated to the United States between 1865 and 1900,
where they furnished much of the labor for various industries in
the mill towns. They early drew the attention of the Home
Mission Society, where speakers described the "very bigoted"
Catholics whose spiritual leaders had openly proclaimed their
mission to subdue New England to papal authority. In one of
the society's meetings as early as 1880, long before anti-Catholicism became rampant among Baptists, a missionary quoted the
words of one priest to his flock: "Providence has sent you here

---

[19] Dwight Spencer, "Divine Adjustments," *Baptist Home Mission Monthly*,
XVII (Sept., 1895), 334-336.
[20] *Ibid.*

to do, in New England, what you have so generally done in Canada, to bring everything into subjection to our Holy Father the Pope." [21] Repeatedly over the next twenty years Baptists accused the French Canadian clergy of urging American citizenship upon their people so they could vote and thus get a share of public educational funds for parochial schools. Every year alarmists warned the annual meeting of the Home Mission Society that a foreign Catholic invasion would debase New England life, corrupt politics, increase crime and intemperance, and boycott non-Catholic businesses. Because French Canadians were reportedly a most prolific race, Baptists feared that they would outnumber the descendants of the Pilgrims more readily than had the earlier influx of Irish immigrants, and both groups would soon threaten to oust Protestants from positions of prominence and power.[22]

Baptist efforts to evangelize the newcomers from Canada revolved around the career of the Home Mission Society's director of this work from 1873 to 1915, James N. Williams, who personified the spirit so evident in many missionaries working under him. Born in Quebec in 1829, Williams studied Catholicism in detail under former priests at the Protestant Grand Ligne Mission and learned still more about the church at Rochester Theological Seminary. As pastor of the St. Helen Street Baptist congregation in Montreal, the young Williams debated with Catholic clergymen with such success that the local bishop forbade his priests to have further encounters. In the mid-1860s, while publishing a French-language Protestant newspaper in that city, he visited the United States and soon emigrated to preach among a group of French immigrants living in Stryker, Ohio. Many of these people from the northeastern provinces of France disliked the unfamiliar Baptist sect and its apostle, and at first only two families supported Williams by providing the necessities of life. His appeal to the Ohio Baptist State Con-

---

[21] James N. Williams, "French Canadians in New England," *Baptist Home Mission Monthly*, II (Feb., 1880), 25–27. The date of this article is significant, for the intense anti-Catholicism of the 1890s was portrayed much earlier in this one area as Baptists came into contact with French Canadians.

[22] *Ibid.*; 64th Annual Report, ABHMS (1896), 18, 92–100; C. E. Ameson, "The Work of French Evangelization in New England," *Baptist Home Mission Monthly*, IX (Oct., 1887), 262.

vention was successful, but after two years the discouraged missionary left Stryker for Chicago. An unsolicited letter offering appointment as the Baptist Home Mission Society's evangelist among the French Canadians in New England began in 1873 a long relationship that terminated only upon his death.[23]

Williams at first adopted the circuit idea of preaching, visiting monthly the cities of Lowell, Salem, Haverhill, Fall River, Worcester, Providence, and Woonsocket. He evidently made a few converts, for the number of Canadian immigrant missionaries sponsored by the Home Mission Society grew from five in 1883 to fifteen in 1890, all of whom had French names except their leader. By the mid-1890s, when this work reached its high-water mark, these Baptist clergymen resided in or visited regularly Lynn, Marlboro, Lowell, and Boston in addition to those places where Williams had begun his ministry. Outside of Massachusetts, French-speaking Baptists preached at Waterville, Lewiston, and Biddeford in Maine and at smaller towns in Connecticut, New Hampshire, and Rhode Island. Even the far-off coal region near Pittsburgh, where immigrant miners had settled, had a Baptist emissary who spoke the language heard on the streets of Paris. Financing of these activities came not only from the Home Mission Society but in some cases from the Baptist state conventions in the states involved. Throughout the 1890s the Newton Theological Seminary maintained a French Department for the training of missionaries, which ceased to operate only when the results of the work diminished at the end of the decade.[24]

Everywhere, according to Williams's testimony, Catholic religious leaders obstructed Baptist efforts by intimidating their congregations from attending Protestant meetings. The "gospel wagon," a carriage that served as a pulpit for preaching and a

---

[23] Biographical information on Williams is found in Walter S. Stewart, *Later Baptist Missionaries and Pioneers*, 2 vols. (Philadelphia, 1928–29), I, 35–61. The fact that Williams appears in this volume, whose early section included such notables as Adoniram Judson, indicates the high esteem in which he was held both throughout his lifetime and after his death.

[24] Various annual reports of the ABHMS: 51st (1883), 44; 55th (1887), 58; 56th (1888), 64–65; 57th (1889), 50–51; 58th (1890), 52–54; 59th (1891), 48–49; 60th (1892), 64–65; 61st (1893), 63–66; 62nd (1894), 87–88, 91–92; 63rd (1895), 99–107; 67th (1899), 90–99. Most of these reports were written by Williams.

storehouse for tracts and Bibles distributed from house to house, was the object of much derision. When a former priest aided Williams during meetings at Putnam, Connecticut, in 1874, the outbuildings of the home where both were staying burned to the ground, and the missionary's account left little doubt about who was responsible.[25] Years later flying eggs greeted an evangelist giving an outdoor sermon at Waltham, Massachusetts. In Danielsonville, Connecticut, a riot nearly erupted in the course of a Baptist worship service. Members of the crowd there threw eggs, sticks, and stones and heckled the speakers with hisses and insults. Mobs sometimes attacked the missionaries, followed by arrests of unruly individuals. Baptists reported these incidents of hatred and violence each year in the national organizations and described boycotts initiated upon the orders of priests against Catholic businessmen who became Protestants.[26] Williams told his colleagues in the Home Mission Society that "it requires iron-clad courage and almost iron-clad throats to labor amidst the dangers and din of such gatherings of ignorant and prejudiced masses." [27]

Smarting from such opposition, the letters of French Canadian Baptist evangelists to the society are replete with stories designed to illustrate the "hateful features" of Catholicism. Gideon Aubin of Fall River, Massachusetts, asked, "If Romanism is not Paganism, what is it?" As evidence that the two were synonymous, Aubin recounted how a priest once advised a sick woman to eat small pictures of the Virgin Mary if she desired to recover. In another instance a clergyman allegedly forced the parents of a Catholic girl who converted to Protestantism to close their door to her because she refused to return to the church. The Baptist observer concluded, "The priest is the cause of that savage and unnatural conduct of her parents." [28]

[25] Stewart, *Later Baptist Missionaries and Pioneers*, I, 35–61.
[26] "Rampant Romanism in New England," *Baptist Home Mission Monthly*, XVII (Sept., 1895), 344–345; Henry L. Morehouse, "Baptist Mission to the French in the United States," *ibid.*, XV (Dec., 1893), 407–412.
[27] 62nd Annual Report, ABHMS (1894), 87–88.
[28] Letter of Gideon Aubin, in *Baptist Home Mission Monthly*, IV (Dec., 1882), 327; Gideon Aubin, "Evangelization of Romanists," *ibid.*, XVIII (Apr., 1896), 134–135.

To win people away from such an "evil" religion, Aubin wrote and distributed 5,000 copies of a tract entitled "Lectures on the Principal Doctrines of the Roman Catholic Church." This pamphlet criticized such Catholic beliefs as transubstantiation, the worship of Mary, confession, purgatory, and the idea of the mass on the ground that these articles of faith were diametrically opposed to the Bible. Proclaiming that "the Church of Mohammed is not more openly and directly at war with God than the Catholic Church," Aubin portrayed Roman Catholics as forever hovering on the brink of the gulf of perdition.[29]

The accounts relating experiences with French Canadian Catholics especially emphasized their hostility to the public schools and to the Scriptures. Reverend J. D. Rossier of Burlington, Vermont, claimed that a priest had forced a family in his parish to return both Catholic and Protestant copies of the Bible that Rossier had left with them. James Williams reported a tale of two boys who were made to kneel in penance for two hours as punishment for obedience to their father's command to attend a public school. A similar act on the part of another parent brought a refusal of the priest to instruct his children in religion and advice to the wife to leave her husband if he did not remove the youngster from the secular institution. Whether or not such stories were exaggerated is not as important as the fact that Williams and others wrote and spoke repeatedly about them. The effects must have impressed the wide audience of Baptists who read and listened to these variations on the anti-Catholic theme.[30]

One influential Baptist leader who listened to Williams gradually began to accept a theory of racial superiority that demanded immigration restriction. Henry L. Morehouse, for many

[29] *Ibid.*; Gideon Aubin, "French Evangelization, the Importance and Promise of This Work," *Baptist Home Mission Monthly*, VII (Aug., 1895), 199–203.

[30] Letter of J. D. Rossier, in *Baptist Home Mission Monthly*, IV (Feb., 1882), 51; James N. Williams, "What I Know about Romanism," *ibid.*, II (Dec., 1880), 239–240. In fairness to Williams, it must be emphasized that the feelings of hatred between Baptists and Catholics were mutual; the Baptist reaction did not occur in a vacuum but was in part brought about by the hostility of Catholic immigrants that Williams described.

years the distinguished secretary of the Home Mission Society and one of the architects of the Northern Baptist Convention, expressed alarm over the French Canadian problem in 1896. Experience had indeed shown that "they were the most bigoted and ignorant Roman Catholics, almost inaccessible to evangelical efforts and persecutors of missionaries and converts to our belief." These people, who now overran New England, thus threatened to lower the quality of the native American stock. Morehouse began to make the distinction that was becoming popular in the 1890s: while the Swedes and Germans were generally "desirable," the French Canadians were not. This latter group, he claimed, proved themselves very inferior to New England–born citizens—in physical strength, in intellect, and in moral and religious ideals of manhood, civilization, and Christianity. Until the present, contact with Americans had changed them for the better, but now the danger arose that they would adversely affect white Protestant culture.[31]

Like Baptist writers and thinkers of the eighties, Morehouse proposed that the evangelical gospel could save both souls and civilization from undemocratic and un-American Roman Catholicism, by which foreigners "spread a creeping paralysis over the land." But now this was not enough. The Baptist leader quickly added that Senator Henry Cabot Lodge wisely advocated restricted immigration to counter the possibility of a great and perilous change in the fabric of the American race. Over twenty years of negligible progress in converting French Canadians, as enunciated annually by exasperated missionaries, had somewhat dimmed the optimism of the Home Mission Society and its field secretary about the plan of providence. Now Morehouse easily placed these "bigoted and ignorant Catholics" in Lodge's category of undesirable ethnic groups, with refusal to convert to Protestantism the chief criterion of inferiority. Where Baptists in 1881 could envisage the citizens of France joining in a spiritual rebirth as the result of Protestant success

[31] Henry L. Morehouse, "New England's Duty," *Baptist Home Mission Monthly*, XVIII (May, 1896), 154–160; report of Morehouse in 64th Annual Report, ABHMS (1896), 112–113.

with their countrymen in the New World, by the mid-1890s such hopes had cooled, and the atmosphere of gloom pervading the Home Mission Society led its secretary to advocate restriction.[32]

Late nineteenth-century anti-Catholicism culminated in the American Protective Association, which reached its zenith about 1893. Requiring its members to pledge never to vote for any Catholic for public office, the APA blamed current social and industrial unrest on subversive papal designs and warned of Rome's influence in politics. The most prominent Baptist who joined this organization, Thomas J. Morgan, won its approval in 1889 when, as President Harrison's Indian Commissioner, he sought to end the federal policy under which church missionaries operated Indian schools through annual contracts with the government. Catholics involved in such missions bitterly attacked Morgan, and some even held him responsible for Harrison's defeat in 1892. Because anti-Catholics regarded Cleveland's victory as a blow to their cause and a triumph for "political Romanism," Morgan soon became the darling of the APA press, which now turned the cessation of government appropriations for Indian contract schools into a rallying cry. Only moderately anti-Catholic before his service under Harrison, he now joined the organization and described his experiences with Catholics before widespread audiences.[33] John Quincy Adams Henry, another Baptist lecturer for the APA, addressed as many as 2,000 persons at a time on the West Coast and became editor of the San Francisco *American Patriot*. Henry's extreme denunciations of Catholicism, together with those of Baptist former priest Joseph Slattery in the Bay area, called forth criticism by clergymen both within and without the denomination.[34]

The Baptist reaction to the American Protective Association varied from outright condemnation of its goals and methods to

[32] *Ibid.* See also 49th Annual Report, ABHMS (1881), 21.

[33] Donald L. Kinzer, *An Episode in Anti-Catholicism: The American Protective Association* (Seattle, 1964), 74–79, 99, 108–110.

[34] *Ibid.;* "Anti-Romanism," *Pacific Baptist*, XVIII (Apr. 12, 1894), 2.

actual endorsement of the organization. Its pattern does not sustain assertion by the historian of the association that support usually came from "fundamentalist" ministers and opposition from many other Protestants.[35] The *Examiner* of New York City, then conservative and for many years the major organ of Baptist fundamentalism after its merger with the *Watchman* in 1913, characterized the APA in 1894 as the one secret organization "against which we should set our faces as a flint." This paper affirmed that every Baptist ought to reject the APA because its principles were hostile to the New Testament, to the spirit of Christ, and to the fundamental law of the land. No one could join without repudiating the traditional Baptist concern for the equal liberty of all men in matters of religion. The APA might be justly alarmed by the aggressions of Romanism, the *Examiner* admitted, but its remedy was an equally intolerant and persecuting Protestantism. The program of placing Protestants in political office, moreover, flatly contradicted the prohibition of religious tests by the federal and state constitutions. In short, the APA's prejudicial oath regarding voting and the employment of Catholics smacked of the Inquisition and the spirit of the devil in its pretended zeal of pure religion.[36]

The *Pacific Baptist*, most proximate to the West Coast rantings of Morgan, Henry, and Slattery, issued a more qualified criticism of the American Protective Association than the *Examiner*'s. The Portland journal refused to countenance unlimited vituperation and intemperate malediction even against Catholicism, and it warned that fanatical methods would defeat the APA's goals. But the organization's purposes of protecting

[35] Kinzer, *An Episode in Anti-Catholicism*, 86–87, 97–98, 244–245. Kinzer uses the term "fundamentalism" even though it was not in use in the 1890s. Then one might have spoken of a "conservative" or "orthodox" Baptist, but only in the 1920s did the word "fundamentalist" become well known.
[36] Editorial: "Anti-American, Anti-Christian, Anti-Baptist," *Examiner*, LXXII (May 3, 1894), 4. The *Examiner* especially objected to the pledge required of APA members not to employ a Roman Catholic when any Protestant was available and not to support the nomination or election of Roman Catholics for office. Here the Baptist principle of the separation of church and state came into operation to prevent a wholesale endorsement of the APA, whose religious test was as odious to Baptists as the alleged Catholic attempts to control the government.

American institutions from the political machinations of the Roman hierarchy were sound: the Catholic church must be held in check by wise legislation against religious interference in the affairs of state. "Will the people and papers in opposition to the American Protective Association," asked the editor, "admit that whatever objectionable features that organization may possess its influence has been positively and mightily in the direction of good government?" Pointing to the corruption of Romanism as a system, as evidenced by its alliances with institutions like Tammany Hall, the paper affirmed that if Catholicism "were eliminated from our politics altogether the largest problems of the day would be solved." Nevertheless, asserted a later editorial, Baptist concern for the public school system ought not to obscure the plausibility of Catholic charges that these institutions were unreligious. Rabid, unrestrained, and unreliable APA statements about the Church of Rome, despite their noble aims, would not effectively combat the real menace.[37]

One of the strongest Baptist endorsements of the association came from Heman L. Wayland, son of Francis Wayland and editor of the *National Baptist* of Philadelphia. In 1894 he denounced critics of anti-Catholic groups: while the Know-Nothings and the APA had possibly used questionable methods, organized opposition to the Roman Catholic church was indeed necessary. The Philadelphia clergyman charged that to equate the APA with the Inquisition and the Star Chamber was reckless and untruthful defamation, because the failure to resist popery allowed the church privileges in such areas as appropriations for Indian mission schools. Wayland professed respect for the rights of Roman Catholics to build churches, convents, and educational institutions and to vote. But those who differed from them had the equal privilege of casting their ballots as a unified body. "I fully believe that the time is coming when everyone who possesses the American spirit," he prophesied, "whether of native or foreign birth, will find himself compelled to stand in opposition, not to the Catholics, but to the

[37] Editorials: *Pacific Baptist*, XVIII (Oct. 18, 1894), 1; (Nov. 15, 1894), 1; (Dec. 13, 1894), 1; XIX (Oct. 31, 1895), 1.

spirit of the Catholic Church." Wayland could not understand why any intelligent and patriotic citizen should object to any of the principles of the APA platform.[38]

Contemporaneously with and in large part because of the rising tide of anti-Catholicism, Baptists began to rethink their position of the 1880s on immigration restriction. In the earlier decade enough Baptists believed in the providential gathering of nations in America to keep them from advocating a closing of the doors. Both the Home Mission Society and the major Baptist papers, except the *Journal and Messenger*, would not consider taking such a step until 1888. The *Watchman* in 1880 urged that Europe be required to take care of its own paupers, criminals, and insane but refused to go further and support any "policy of repression." [39] As late as 1887 the *Standard* appeared gratified that politicians were discussing the immigration problem, but it argued for legislation to encourage the honest immigrant to come to the United States by protecting him from sharpers and monopolists.[40] The *Examiner*, in the same year in which it proposed the exclusion of anarchists, nevertheless rejected any tests of property, education, or political views designed to discriminate among the newcomers. Having opened the gates in recognition of the importance of workmen and artisans in national development, shutting them would not be easy. "Any restriction of immigration beyond fair self-protection would reverse the principles we have always held," noted the paper.[41] The big question obviously was what constituted "fair self-protection," a criterion that became enlarged as time went on.

[38] Heman L. Wayland, "About the A.P.A.," *Watchman*, LXXV (Aug. 9, 1894), 1. While the account of these three commentaries on the APA reveals that Baptist nativism was limited, the criticism of the organization by the two papers indicates not a tolerance of Catholicism but, rather, a realization that the APA was so extreme as to hurt its own cause and was inconsistent with the Baptist reverence for freedom of religion. Both the *Examiner* and the *Pacific Baptist* affirmed either explicitly or implicitly the rightness of opposition to Catholicism, but both disagreed with the methods of the APA.

[39] Editorial: "Foreign Emigration," *Watchman*, LXI (Nov. 25, 1880), 1.

[40] "A Religious Question Become National," *Standard*, XXIV (July 7, 1887), 1.

[41] Editorials: "The Question of Immigration," *Examiner*, LXIV (Dec. 22, 1887), 1; "The Immigration Problem," *ibid.* (July 21, 1887), 1.

In 1888 the Baptist Congress for the Discussion of Current Questions, a nationwide organization, made the first denominational attempt to grapple with this problem since the fiftieth anniversary meeting of the Home Mission Society had spurned immigration restriction in 1882. In the congress's discussion of "The Limits of Immigration," which, significantly, preceded a consideration of "The Political Aspects of Romanism," one of the participants called attention to the change that had taken place since the Baptists had "beat down and overwhelmed poor [Granville] Abbott" six years before.[42] Now more Baptists favored some sort of regulation than opposed it. The keynote speaker, layman John G. Sawyer from Albion, New York, argued persuasively that new conditions called for a modification in immigration policies. He explained that when America was undeveloped, with limitless resources, she needed the assistance of laborers from other countries, but now much agricultural land had been occupied, and an enlarged population could furnish nearly all the helping hands. Sawyer emphasized that he would not prohibit the entry of any person of good character who came here to make his home and who identified with the American way. Because of this, most of his proposals were moderate: exclusion of paupers, criminals, and the insane. But in the concluding portion of his speech the western New Yorker added a criterion of admission that foreshadowed later national feelings: he would shut out any aliens who came from "a country of a lower civilization than our own, whose habits, customs, and modes of life are entirely dissimilar to ours . . . who do not assimilate with our people or become Americanized in feeling or action." While he mentioned only the Chinese as fitting into this category and the Germans and Irish as specifically exempt from it, Sawyer's assertion that "large accession[s] to our population [in] the last few years" were of a "lower civilization" implies that his undesirables were not just Orientals.[43]

A number of Baptists rose to answer Sawyer. Walter Rauschenbusch, as yet the little-known pastor of Second German

[42] E. H. Johnson, in *Baptist Congress Proceedings* (1888), 83.
[43] John G. Sawyer, "Limits of Immigration," *Baptist Congress Proceedings* (1888), 69–74.

Baptist Church in New York City, was convinced that the act of restriction would be basically wrong. "I believe in throwing open this country for all who will come, for I believe God made it for all," he exclaimed. Pointing out that every American derived from foreign ancestry, Rauschenbusch claimed that it was easier for Christians to scorn the stranger abstractly than as an individual. He refused to endorse the most modest barriers, noting that "even the anarchists are a boon to us, for the explosion of a dynamite bomb has set us thinking. We have been turning our attention to social questions in a way we have never done before." [44] Reverend H. A. Delano of Connecticut agreed that to take just one step toward closing the door would confess failure of the republic's traditional assumption that diverse nationalities could be brought together under a single flag. "I believe our government is large enough to take in these [undesirable] classes," he affirmed. The refusal of entrance to anyone, he concluded, would hinder mission work and thus might cause Baptists to miss the God-given opportunity of all the ages of founding a Christian republic encompassing all the peoples of the earth.[45] Two Southern Baptist ministers added their support to Rauschenbusch and Delano, attesting to their great faith in the educational force of free government to lift up all under its beneficence. In the South, they noted, people attempted to promote immigration rather than prevent it. Even if fixing the quality of the influx was justifiable, a general closing of ports would constitute a libel on America's record.[46] Thus two years after Haymarket a few Baptists could still hold the cosmopolitan interpretation of the all-inclusive Anglo-Saxon race.

But Sawyer's supporters had the last word that was denied to Granville Abbott in 1882. If the western New York layman had left any doubt about the specifically inferior races, his ad-

[44] Walter Rauschenbusch, in *Baptist Congress Proceedings* (1888), 86–87.
[45] H. A. Delano, in *Baptist Congress Proceedings* (1888), 80–81.
[46] Henry McDonald (Atlanta) and W. E. Hatcher (Richmond), in *Baptist Congress Proceedings* (1888), 91–92, 94–95. Southern Baptists were always invited to the annual meetings of the Baptist Congress, which was the only forum in which northern and southern members of the denomination conversed together after the schism of the Civil War period.

vocates did not. Professor E. H. Johnson of Crozer Theological Seminary in Chester, Pennsylvania, combined his Anglo-Saxonism with intense nativism, setting the predominant pattern of Baptists and the nation for the next decade. Until recently, he said, the Anglo-Saxon race had absorbed and assimilated other groups, but this could not go on indefinitely. To Johnson, as well as to others present, the melting pot was not amalgamating rapidly enough; therefore, the dregs of society should be denied admission. The foreigners in northern cities threatened to create a race problem as serious as that in the South. With emotion the Crozer professor related his impression upon seeing the undesirables at the port of New York:

I have stood near Castle Garden and seen races of far greater peril to us than the Irish. I have seen the Hungarians, and the Italians and the Poles. I have seen these poor wretches trooping out, wretches physically, wretches mentally, wretches morally, and stood there almost trembling for my country, and said, what shall we do if this thing keeps on? In the name of God, what shall we do if the American race is to receive constant influx of that sort of thing, with such a history as they had had.[47]

Johnson's answer to alleviate this situation was the exclusion of all laboring men who had no handicraft or trade. Long before the Dillingham report of 1907, he accepted the notion that most of the southern and eastern Europeans were unskilled. "On that plan," he was confident, "I can see how we may exclude these fatal Poles, these deadly Hungarians, these murderous and low-lived Italians." In closing, Johnson begged the Baptist Congress members to ask themselves whether Anglo-Saxon power over American industrial notions had the ability to receive without limit the influence of alien ideas.[48]

[47] E. H. Johnson, in *Baptist Congress Proceedings* (1888), 83–84. Reverend Frank M. Ellis of Baltimore also asserted that the assimilating power of America was weakening faster than the newcomers were becoming amalgamated. Because Americanization was thus not taking place at a satisfactory rate, Ellis agreed with Johnson that American citizens, through the policy of their government, should now demand a cessation of the influx of the dregs of European society (*ibid.*, 89–90).
[48] E. H. Johnson, in *Baptist Congress Proceedings* (1888), 87–88.

Several very prominent Baptists buttressed Johnson's arguments. George E. Horr, Jr., soon to become editor-in-chief of the Boston *Watchman,* denied that God had providentially increased migration to the United States but attributed the rise in numbers to the "very human device of steamship companies to enlarge their revenues." [49] He, too, believed that the ideal of developing a perfect type of Christian civilization here justified the closing of both the eastern and western gates. Undesirable classes would only complicate the process of firmly establishing free institutions, and the gamble was not worth taking. Leighton Williams, shortly to become active in Rauschenbusch's social gospel group known as the Brotherhood of the Kingdom, agreed: "The scripture gives me the warrant to keep out these heathen nations of the world. Let us first hold up the candle of a right civilization and true liberty here. In order to do that we cannot welcome the heathen into our homes nor into this country." [50]

By 1888 the providential view, with its concomitant opposition to immigration restriction, seemed to be disappearing from Baptist expressions of opinion. The *Journal and Messenger,* always anti-immigrant, led the way in the crusade to erect barriers with demands in 1887 and 1888 for legislation requiring a certificate from the U.S. consul in foreign countries attesting to the acceptability of each prospective American about to emigrate. Editor Grover P. Osborne stated that because the national development had now reached the stage where very few immigrants were desirable, federal policy should attempt to reject persons from Italy, Austria, and Hungary. To achieve this end, he suggested the imposition of a head tax of $100 on every immigrant.[51] Other Baptist periodicals shortly fell into line. The *Watchman* and the *Standard* concurred with Osborne on the advisability of examination by American officials in the nation of origin to screen out those who might not make good citizens.

---

[49] George E. Horr, Jr., in *Baptist Congress Proceedings* (1888), 87–88.

[50] Leighton Williams, in *Baptist Congress Proceedings* (1888), 93–94.

[51] *Journal and Messenger,* LVI (June 8, 1887), 1; (Sept. 1, 1887), 1; "A Tax on Immigrants," *ibid.,* LVII (Aug. 30, 1888), 1; LIX (Jan. 16, 1890), 1.

The *Examiner* recommended that since many poor Italian laborers came here under falsely induced hopes of making an easy fortune, the government ought to bar them in their own interest as well as that of native-born workers.[52]

In 1891 both the *Watchman* and the *Examiner* praised the new congressional codification of existing federal immigration statutes that added to the excluded classes paupers, persons suffering from a loathsome or contagious disease, polygamists, and most of those who had not paid their own passage. The provisions of the 1891 legislation, which forbade steamship companies to encourage or solicit migration to the United States and forced them to bear the expense of returning illegal entrants, especially pleased the Baptists. The *Examiner* rejoiced that the country now had "but one opinion on the propriety of opening our ports to the indiscriminate, pauperized, diseased scum of foreign lands."[53] In a revealing paragraph the *Watchman* wished this law had been passed twenty years earlier and indicated that Baptist attitudes had changed greatly since that time: "An immense amount of twaddle has been uttered on this immigration question. Speakers at our National Anniversaries have time and time again referred to the 'Divine Providence' that has brought the scum of Europe to our shores. It would be well for these gentlemen to distinguish between 'Divine Providence' and the cupidity of steamship and railroad companies. The new law will do something to illuminate the distinction."[54]

The *Journal and Messenger*, however, was dissatisfied. Grover P. Osborne had his watchful eye on events in New Orleans, where a mob had executed several Italians recently acquitted of murder charges. This incident would prove sufficient to wake up the country to the great Italian danger, hoped the Cincinnati editor. For all his readers, Osborne painted a lurid picture

[52] Editorials: "Foreign Emigration," *Watchman*, LXX (Apr. 18, 1889), 6; "The Immigration Problem," *Standard*, XXXVI (Aug. 15, 1889), 7; "Italian Immigrants," *Examiner*, LXV (Aug. 2, 1888), 1.

[53] Editorials: "A National Question," *Examiner*, LXVIII (Jan. 2, 1890), 1; "To Regulate Immigration," *ibid.*, LXIX (Jan. 8, 1891), 2; "Immigration to Be Regulated," *ibid.* (Apr. 16, 1891), 1.

[54] Editorial: "The New Immigration Law," *Watchman*, LXXII (Apr. 2, 1891), 1.

of the "Dagoes," who drank excessively, lived in a state of filth, and used the knife at the slightest provocation. Because of their propensity for violence and tendency to retaliate against fancied wrongs, the *Journal and Messenger* advocated special measures to keep out the sons of Italy.[55] The *Pacific Baptist* also viewed daily happenings with alarm, pointing to the strange syllables of the names of strikers involved in riotous labor disputes and asserting that anyone unfit to identify with American institutions should not be admitted.[56]

Baptists, like other Americans, were rapidly developing a theory of the changing character of immigration that made invidious comparisons between immigrants from northern and western Europe and those from that continent's southern and eastern nations. Historians have discerned the roots of this belief, which ultimately found its way into the National Origins Act of 1924, in the Anglo-Saxon race ideas that combined with nativism in the 1890s. These concepts, which held that the inhabitants of the Mediterranean region suffered from an inherent inferiority of blood that made them biologically different from northern and western Europeans, gained wide currency among a group of intellectuals in the United States around the turn of the century.[57] Many Baptists accepted this version of Anglo-Saxonism, yet a number of clergymen separated themselves from the "scientific school" of racism by emphasizing a religious criterion of inferiority—unwillingness to convert to Protestantism—over physical and racial criteria. Those who feared that immigration would destroy the perfect white Anglo-Saxon Protestant civilization often named the specific "most turbulent and dangerous races"—Russians, Hungarians, Italians, and Poles.[58] Henry L. Morehouse, however, did not use the term

---

[55] Editorials: *Journal and Messenger*, LX (Jan. 8, 1891), 1; "The Problem of the Foreigner," *ibid.*, LXII (Dec. 28, 1893), 4.

[56] Editorials: *Pacific Baptist*, XVI (Sept. 8, 1892), 1; XVII (Jan. 12, 1893), 1; XVIII (Aug. 2, 1894), 1.

[57] Handlin, *Race and Nationality in American Life*, 96; Higham, *Strangers in the Land*, ch. 6 ("Toward Racism: The History of an Idea"), 131–157.

[58] See Hubert C. Woods, "Home Missions: The Hope of the Country, the Opportunity and Obligation of the Church," *Standard*, XXXVII (Nov. 29, 1889), 2, and E. H. Johnson, in *Baptist Congress Proceedings* (1888), 83–

"Anglo-Saxon" when he concluded in 1896 that French Canadians and Irish were of a lesser breed than Germans and Swedes.
Rather, the influential secretary of the Home Mission Society
based his views on the frustration Baptists had experienced in
attempts to convert the immigrants from Quebec; inaccessibility
to evangelical effort was what determined the undesirability of
a national group.[59]

Kerr B. Tupper, the pastor of a large Baptist church in
Denver who first brought the difference between "old" and
"new" immigration to the Home Mission Society's attention in
1891, revealed the tension between the Anglo-Saxon and religious criteria of ethnic inferiority. Speaking of the Bohemians,
Poles, Hungarians, and southern Italians, Tupper advocated
rejecting them all because they were ignorant of "Anglo-
American ideas of civil liberty" *and* of "spiritual religion." The
right of any nation to develop a model society that would
enrich the world, Phillips Brooks had said, justified the enactment of legislation to guard that ideal. Showing special contempt for the Italians, Tupper pointed to the arrests of some
of these immigrants in New Orleans for murder of the superintendent of police, but he conveniently neglected to tell of the

84. Unfavorable comparisons were made by Baptists before it was generally
realized that southern and eastern Europeans were becoming predominant.
In 1880 the *Examiner and Chronicle* noted that German and Scandinavian
immigrants, most of whom were skilled artisans or farmers, were least a
charge to the authorities of all groups. The Italians, it was said, came in
fewer numbers but were often a burden to the state. They seemed to settle
in large cities as rag pickers and assistants to the regular scavengers—thus
they were the least desirable immigrants of all (*Examiner and Chronicle*, LVII
[July 1, 1880], 4).

59 Henry L. Morehouse, "New England's Duty," *Baptist Home Mission
Monthly*, XVIII (May, 1896), 154–160; 64th Annual Report, ABHMS (1896),
112–113. Baptists were either unaware of or chose to ignore the fact that
some Protestants were found in the peoples of southern and eastern Europe,
especially among Hungarians and Czechs. Not until 1905, when Howard B.
Grose described the Slavic nationalities one by one, was there a recognition
of the religious pluralism of the new immigration; see "The Slav Invasion,"
Baptist Home Mission Monthly, XXVII (Mar., 1905), 89–107. This failure to
acknowledge the different religions of eastern Europe, including the Eastern
Orthodox, tends to substantiate the argument that anti-Catholicism, which
dwelt upon the preponderant Catholic element of the new immigration, was
a major factor in leading Baptists to advocate immigration restriction in the
1890s.

acquittal of the suspects and their subsequent lynching by an angry mob unchecked by local officials. The Denver minister contributed to what was to become the Italian stereotype: Italy was now flooding the United States with a torrent of peanut venders, organ grinders, and dangerous criminals. Tupper's suggestion for a law requiring each prospective citizen to prove his genuine sympathy with American civilization and his ability to read and write in his native tongue was the first mention of the literacy test in an official Baptist body, probably deriving from Henry Cabot Lodge's advocacy of it early in the same year.[60]

When the Baptist Home Mission Society formally stated its acceptance of the differentiation of persons according to nationality in 1896, the religious criterion of inferiority seemed paramount. The annual report of that year flatly asserted that immigrants from England, Scotland, and Scandinavia readily assimilated because they adopted Protestant principles, while those from Poland, Austro-Hungary, and Italy stubbornly resisted the appeals made to them by Protestant missionaries as well as the political influences of liberty. Affirming that "multitudes, indeed the mass of them, have been born and reared in the Roman Catholic faith," the Home Mission Society lamented the fact that Baptist emissaries had sought largely in vain to win these foreigners "from their errors, their superstitions, [and] their image worship." Undoubtedly impressed by Secretary Morehouse's arguments concerning the French Canadians, the organization that he led now officially applied his reasoning to

[60] Kerr B. Tupper, "Immigration and Christianity," *Baptist Home Mission Monthly*, XIII (Sept., 1891), 247–253. See also Marsena Stone, "Immigration," *Standard*, XXXIX (July 14, 1892), 2. Stone called attention to the "decay of popery" in southeastern Europe, resulting in the emigration of the "useless and low down" classes to America. "Most of the immigrants of late are Romanists," he averred, "able neither to read nor write, yet they are solid for the saloon, and are sure to furnish large recruits for the poor-houses and prisons." Stone believed that no one should be allowed to vote unless he could read and write English, and he concluded his article with the recommendation that the United States would do well to discourage all immigration that did not propose to adopt American citizenship, after suggesting that Americanization helped rid the immigrants of the false ideas under which they had been reared.

other appropriate groups.[61] Perhaps many of its members had read an article in the *Baptist Home Mission Monthly* two years earlier attempting to prove that something inherent in the natives of southern and eastern Europe precluded their conversion to evangelical Protestantism. A Swedish-American pastor had carefully calculated the proportion of Baptists in Holland, Germany, Denmark, and Sweden compared with the very few adherents to this faith in France, Italy, Spain, and Greece. From this observation, he concluded that the greater the preponderance of Gothic blood in a people, the more congenial was the soil for the unadulterated tenets of the New Testament and for the free, democratic order as practiced by Baptist churches.[62]

Two other features of the Baptist rationale for immigration restriction in the 1890s indicate that the religion of the immigrant was more important than the relation of his ethnic origins to Anglo-Saxon culture. One is the severe criticism of Scandinavian Lutheranism common throughout the decade. The general missionary to the Norwegians in Iowa told the Home Mission Society in 1893 that large numbers of Lutheran ministers and laymen had never experienced a true religious conversion. Many of these people, he said, showed all the natural results of ecclesiastical ritualism—lack of spirituality, of interest in missions, of knowledge of the Bible. Worst of all, they believed in baptismal regeneration, a sacramental view opposed to the Baptist doctrine that the new birth into the kingdom of God came only from a deliberate act of faith. Baptist literature at this time is replete with references to "dead Lutheran formalism," with some going so far as to brand this faith as "half Catholic." [63]

[61] 64th Annual Report, ABHMS (1896), 41–42.
[62] A. P. Eckman, "The Religious Status of the Scandinavians," *Baptist Home Mission Monthly*, XVI (Sept., 1894), 374–377.
[63] 61st Annual Report, ABHMS (1893), 70. For a good example of this type of anti-Lutheran feeling, see the *Pacific Baptist*, XVI (Jan. 28, 1892), 1. This sentiment proves that the religion of the immigrants did not *have* to be Catholic to be condemned—only not of the free evangelical church tradition. The Baptist description of Lutheranism as "half Catholic" indicates that even if the Baptists had acknowledged such religious groups of the new immigration as the reformed Hungarians and the Lutheran and reformed Slovaks,

The other attribute revealing that Baptists were not primarily concerned with ethnicity or race as the criterion of an immigrant's desirability is the virtual absence of anti-Semitism in all their utterances of this period. The failure of Baptist clergymen to adopt this characteristic feature of "scientific" racism at this time clearly separates them from other intellectuals. Many of the newcomers from eastern Europe were Jewish, but only once in the decade did a Baptist paper even mention this fact, let alone pass judgment on it. The *Journal and Messenger* in 1892 charged that many of the Jewish refugees aided by Baron Hirsch in their exodus from Russia to America would enrich themselves by exploiting others, selling poor goods at high prices. Polish Jews were equally objectionable, asserted editor Grover P. Osborne, pointing to the decline in property values whenever these people entered a neighborhood. But the very isolation of Osborne's advocacy of prohibiting Jewish immigration, for the same reasons as for barring Italians, makes it the exception that proves the rule. Even the *Journal and Messenger* spoke of this issue only once, and then as one small facet of a consistent forty-year campaign to restrict immigration.[64]

Osborne shortly deserted the Jews to return to attacks upon the Italians and to urge that the discrimination between northwestern and southeastern Europeans be enacted into legislation to keep out the latter. "An Irish Catholic is preferable to an Italian Catholic," he exclaimed, "an Irish shillalah to an Italian knife." Poles, Hungarians, Jews—undesirables all—might be eliminated from America by the imposition of a head tax of $10 on individuals coming from Britain, France, Norway, and Sweden and $100 on those from all other countries. The editor of the *Journal and Messenger* was indeed happy to hear of the activities of the Boston Immigration Restriction League, and by 1895 he rejoiced that most of the nation's religious newspapers agreed with him upon the advisability of restriction. Only a few years before, he recalled, the *Journal and Messenger* had

these groups would still have been found wanting because, to use Tupper's phrase, they were ignorant of "spiritual" religion.
[64] *Journal and Messenger*, LXI (Jan. 7, 1892), 1.

stood quite alone in demanding the closing of the gates. In his elation that now other Baptists had joined the crusade, Osborne could not foresee that in a short time his denomination would again reject his views while the nation at large accepted them.[65]

That Baptists were in virtual accord by the mid-1890s, however, is evidenced by their response to Henry Cabot Lodge's proposal for a literacy test. Late in 1895 the Massachusetts senator had introduced a bill in Congress which had been drawn up by the Immigration Restriction League of Boston. Designed to distinguish clearly between Anglo-Saxons and southern Europeans, Lodge's recommendations called for the exclusion of persons between the ages of fourteen and sixty who could not read and write some language. Both houses of Congress passed the Lodge bill near the end of 1896, but President Grover Cleveland vetoed it early in 1897 on the grounds that such a law would upset tradition and appear hypocritical to the world. When later introduced in 1897 and 1902, the literacy test was rejected by Congress; not until 1917 would anti-foreignism again be at sufficient strength to pass it over Woodrow Wilson's veto.

Throughout the discussions of this much-publicized idea, the *Journal and Messenger* led the Baptist press in expressions of satisfaction with a measure that would shut out the millions from Italy, Hungary, Austria, and Russia because of the high rate of illiteracy in these nations. The Cincinnati paper howled in protest upon Cleveland's veto, blaming the president's action upon his desire to win the Catholic vote and on his connections with the New York financiers who had ties with the steamship companies. When Congress refused to pass further literacy tests

[65] Editorials: "Practical Methods of Limiting Immigration," *Journal and Messenger*, LXIII (Mar. 15, 1894), 1; LXIV (Mar. 21, 1895), 1. Osborne's apparent preference for an Irish Catholic over an Italian Catholic might make it appear that the ethnic factor was indeed more important to him in drawing the lines of restriction. But this must be balanced with the statement of Henry L. Morehouse that both the French Canadians and the Irish were inferior because they were bigoted Catholics who would not convert. Morehouse, who was more influential in the Home Mission Society than Osborne, thus gave priority to the religious criterion when he called for the restriction of immigration (Morehouse, "New England's Duty").

in 1898 and 1902, the *Journal and Messenger* failed to realize
that a decline in nativism was responsible, clinging instead to
its argument that "the future of the United States rests largely
on this question." [66] The *Standard* followed the progress of
Lodge's proposal with interest, maintaining that it deserved
bipartisan support from all good citizens. The Chicago journal
clearly perceived the effects of such a law, which would still
exclude those of no use to this country. Casting off its skep-
ticism of the previous decade, the *Standard* now endorsed commentaries by correspondents who called for restriction designed
to prevent the flow from southern and eastern Europe from
dominating American cities. In 1895 the paper showed at least a
degree of sympathy for the American Protective Association by
reprinting from its *American Patriot* an article entitled "Twenty
Reasons Why Immigration Should Be Restricted in the United
States," the first of which was the deteriorating quality of the
new arrivals. [67] The *Examiner* agreed that the Immigration Restriction League's program, for which Lodge campaigned, had
been essentially right. Over 40 percent of the immigrants above
fourteen years of age who landed in 1895, claimed the New
York paper, were illiterate and hence undesirable. [68]

Appropriately, a prominent Boston Baptist spoke eloquently
for his denomination in defense of the literacy test. George
E. Horr, Jr., editor of the *Watchman* and later president of
Newton Theological Seminary, showed that the ideal of a perfect civilization was yet very much alive among Protestants.
Lodge's plan reflected a growing spirit of nationalism, Horr
asserted, with a nod of approval to the senator's belief that the
wholesale infusion of races with alien traditions, thoughts, and

[66] Editorials: *Journal and Messenger*, LXIV (Dec. 12, 1895), 1; "A Great
Victory," *ibid.*, LXVI (Feb. 25, 1897), 1; "The Veto of the Immigration Bill,"
ibid. (Mar. 11, 1897), 1; LXVII (Jan. 20, 1898), 1; (May 19, 1898), 1; LXXI
(June 5, 1902), 1.

[67] Editorials: *Standard*, XLII (Feb. 14, 1895), 7; XLIII (Dec. 14, 1895), 1;
(May 30, 1896), 1; XLIV (Apr. 10, 1897), 1; XLV (Jan. 29, 1898), 1; XLVI
(Dec. 24, 1898), 1. See also E. E. Lewis, "Our Perils from Immigration,"
Standard, XLI (Jan. 4, 1894), 1; "The Immigration Peril: Comment on E. E.
Lewis' Article," *ibid.*, 4.

[68] *Examiner*, LXXIV (Nov. 26, 1896), 1–2.

ideas endangered the quality of American citizenship. The United States still stood as the refuge of nations, but recent developments indicated that liberty remained on trial. Horr enunciated the nationalist rationale for restriction: America was to lead the world by example, and nothing must be allowed to mar the pattern she should set. "If we should fail, or not achieve success at which we aim," he wrote, "the human race itself would suffer in our disaster. The question with us is . . . whether we have not reached a point in our national development at which the success of free institutions and the welfare of government throughout the world may not be too seriously imperilled by our continuance in our present course." In Horr's view "the largest and truest recognition of the brotherhood of man may lead us to restrict or prohibit further immigration of the least desirable classes in order that our institutions may ultimately be of the largest advantage to the whole world." [69]

The sympathy for Henry Cabot Lodge's reasoning behind the literacy test professed by George Horr reveals that although many Baptists used strictly religious criteria to determine "desirability," others accepted the broader grounds of a superior Anglo-Saxon race threatened by those inferior in ways that went beyond religion. Certain foreigners posed dangers to the ideal that America was to lead humanity forward not only in the enjoyment of individual freedom and popular government but also in the "higher spiritual ends" of "universal righteousness, love, peace, and joy." These dangers now justified the exclusion of those who did not qualify for citizenship in the kingdom! [70] Many Protestants had taken seriously the words of Lodge and his supporters, while in the Baptist denomination some had learned their lessons of the 1890s from bitter experience in attempting to convert such "bigoted and ignorant Romanists" as the French Canadians. But whatever its origins, from current racial ideas or from unsuccessful encounters with

[69] Editorial: "Unrestricted Immigration," *Watchman*, LXXVII (Mar. 24, 1896), 7–8.
[70] Edward H. Brooks, "An Outlook upon the Nation," *Standard*, XLI (Aug. 2, 1894), 2.

immigrants, the conclusion of the nineties was the same for Baptists and many other Americans. Political action based on discriminatory standards of race and religion appeared to be the answer that would cut off the flow of newcomers. Nothing was to be allowed to get in the way of God's plan for a Protestant Christian nation in North America, where the United States was destined, in the words of one Baptist, "to extend the zone of human liberty, and to take [its] place along with Great Britain as an agent of civilization, and a harbinger of peace." [71] Nevertheless, as Baptists traveled along this road to restriction and nativism in the 1890s, their traditional principles helped to mitigate the influence of experience and prevalent Anglo-Saxonism. The ancient doctrine of the separation of church and state, which made their anti-Catholicism more rational and explainable than that of other Protestants, in fact kept most Baptists from supporting such an organization as the American Protective Association because of its religious test for officeholding, thus drawing limits about their anti-foreignism.

For the most part, the Baptist reaction to immigration in the 1890s paralleled a similar response in other denominations. Articles in Presbyterian religious papers pointed to the deteriorating quality of the new arrivals, characterizing the Scotch and Germans, and even the Irish and French, as more desirable than others. In this branch of Protestantism also the suggestion appeared that it would be wise to discriminate on the basis of nationality in shutting out unwanted aliens.[72] Methodists likewise called for a limit on the foreign influx, one churchman going so far as to advocate total exclusion for extended periods. In the 1890s they, too, looked to Congress to deal with immigration by political means.[73] The only exception to this pattern is visible in the Congregational church, where amidst the storm

[71] Thomas J. Morgan, "The New Republic and Its New Duties," *Standard*, XLIV (July 23, 1898), 4.
[72] "Foreigners," *Church at Home and Abroad*, XXII (Aug., 1897), 134–137. See also D. J. McMillen, "Our Foreign Population," *ibid.*, IX (May, 1891), 402.
[73] *Zion's Herald*, LXVIII (Sept. 3, 1890), 1; LXIX (June 10, 1891), 1; LXX (Feb. 17, 1892), 1; (Dec. 7, 1892), 1.

correspondents to denominational journals took up the cause of the stranger. In this segment of Protestantism one may observe pronouncements that most of the current charges against the foreign populations were "worthless as material for serious judgement." [74] While other Protestants trembled in terror, Congregational spokesmen assured Americans that the prevailing outcry against immigration was exaggerated and not sustained by the facts, expressing confidence both in the improving quality of the newcomers and in the vast assimilative powers of the native stock. This contrasting point of view placed more blame on American negligence for any existing danger to the republic, affirming that any exclusion should be against bad character rather than nationality.[75] Even here, however, one Congregational paper made clear that anarchists and socialists, along with "densely ignorant immigrants" and those who had no desire to become naturalized, should be barred from entry into the United States.[76]

No such deviations from the norm, except the earlier position of Walter Rauschenbusch and his friends at the Baptist Congress in 1888, marred the evolution of Baptist thought in the 1890s. The Baptist conviction that unwillingness to convert to evangelical Protestantism constituted a badge of inferiority for the alien shows the deeply religious roots of the increasingly popular distinction between southeastern and northwestern Europeans. When such a belief led them to demand the barring of certain immigrants by federal policy, Baptists came perilously close to deserting the principle of the separation of church and state. Formerly they had asserted that a pure Christianity would mould all who became acquainted with it; now they reversed the argument by saying that only those predisposed to accept the spiritual religion should be given a chance to do so. Once they had believed that a relentless campaign to spread the gospel could alone accomplish the desired goal; now they had to call

[74] A. A. Berle, "A Plea for the Immigrant," *Congregationalist*, LXXVI (July 30, 1891), 254.
[75] *Ibid.* See also M. W. Montgomery, "Immigration," *Congregationalist*, LXXIV (Mar. 21, 1889), 97.
[76] "Immigration and Infection," *Independent*, XLIV (Dec. 22, 1892), 11.

on the government to assure its fulfillment. But the Baptist endorsement of restriction was only partially due to a loss of faith. When Leighton Williams requested the closing of the gates to allow America time to hold up a candle to the whole world, he revealed that Protestant idealism was not dead. The failure to convert French Canadian Catholics did not end the efforts of the Baptists among the foreign-born, nor did meager results with other groups lead to such a hostile reaction. While many Baptists traveled the highway of boisterous nativism, with all its anti-Catholicism, anti-radicalism, and Anglo-Saxonism, others walked more slowly along another road. Behind the scenes, Baptist missionaries who worked with various nationalities of the new immigration shortly discovered that if one experience could dim the vision, personal acquaintance with the newcomers could lead to a renewal of hope and a change in outlook.

4

From Fear to Friendship: Baptist Work
among Immigrant Groups

While the Baptist press and the Home Mission Society debated the problem of immigration and how to resolve it, the latter organization quietly continued its campaign to win as many of the strangers as possible to the Baptist faith. Founded in 1832, the society's missionaries followed the pioneers westward throughout much of the nineteenth century. During the first fifty years of its existence, they ministered primarily to the white settlers on the frontier, with supplementary work among the Indians and considerable activity among the freedmen of the South following the Civil War. Baptist emissaries of the gospel repeatedly set forth the *raison d'être* of their efforts. As one of the society's district secretaries succinctly expressed it, the perpetuity of free institutions and the preservation of American civilization depended upon the evangelization of the entire country. Unless many of its citizens believed in Protestant Christianity, the government would fail and the nation perish, resulting in a devastating blow to the hopes of mankind for human freedom and to the prospects of spiritual religion. Applied to the immigrant, this belief stated that conversion and concomitant Americanization were necessary for the safety of the American republic as well as for his individual benefit. Beginning with the Welsh, therefore, in 1836 the Home Mission Society began a long history of evangelistic endeavors among peoples who made the United States their adopted home.[1]

[1] White, *Century of Faith*, 129–131; C. P. Sheldon, "Home Missions: Their

Over the years Baptists faced many difficulties in this work. In its early stages the ministry aimed at such groups as the Germans and Scandinavians, both of which had a Protestant heritage. But near the end of the nineteenth century, an autonomous, decentralized denomination confronted the prospect of winning converts from one of the most hierarchical religious organizations in all of modern history. What would the Baptist approach to this situation be? In what ways would Baptists appeal to Catholics? Would they emphasize the negative aspects of the immigrants' religion and culture, as in the case of the French Canadians? Or would the failure of such a method lead them to search for the positive attributes of the new immigration? To what extent would the Baptist campaign show numerical results? How would native Americans receive those who did come into the denomination, and what impact would they have upon it? Would the Baptists, in the course of their efforts, change their attitudes toward the stranger and become more sympathetic to his plight, or would hostility and demands for restriction increase in the face of frustration in effecting mass conversions? The religious literature of the day, replete with accounts of mission work among the foreign-born, yields answers to each of these questions.

The Home Mission Society gradually assumed more and more of the responsibility for immigrant evangelization toward the end of the nineteenth century, but it never became exclusive in this regard. Baptist state conventions and city mission groups, often aided in finance and direction by the national agency, cooperated in the work among new Americans. The two Women's Baptist Home Mission Societies, which ultimately merged, engaged in activity among foreign-speaking women and children. The American Baptist Publication Society, founded in 1840, printed religious pamphlets and Bibles in various lan-

Fields and Work," pamphlet bound with the 51st Annual Report, ABHMS (1883). For a study of Protestant mission work in the West, see Colin B. Goodykoontz, *Home Missions on the American Frontier* (Caldwell, Idaho, 1939). For a very brief general introduction to the nature of Protestant approaches to Catholic immigrants, see Theodore Abel, *Protestant Home Missions to Catholic Immigrants* (New York, 1933).

guages for distribution to prospective converts. In this way the drive to bring the alien into the church went forward simultaneously on a variety of fronts.

Fairly successful efforts with the Germans and Scandinavians before 1880 set significant patterns for work among other immigrants. Both of these groups established the organizational relationship that foreign-speaking churches would have in the Home Mission Society, and defended the character of their entire nationalities to native American Baptists. Both founded special institutions to train men for a bilingual ministry, and the Germans especially led the fight to use their own language in preaching to their countrymen. Baptists drawn from the "old" immigration often took the first steps in the winning of persons from the "new" to the faith, thus breaking down ethnic hostility to a greater degree than otherwise would have occurred.

Because of several major hindrances to the Baptist movement in Germany, only 1,500 adherents to this faith could be found there as late as 1845.[2] Nevertheless, a clergyman already converted in his homeland initiated mission work among the Germans in America. In 1840 Konrad Fleishmann journeyed to Reading, Pennsylvania, and for nearly three years preached to the residents of an area that had been settled by Pietists, Mennonites, and Dunkards. In 1843 he organized a German Baptist church in Philadelphia, and five years later a religious newspaper, *Der Sendbote des Evangelium*, began to publish under his direction. With the help of another German immigrant, John Eschmann, Fleishmann established another congregation in New York City in 1847. As members of these early parishes traveled west, they united with other German Baptists in such growing cities as Newark, Albany, Rochester, Buffalo, Milwaukee, Chicago, Springfield, Peoria, and St. Louis. By 1851 the existence of these groups justified the formation of a German Baptist Conference in Philadelphia, which later divided into

2 Torbet, *History of the Baptists*, 193. Torbet lists these hindrances as follows: (1) longstanding German antipathy to Anabaptists; (2) the Lutheran clergy's resentment of Baptist growth among the common people; and (3) a government policy of intolerance, by which Baptists suffered indignities and loss of property.

eastern and western agencies that remained separate from American Baptists for twenty years.[3]

The appointment of George A. Schulte as general missionary for the East German Conference in 1870 by the Home Mission Society began a successful fifty-year relationship between these foreign-speaking Baptists and their American brethren. The society commissioned missionaries upon recommendation of the conferences, and both organizations contributed to their financial support. After the Western German Conference subdivided into three parts in 1881, the work spread rapidly. German Baptists soon appeared from New England to Texas, from North Dakota to Tennessee, and their representatives attended the Home Mission Society's annual national meetings. A separate Publication Society opened in Cleveland in 1870, and ethnically oriented orphanages, hospitals, and homes for the aged sprang up in various places. By 1882, 10,334 persons had memberships in German Baptist churches across the land.[4]

Special education for Baptist emissaries to the Germans commenced in 1858 when Augustus Rauschenbusch arrived as a new faculty member at Rochester Theological Seminary. In 1872 Hermann M. Schaeffer of New York City came to Rochester to become Rauschenbusch's assistant. The German Department grew under the tutelage of a number of men—Jacob S. Gubelman, Frederick W. Meyer, and Albert J. Ramaker. Its most outstanding instructor, Walter Rauschenbusch, taught from 1897 to 1902 in the program his father had founded. Much of the curriculum consisted of pre-theological studies because most of the students had no high school or college background. From its inception to the year 1924, this institution trained 494 men to preach the gospel in the tongue of Schiller and Goethe. That year one of its professors estimated that of 224 clergymen presently serving German Baptist churches in the United States and Canada, all but 31 had completed their education at Rochester.[5] Many of these pastors carried on a bilingual ministry, and

[3] White, *Century of Faith*, 129–132; Albert J. Ramaker, *The German Baptists in North America* (Cleveland, 1924), 14–36.

[4] White, *Century of Faith*, 133, 135–136; Ramaker, *German Baptists in North America*, 71.

[5] Ramaker, *German Baptists in North America*, 81–89.

over the years various congregations united with English-speaking Baptist associations. But by 1920 the German Baptist Conference was so strong financially that it could declare itself independent of the Home Mission Society in that respect.[6] The pattern of separate foreign-language parishes, with special training programs to supply them, remained consistent with Baptists in the light of the German example. In 1923 the Baptist gospel went forth in German to 31,826 members of 284 churches in 27 states and the Dominion of Canada.[7]

The question of preaching to the Germans in their own tongue became contentious at times, because some native Baptists feared that such a policy would hinder Americanization by perpetuating an alien culture. The *Examiner* voiced this apprehension in 1889 when it recognized the need to use German in ministering to the elderly, but it doubted the value of linguistically distinct churches and seminaries.[8] The *Standard* later agreed that during an immigrant's first years in his new land he should be able to hear the gospel in familiar syllables, but it emphasized that this practice should be temporary. As long as recent arrivals predominated in a given congregation, German might be spoken. But all foreign-speaking parishes should aim either for merger with English-speaking Baptists or for the adoption of the American language, said the Chicago paper. Accordingly, the *Standard* praised the use of English by the young people of many German Baptist churches, contenting itself not to force the issue further.[9]

When the matter came up for debate in the Home Mission Society in 1882, Professor Hermann Schaeffer of Rochester Theological Seminary argued vigorously that only the native language of the immigrant would reach him effectively. The church must give religious truth to the hearer in the sounds with which the mother first imbued her child with Christian precepts, he asserted. Sensing the misgivings American Baptists might have over such a policy, Schaeffer drew their applause

[6] White, *Century of Faith*, 135–136.
[7] Ramaker, *German Baptists in North America*, 37–42.
[8] *Examiner*, LXVI (May 2, 1889), 4.
[9] *Standard*, XLIII (Oct. 19, 1895), 2.

when he affirmed that "we do not so much wish to perpetuate the German tongue in America as we wish to perpetuate American ideas by means of the German tongue." [10] For the next few years the Rochester professor and other German Baptist clergymen insisted that the evangelization of the foreigner, best attempted in words he could understand, would automatically Americanize him. Assimilation, they claimed, depended more on principles and attitudes than on speech or habits. Wisely noting that nationality was "too great a force to be changed like a coat," [11] these men gradually convinced Baptists that foreign-speaking churches were agencies for the slow, healthy, and organic assimilation of the Germans in this country. The acceptance of this argument undoubtedly accounts in part for the willingness of white Protestant Americans, at least in the case of the Baptists, to delay the development of more elaborate Americanization programs until after World War I.

The presence of German leaders in American Baptist organizations such as the Home Mission Society had another impact that established a pattern of response to many of the new immigrants. In these Baptist groups and in the religious press the tendency of representatives of each nationality to defend their heritage helped to mitigate the harsh views of the stranger held by so many people in the late nineteenth and early twentieth centuries. German Baptists continually drove the point home that criticism of a particular ethnic group, even on religious grounds, would do more harm than good. Professor Jacob S. Gubelman, the grandson of German Pietists, told the Home Mission Society that its duty was to enlighten and save his people rather than condemn their religion or customs. George Schulte

[10] Hermann M. Schaeffer, "The Problem before American Christians," speech to the ABHMS, in *Baptist Home Missions in North America*, 129–133.

[11] Jacob Meier, "Mission Work among the Germans in America," *Standard*, LI (Oct. 17, 1903), 7–8. See also "What Shall We Do with the Germans," *Examiner*, LXXIII (Jan. 19, 1895), 12–13; Julius C. Haselhuhn, "Work among the Germans," *Baptist Home Mission Monthly*, IV (Nov., 1882), 296–300; and Hermann M. Schaeffer, "Does the American Baptist Home Mission Society Americanize Germans?" *ibid.*, XIII (Nov., 1891), 312–314.

agreed that too much emphasis on German faults would only widen the breach between the immigrant and his adopted countrymen. He chided Daniel Potter of New York for his assertion that Baptist work among Germans in that city was unsuccessful and for his derogatory remarks about aliens. In like manner, many others stressed the positive attributes of the Germanic peoples: industry, intelligence, thrift, gregariousness, and respect for law.[12]

The influence of German Baptists upon their American brethren went beyond periodic articles and speeches to the Home Mission Society. As members of that body listened, the effects were pronounced. The forcefulness of Professor Schaeffer of Rochester during the 1882 meeting must have shaken a number of individuals. At his request the Committee on Missions among Non-English-Speaking People deleted the last clause of an affirmation that foreigners "cling to the language of their native land and insist upon its study in our public school *contrary to the best interests of the body politic.*"[13] Only the year before, in 1881, the same committee's report had said that the Germans introduced a secular, unchristian element into American civilization that endangered some of its most sacred institutions. But the annual statement of 1883, after Schaeffer had argued for his countrymen, claimed that the Germans deserved special religious attention because of the fine character, love of family life, and intellectual abilities with which they would enrich Christianity if converted.[14] Henry L. Morehouse, for many years the Home Mission Society's most prominent leader as its corresponding secretary, praised the German Bap-

[12] Jacob S. Gubelman, "The Demands and Needs of the German Mission Field in America," address to the ABHMS, in *Baptist Home Mission Monthly*, II (July, 1880), 130–132; George A. Schulte, "The Other Side of the German Question," *Examiner*, LIX (July 6, 1882), 2; A. P. Mihm, "German Immigration," *Baptist Home Mission Monthly*, XX (Sept., 1898), 305–308. For a sample of Daniel C. Potter's views, see "What to Do with the Foreigner," *Examiner*, LXVI (Jan. 17, 1889).

[13] A. F. Mason, speech on the need for the unification of German and American work, in *Baptist Home Missions in North America*, 133–135. The italicized clause was deleted at Schaeffer's request.

[14] 49th Annual Report, ABHMS (1881), 22; 51st Annual Report, ABHMS (1883), 13–15.

tists for their orthodoxy and added that German-speaking peoples were especially susceptible to the gospel.[15]

Within the Baptist ranks the Germans helped to keep ethnic friction at a minimum by initiating evangelistic work among several other nationalities, particularly the Bohemians, Poles, Slavonians, Hungarians, and Slavs. The First German Church of Chicago began a ministry to the Bohemians and Poles in that city and fostered this endeavor for several years. In Buffalo a German Baptist group set up the charter congregation of Polish Baptists. The same arrangement was used to establish a mission among the Letts of Philadelphia and the Slavonians and Hungarians of Pittsburgh. In a very real sense, wrote the official historian of the American Baptist Home Mission Society, "the Germans thus became the Society's leading agent in giving the gospel to other national groups in America." [16]

It is difficult to ascertain how many German Baptists in the United States at any one time were already in the fold upon arrival and how many were converted here. Albert J. Ramaker, the chronicler of their history, felt that immigration from the homeland had its greatest impact in the early years and played a less prominent role in the increase of the late nineteenth and early twentieth centuries. Before the Civil War, he pointed out, the German influx divided about equally into rural and urban areas. But after 1865, when a greater proportion went to the agricultural sections of the central, northwestern, and southwestern states, most of the German Baptist churches in these sections were apparently founded either by the Home Mission Society or by older families of the East. If those already Baptist in Germany did contribute significantly here after 1865, he believed, this occurred primarily in the cities.[17]

This question is more readily answered with respect to the origins of the Swedish Baptists in America. George M. Stephenson, who has studied the matter in detail, asserts that the foundations of the Baptist religion in Sweden were laid in the United

[15] Henry L. Morehouse, "German Baptists in America," *Baptist Home Mission Monthly*, XIII (Nov., 1891), 301–306.
[16] White, *Century of Faith*, 134.
[17] Ramaker, *German Baptists in North America*, 37–42.

States, not vice versa.[18] In 1845 a Swedish sea captain, Gustavus Schroeder, became a Baptist at Mariners' Temple in New York City. Upon his return to Sweden, Schroeder met another individual who had been converted in the same place, F. O. Nilsson. Banished from his native land on account of his religious views, Nilsson brought a small group of followers to Houston, Minnesota, in 1853. Meanwhile, in 1852 a Swede of similar persuasion, Gustaf Palmquist, had set up a church at Rock Island, Illinois. The Home Mission Society at once took notice of these rather unexpected activities and hired Palmquist to preach in Illinois, Ohio, and New York. By the time the Rock Island pastor went back to Sweden in 1857, eight congregations in America boasted a total of over 200 members in the areas where he and Nilsson had worked.[19]

Swedish Baptists often led the way in attempts to convert other Scandinavian nationalities, but these ultimately established separate conferences, though they cooperated in training men for the ministry. Norwegian immigrants gathered their first Baptist congregation in Illinois in 1848, and a Danish-Norwegian church came into being in Wisconsin eight years later. The Home Mission Society sent out a missionary to Finnish people at Rockport, Massachusetts, in 1891, and organizations shortly formed at Worcester and at Duluth, Minnesota. While the principal area of Baptist activity among Scandinavians was always the northwest Mississippi region where they were concentrated, Swedish mission stations and churches also exercised influence in Connecticut, Massachusetts, New York, New Jersey, and Pennsylvania. By 1920 the Norwegian Baptist Conference counted 4,038 members in 46 congregations; the Finnish Baptist Union, 712 persons in 17 groups; and the Swedish Baptist Conference, approximately 31,000. All of these foreign-speaking Baptists founded their own hospitals, schools, orphanages, and homes for the aged.[20]

[18] George M. Stephenson, *The Religious Aspects of Swedish Immigration* (Minneapolis, 1932), 74, 83.

[19] White, *Century of Faith*, 138.

[20] *Ibid.*, 138–139; Charles H. Sears, "The Establishment of the First Norwegian-Danish Church in the East," *Baptist Home Mission Monthly*, XXXI (Feb., 1909), 89–90. The "official" histories for each of the Scandinavian

Following the example of their German Baptist brethren, the Scandinavians set up a seminary to supply their own pastorates. The founder of this school, John A. Edgren, came to America in 1862 and for several years served as a colporteur and missionary of the Baptist Publication Society. In 1871 he began to teach Scandinavian students separately in the Baptist Union Theological Seminary of Chicago. The department that Edgren established continued its association with this American institution until 1914, except for a vain attempt at independence from 1884 to 1888. In 1914 it became a part of Bethel Academy in St. Paul, Minnesota, which the Swedish Baptists had set up in 1905. Edgren, who often differed with American Baptists, nevertheless could not get on without their financial support. In search of money, he and his Swedish colleagues often approached the American Baptist Home Mission Society and appealed to its members through articles in the *Baptist Home Mission Monthly*.[21]

The influence of the Scandinavians upon Northern Baptists showed a remarkable similarity to that of the Germans. As immigrant pastors defended their countrymen to Americans, the latter began to develop a favorable view of the former. This interaction, coupled with the relative success of Baptist work among Swedes, Danes, and Norwegians in the eighties and nineties, helped lead Baptists to the belief that northern and western Europeans were superior. Two professors at the Scandinavian seminary in Chicago, Edgren and Nels P. Jensen, wrote of the industrious, frugal, and good moral character of these hardy farmers who were turning the American Northwest into a well-settled and prosperous land. Both argued that their own people were better educated and more enlightened than other newcomers, even if many from Scandinavia professed a dead, nominal Christianity that Baptists regarded as only a short step

Baptist groups are: M. C. Carstensen *et al., Seventy-five Years of Danish Baptist Missionary Work in America* (Philadelphia, 1931); P. Stiansen, *History of the Norwegian Baptists in America* (Wheaton, Ill., 1939); and Adolf Olson, *A Centenary History* (Chicago, 1952). The last volume, which deals with the Swedish Baptists, is by far the best documented and researched of the three.
[21] Olson, *Centenary History*, 153–173, 483–500; Stephenson, *Religious Aspects of Swedish Immigration*, 246–256.

from Catholicism. Although under the control of Lutheran priests who kept their parishioners ignorant of "revealed truth," said Edgren, the Scandinavian mind had been open to God's spirit and word for some time.[22]

Frank Peterson, the immigrant pastor of First Swedish Church of Minneapolis and later a district secretary for the Home Mission Society, affirmed that the arrivals from northern Europe were among the best foreigners in America. Because they loved liberty and religion, adjustment to the institutions of their adopted land came easily. Their faith, even if predominantly Lutheran, was Protestant; therefore they did not seek to dishonor the sabbath or engage in socialist or Communist plots. Peterson's whole argument was designed to prove the compatibility of his people: persons from Scandinavia had manners and customs, political and religious instincts, similar to Americans, as well as a cosmopolitan character. In contrast to other aliens, he pointed out, they furnished few peddlers, organ grinders, or beggars. This obvious reference to the Italians reveals that many of the invidious comparisons made between the "old" and the "new" immigrants often originated with the former groups themselves.[23]

Again American Baptists responded with an acceptance of these laudatory views. The 1880 report of the Home Mission Society stated that the Scandinavians were generally more intelligent and easier to Americanize than other newcomers, and the next year's report added that they distinguished themselves by simplicity of habit, thrift, and respect for law.[24] William M. Haigh, its district secretary in the Midwest, verified these

[22] John A. Edgren, "The Scandinavians," *Baptist Home Mission Monthly*, II (Feb., 1880), 23-25; Nels P. Jensen, "The Scandinavian Nationalities," *ibid.*, IV (Jan., 1882), 7-9; "The Scandinavians," *Tidings*, I (Aug., 1881), 2.

[23] Frank Peterson, "Scandinavia in America," *Baptist Home Mission Monthly*, VIII (Oct., 1886), 233-237; Peterson, "The Swedes in America," *ibid.*, XVIII (Apr., 1896), 126-133. Identical views to those of Peterson, together with the references to organ grinders and peddlers, were set forth by C. P. Johnson, district missionary for the Home Mission Society to Norwegians in Iowa; see "The Norwegians in Iowa," *ibid.*, XIV (June, 1892), 181-182. See also J. A. Jensen, "The Danes and Norwegians of Nebraska," *ibid.* (May, 1892), 155-156.

[24] 48th Annual Report, ABHMS (1880), 34; 49th Annual Report, ABHMS (1881), 22.

thoughts by experience. Rejoicing that these people were "Protestant through and through," his supervision of the work with them convinced him that the Scandinavians assimilated and adapted to their new country, readily identifying with its interests and privileges.[25] In fact, successful results in the Home Mission Society's efforts among the Swedes helped shape the racial distinctions between nationalities that its leader, Henry L. Morehouse, gradually came to espouse. Just as the negative response of the French Canadians caused them to be regarded as inferior, the conversion of many northern Europeans to the Baptist faith made them appear superior. Speaking on the occasion of the fiftieth anniversary of the first Swedish Baptist church in America, Morehouse commended his foreign-speaking brethren for their zeal and consecration in the evangelization of persons from their homeland. He attributed part of their accomplishment to the added strength brought by the immigration of about 7,000 Swedish Baptists to the United States in the last quarter of the nineteenth century. Satisfied that the Scandinavian churches constantly contributed to English-speaking congregations, the secretary of the Home Mission Society expressed confidence in the sound doctrine and spirituality of the group whose representatives he addressed.[26]

At this point Morehouse added the *coup de grâce* to his argument: Baptist achievements among the Scandinavians had been notable because of the good qualities in the racial stock, for the same evangelical effort with different peoples did not always yield equal results. In northern Europe a more strenuous life brought out robust elements of character. Unlike southern Europeans, who spent warm nights lounging about the streets, the Swedes sat around a hearth and thus proved themselves true homemakers. Now a thorough-going social Darwinist unawares, the Baptist leader concluded that "to us they [Scandinavians]

[25] William M. Haigh, "Record of Baptist Mission Work among the Scandinavians of the United States," *Baptist Home Mission Monthly*, XIX (Nov., 1897), 374–377.

[26] Henry L. Morehouse, "Swede-American Baptists," speech on the First Swedish Baptist Church fiftieth anniversary, in *Baptist Home Mission Monthly*, XXIV (Dec., 1902), 318–323.

bring also that physical vigor which is replenishment to the American stock of vitality." This feature, when combined with the native population, would produce a magnificent American type with strong physical, mental, and moral fiber. By now the cause-effect relationship between racial and religious criteria of inferiority had become completely blurred in Morehouse's mind, yet the order of presentation of his speech indicates that he still gave priority to the latter. This is further proven by his emphatic statement that the Scandinavians had contributed much to American industry and manufacturing and fitted into political life here because they had never been under "the deadening influence of a medieval Romanism." Whether inherent racial characteristics caused men to reject Protestantism or their religion of "errors" brought about the undesirable traits, such Baptists as Morehouse always began their train of thought with the observation that those who accepted the superior Protestant faith *were superior;* those who were reluctant or refused the gospel were of a lesser breed.[27]

Nevertheless, immigrants from southern and eastern Europe now constituted a significant force in America, and efforts to win them had to be made. Concerned for the welfare of the nation, which they regarded as intimately bound up with its evangelization, even the most anti-immigrant Baptist spokesmen showed enough interest in the individual to support mission work among the new arrivals. The *Journal and Messenger* at the very height of its nativist campaign in 1897 proclaimed the duty of Baptists to go into every community and hold up the standard of Protestant Christianity as man's only hope. The clear-cut difference between an "ancestral religion inherited in Baptism" and one "associated with a personal repentance of sin and the exercise of a living faith in Christ" justified decisively attempts at outright proselytizing from Roman Catholicism. Not only because the religion of the new immigration threatened the country, but because it did not meet the qualification of insistence upon "personal faith in Christ" in Baptist eyes, did the *Journal and Messenger* set the tenor of the evangelization cru-

[27] *Ibid.*

sade. "Proselyting is not the terrible sin which some would have us believe it to be," cried the paper's editorial columns. "Let us have even more of it." [28]

In such a spirit a decentralized and autonomous denomination first confronted the hierarchical structure of the Catholic church in the 1880s. Now the national home mission societies, both women's and men's, assumed more responsibility than ever before. In the early years two approaches were used. One method sought to work among immigrants of all nationalities at once in such places as Ellis Island and the mining towns of Pennsylvania where they were heavily concentrated. The more common arrangement of the Home Mission Society was to appoint missionaries recently converted to the Baptist faith to engage in evangelistic efforts with their own ethnic groups. Neither attempt brought huge numbers of persons into the Baptist denomination, but those who did enter the fold had a profound impact upon the native Americans already within. The presence of foreign-speaking believers from the new immigration in the Northern Baptist organizations ultimately helped to alter attitudes toward the immigrant, just as the Germans and Scandinavians had convinced their English-speaking brethren of the positive attributes of the citizens of their homelands.

As previously mentioned, German pastors often began Baptist missions among the new immigrants. The Home Mission Society's emissary at Castle Garden in New York from 1882 to 1892, John Schiek, initiated his activities immediately upon arrival from Germany. As an immigrant he sympathetically realized that "in no condition of life is man more helpless than when he finds himself a stranger in a strange land." His ministry constantly sought to protect the innocent from the dangers and temptations posed by "treacherous and deceitful countrymen, by imposters and bad characters who would rob them." He not only approached non-Protestants but made the acquaintance of those already Baptist, providing them with a list of churches in which they would feel at home. At one time the ardent mis-

[28] Editorial: "Concerning Proselyting," *Journal and Messenger*, LXVI (Oct. 7, 1897), 8.

sionary acted as sponsor for a group of Russian Stundists about to be returned because they had no set destination in America, thus securing their admission. In the single year of 1889 Schiek greeted 850 Baptists coming from abroad. His work among those not of the faith encompassed even greater numbers: 650 visits to immigrant boardinghouses; 600 testaments and 19,800 tracts, church guides, and magazines distributed; 400 poor and needy persons given financial help; 112 religious meetings held; and 1,003 immigrants reported to his care.[29] After Schiek's death in 1892, the Women's Baptist Home Mission Society sent emissaries to Ellis Island to continue his ministry. One appointee undertook a special assignment among the Scandinavians, with whom she was horrified to find occasional Mormon converts on their way to Utah! Another engaged in humanitarian activities at the port of New York for many years, helping destitute families with food, clothing, and money. Because such women were often the only friends the stranger found when first setting foot on American soil, the colleagues of one missionary could well describe her upon her death as "the angel at the gateway." [30]

In their approaches to the separate nationalities of the new immigration, Baptists followed the pattern of polity set down by the German and Scandinavian experience. The first missions and churches used their own language exclusively in worship services and established conferences quite independent of the American Baptist Home Mission Society, except for its financial aid. The Bohemians provided an early testing ground among the peoples recently arrived from southern and eastern Europe. German Baptists began the work in Chicago in 1887, and the society appointed a native-born preacher to aid them. Soon the cities of Detroit and Cleveland had tiny Bohemian missions. William M. Haigh, head of Baptist efforts in Chicago, attributed

[29] 57th Annual Report, ABHMS (1889), 53; John Schiek, "Our Castle Garden Mission," *Baptist Home Mission Monthly*, IX (June, 1887), 149–150. See also "The Stranger within the Gates," *ibid.*, VIII (Jan., 1886), 13–14.
[30] "Castle Garden and Salt Lake City," *Tidings*, IV (Jan., 1885), 1–3; Mary G. Burdette, "A Visit to Castle Garden," *ibid.*, XI (June, 1892), 9–12; "The Angel at the Gateway," *Standard*, LVI (Mar. 27, 1909), 22–23; L. Lanyi, "The Stranger within Our Gates," *Baptist Home Mission Monthly*, XVI (Feb., 1894), 56–57.

the new interest in Bohemians there to the Haymarket riot, which he claimed did much to quicken and enlarge the activities of Christians for the evangelization of foreigners in urban areas. He asserted that because many of the natives of Bohemia were either Catholics or freethinkers, Baptists experienced difficulty in trying to convert them. As late as 1920 the Czechoslovak Baptist Union counted only 1,799 members.[31]

Attempts to draw Polish immigrants into the fold followed shortly with the setting up of a mission in Detroit in 1888 under the leadership of Joseph Antoshevski, a Baptist who had recently emigrated from Poland. He remained there only briefly, however, and in 1891 the Home Mission Society began an operation in Buffalo, which had a rapidly growing Polish community. Charles R. Henderson, the noted University of Chicago social gospel leader, urged Baptists to make every effort to wean Polish-Americans away from the Roman Catholic church. Henderson, revealing that a liberal outlook in religion did not necessarily imply a pro-immigrant disposition, characterized the Poles as "ignorant, riotous, and dangerous to social peace." [32] The Independent Catholic movement in Poland gave encouragement to some Polish Baptists who pointed to the antagonism the pope had aroused in attempting to crush certain ethnic religious characteristics. In the hopes of one such spokesman, the common love for Polish independence and nationalism shared by Baptists and Independent Catholics, coupled with resentment of Rome, would result in many conversions to the Baptist faith.[33] But this dream never came to realization, for in 1921 only fourteen Polish Baptist churches with approximately 1,400 members existed in America.[34]

[31] William M. Haigh, in *Baptist Home Mission Monthly*, XVIII (Nov., 1896), 379–381; 56th Annual Report, ABHMS (1888), 54; White, *Century of Faith*, 155.
[32] 56th Annual Report, ABHMS (1888), 65–66; 59th Annual Report, ABHMS (1891), 51–52; "Polish Mission in Buffalo," *Baptist Home Mission Monthly*, XIV (Apr., 1892), 135–136; Charles R. Henderson, "The New Polish Mission in the United States," *ibid.*, X (May, 1888), 114–116.
[33] "A Significant Movement," reprinted from the *Standard*, in *Baptist Home Mission Monthly*, XXI (Aug., 1899), 333–334.
[34] White, *Century of Faith*, 152–153.

Subsequent Baptist efforts with several other eastern European nationalities also saw small numerical results. In the polyglot center of Cleveland a Hungarian missionary went from house to house among his people after the German Baptists had made the first converts in 1902. In spite of attempts in Passaic, Brooklyn, Detroit, and elsewhere, Hungarian Baptists numbered only 1,577 in the United States in 1929.[35] Among Roumanians and Russians, failure was equally evident in statistical terms: in 1931 they counted 522 and 668 Baptists respectively.[36] The latter group, drawing on Stundist exiles who settled in such places as Scranton, Pennsylvania, and Liberty, North Dakota, furnished converts for English-speaking Baptist churches. From the beginning, however, Russian Baptists had difficulty with their American brethren because of the activities of William Fetler, an extreme fundamentalist from Petrograd who virtually destroyed the short-lived Russian Baptist Bible Institute in New York City with charges of heresy against the school's trustees.[37]

By 1905 some Baptists recognized the presence of non-Catholic elements in the new immigration. That year, when a writer for the *Baptist Home Mission Monthly* published a lengthy article on "The Slav Invasion," he began by stating that most of the recent arrivals had been trained as Greek (Eastern Orthodox) or Roman Catholics. But in his brief account of the history of Christianity in Bohemia, he noted that many Protestant churches were re-established there during the reign of Emperor Joseph II in the late 1700s. Adding that they were a people with inherited Protestant tendencies and thus open to the work of missionaries, he noted that when the restraints of the old country were removed, natural hostility to the Roman

[35] *Ibid.*, 153–154; L. L. Zboray, "Hungarian Baptists in Conference," *Baptist Home Mission Monthly*, XXXI (Aug., 1909), 363–373.
[36] White, *Century of Faith*, 151, 155–156; Louis A. Gredys, "Ohio Baptist Convention Missionary to Roumanians," *Missions*, IV (Sept., 1913), 704–707.
[37] William Fetler, "The Evangelization of Russians in the United States," *Watchman-Examiner*, III (Aug. 12, 1915), 1045; Gilbert N. Brink, "The Russian Bible Institute," *Missions*, VIII (June, 1917), 472–473; Fetler, "Why I Resigned from the New York Russian Training School and Why I Am Still in the United States," *Watchman-Examiner*, V (Nov. 29, 1917), 1531–32; Charles A. Brooks, "Mr. Fetler and the Russian Bible Institute," *ibid.*, 1532–33.

Catholic church caused many Bohemians to drop their allegiance to it. Magyars from Hungary also had Protestants among them, he observed, with a reference to the Lutheran and Reformed churches. Catholic Hungarians, like Bohemians, lapsed easily from their religion after coming to the United States, he claimed. The entire assessment of Slavic nationalities undertaken by the *Monthly* at this time was in fact designed to prove that each group was different; among them all one found both good and bad.[38] Several years later an article in *Missions*, the successor to the *Home Mission Monthly*, called special attention to the 8,000 Roumanian Baptists in Hungary and Transylvania who bore the label "Pocaiti," or "Repenters," in their homeland.[39] Yet as late as 1907 the official report of the Baptist Home Mission Society emphasized that the majority of recent immigrants came either from Roman Catholic countries or from nations where Protestant Christianity existed as a state religion, while large numbers of them were Jews.[40]

Baptists clearly recognized that the Jews from eastern Europe were to be approached separately from the Catholic immigrants. The Women's Baptist Home Mission Society in 1892 sent Jeanette Gedalius, a Baptist Jewess from Germany, to begin a special ministry at the multilingual Mariners' Temple in New York. There she distributed food, medicine, and fuel to the needy along with religious literature. Even so, the formation of a sewing school for children by Miss Gedalius and the hiring of a clergyman to assist her failed to win many Jewish immigrants to the Baptist faith.[41] Undaunted by such meager results, denominational writers refused to turn to anti-Semitism, instead praising the Jews in America for their thrift and readiness to take advantage of new opportunities. It was unfair, asserted a

[38] "The Slav Invasion," *Baptist Home Mission Monthly*, XXVII (Mar., 1905), 89–107.
[39] Louis A. Gredys, "Pocaiti or 'Repenters,'" *Missions*, V (July, 1914), 542–545.
[40] James M. Bruce, "Among the Foreign Populations," in 75th Annual Report, ABHMS (1907), 101–103.
[41] "Report on Jewish Work," *Tidings*, XII (Jan., 1893), 7; A. M. Collishaw, "The Mariner's Temple Jewish Sewing School," *ibid.*, XIII (July, 1894), 13; "A Voice from the Jews," *ibid.* (May, 1894), 12–13.

1910 article in *Missions*, to cast under opprobrium an ethnic group that furnished hard workers and good citizens who willingly helped their fellow men.[42]

When Baptist ventures among the separate nationalities faltered, the Home Mission Society attempted to attract converts in multilingual centers with a single clergyman. In this area events clearly revealed the ability of German Baptists in breaking down hostility to the new immigration and the failure of native-born missionaries to do so at first. Three individuals, one strictly American in origin, and the others of German background, are cases in point. The activities of John Wallace (1877–1943), Henry Crete Gleiss (1870–1939), and Dan L. Schultz (1872?–1923) plainly reveal how one man could arouse a positive or negative reaction both from the human beings he sought to reach and from the denomination's attitudes toward them.

Into the vast polyglot community of mining villages in Pennsylvania's Wyoming Valley (the Scranton area) came the young John Wallace in 1899, an itinerant missionary sent out by the Home Mission Society. Filled with zeal, Wallace personally visited over 2,000 families and held many evangelistic meetings during that year. Despite these contacts, or more likely because of them, the Baptist preacher took back to his sponsors a view of the valley's foreign-born as a strange mixture of humanity— Poles, Slavs, Russians, and Hungarians—persons who cheapened the value of labor and property, whose ignorance and outlook endangered the fabric of American society. Wallace could only see that these residents of northeastern Pennsylvania were superstitious, poor, and "depraved," having no ability to fit themselves for self-government. He observed that many of the coal towns, with their closely adjoining houses and lack of sanitary facilities, were degenerating into "patches" where liquor, lawlessness, and lust prevailed. Environmentalism had not yet dawned upon this American Baptist's mind in 1899, for he attributed the situation in Pennsylvania to the inhabitants rather than blaming their

[42] Joseph H. Adams, "The Jewish Quarter in New York," *Missions*, I (Sept., 1910), 575–580.

surroundings for the misery they endured. In a scornful manner Wallace wrote in exasperation that "it is sometimes a severe test to one's olfactory nerves to be compelled to remain for any length of time in some of these places, especially among the lower order of Romanists." [43]

In the opposite corner of the Keystone State another multilingual community was growing by leaps and bounds at the time when Wallace visited the region around Scranton. Perhaps few of the new Americans in the vicinity of Pittsburgh paid much heed when a twenty-eight-year-old son of German immigrants in Texas became pastor of the First German Church of the Steel City in 1898. In Henry C. Gleiss foreign-speaking peoples of the lower Allegheny Valley were to find a defender who took their plight before American Baptists, in whose councils he rose to positions of respect and influence. Soon after his arrival in Pennsylvania, he became corresponding secretary of the Pittsburgh Baptist Association, in which he fostered an expansion of work among the foreign-born. Other denominations recognized his capabilities, and he attained prominence in the Pittsburgh Council of Churches while supporting various civic and reform movements. Remaining in this area until 1917, Gleiss ultimately headed the Northern Baptist Convention's Committee on City Missions. A tireless individual, he not only operated at the organizational level but made the personal acquaintance of many immigrants in the course of his pastorate and through his affiliation with the German Baptist Orphan's Home in Pittsburgh.[44]

In 1908 Gleiss gave an address to his fellow Baptists that indicated a response to new Americans in stark contrast to that of John Wallace. Whatever characteristics southeastern Europeans possessed, he asserted, resulted from their native environment as well as their adopted one. In the old country they had been

[43] John Wallace, "Wyoming Valley—Foreign Work," *Baptist Home Mission Monthly*, XXI (May, 1899), 212–213; Wallace, "Winning Benighted Foreigners," *ibid.* (Dec., 1899), 467; Wallace, "The Foreign Population of the Wyoming Valley, Pennsylvania," *ibid.*, XXII (Aug., 1900), 233–234.

[44] For biographical information on Gleiss, see the *Michigan Baptist Annual* (1918), 60; 1925, iv; 1927, 1; 1936, ii; 1939, 24; *Rochester Theological Seminary General Catalogue, 1850–1920* (Rochester, N.Y., 1920), 191; and "An Appraisal of H. C. Gleiss," *Standard*, LXV (Oct. 13, 1917), 172.

kept in perpetual subordination by paternal regimes whose surveillance allowed no chance to develop self-control or self-government. Because they lived apart from the great highways of commerce and thus remained almost untouched by modern culture and its accompanying vices, the new immigrants were not ready to withstand the dangers of a greedy, commercialized world. Nowhere in southeastern Europe was there an adequate educational system to prepare them for life in the modern age, into which they had been thrust upon arrival in America. The common references to these nationalities as the "dregs of society" and the "refuse of Europe" were untrue for the vast majority. Rather, said the Pittsburgh minister, they were "ignorant children of nature, possessed of all the natural evils of such people, but also of all the capabilities of the physiologically well-developed people." When they came to the United States, he pointed out, many persons were waiting to deceive them and take their money. Employers exploited them, and their reputation as "dirty foreigners" or dangerous criminals became a popular notion. In this situation the expected occurred: human beings living in poor housing and unsanitary conditions naturally turned to the saloon for drink and companionship.[45]

The attitude expressed by Henry Gleiss reveals that a person of immigrant heritage himself, even of the "old" immigration, could better understand the problems of cultural shock involved in the transfer from a rural, semi-feudal society to an industrial and urban one, than could an American of native ancestry. Despite the hostile comments of some Scandinavian Baptists concerning southeastern Europeans, within the Baptist framework religion helped to reduce enmity between peoples who had not been the best of friends in the Old World. Because Gleiss had a clear grasp of the role of the environment, his solution to the "dangers" of immigration placed the responsibility squarely on Americans themselves. The newcomers had never had the chance for a free Bible or self-government, yet their desire to rise in society held out the promise that they would

[45] Henry C. Gleiss, "Southeastern Europe in Southwestern Pennsylvania," *Baptist Home Mission Monthly*, XXX (June, 1908), 267–270.

one day enter the mainstream of domestic life. Only if neglected or ignored, if left unevangelized by Protestant denominations, would the strangers become a national menace. Native-born citizens could best assist them by teaching through example and precept. In addition to the traditional pleas for missions in their own language, Gleiss advocated institutional church methods such as sewing and carpentry schools for children. Beyond the realm of religion, he urged public-spirited individuals to campaign for the closing of the saloons and the prohibition of Sunday work for the laboring classes.[46]

Concern for the immigrant workingman shortly became the major preoccupation of another Baptist clergyman of German background in Pittsburgh. Dan L. Schultz, pastor of the Lorenz Avenue Church when the great Westmoreland County coal strike began in 1910, viewed with alarm the eviction of families from their homes and their subsequent relocation in camps set up by the United Mine Workers. After seeing the suffering with his own eyes, Schultz wrote articles in Pittsburgh newspapers and toured the entire state making appeals for food, clothing, and money to relieve the distress. Everywhere the minister who had spent his youth working in a glass factory spoke to immigrants of different nationalities about the church and its attitudes toward labor. His efforts helped in the distribution of over ninety tons of clothing and $27,000 to the strike-bound miners.[47]

Schultz's deeds greatly impressed the local American Federation of Labor, which promptly requested the Home Mission Society to ask him to devote full time to the working classes of the United States. The United Mine Workers also wrote the Baptist organization, saying that Schultz's activities had convinced thousands of laborers that "the religious bodies of our country are interested in the social and moral uplift of the common people." In a rare instance of tribute to Protestantism, the

[46] *Ibid.*

[47] Coe Hayne, *Old Trails and New* (Philadelphia, 1920), 177–182; James M. Bruce, "A Labor Evangelist," *Missions*, II (Mar., 1911), 158–162.

UMW resolution stated, "During industrial conflicts there are many who go among our people denouncing religious denominations as being antagonistic to labor interests. The work of Reverend D. L. Schultz in this instance has done much to correct this impression." By now the Home Mission Society had appointed a director of foreign-speaking work, James M. Bruce, who visited the strikers' camps upon Schultz's request and was appalled by the scenes of human misery. Even though he still questioned the "wisdom of the methods by which they sought to obtain their rights," the way in which the miners endured their hardship convinced Bruce that they needed the services of a special clergyman. After consultation with Pittsburgh businessmen and the United Mine Workers' representatives, both of whom approved of Schultz's performance during the strike, he urged the Home Mission Society to create a Baptist labor bureau with the Pennsylvania clergyman at its head. Perhaps because of a traditional Baptist reluctance to appeal to the workingman, the society rejected the organizational proposal as too "formal and ambitious," but it nevertheless acted jointly with the Pittsburgh Baptist Association to name Schultz as "Labor Evangelist." [48]

Bruce knew that the mind of a denomination that had delayed such a step until 1911 (the Presbyterians had set up their Board of Immigrant Ministry under Charles Stelzle in 1903) had to be put at rest. In addition to soliciting the support of Pittsburgh businessmen for this appointment, he wrote that Schultz's task was solely to "preach the gospel." The Home Mission Society specifically instructed their new missionary to "carefully refrain from partisanship in respect to men or policies in labor movements." [49] In spite of the attempt to restrict him, Schultz achieved remarkable success because he constantly asserted that the church stood with labor in its demands for the abolition of sweatshops, a universal education system, and the relief of poverty by as equal a distribution of wealth as possible. Unions from Colorado to Massachusetts invited him to speak on religious

[48] Bruce, "A Labor Evangelist," 158–162.
[49] *Ibid.*, 162.

topics at their conventions and to conduct services among their members. Most of his talks were given to immigrants, and more Catholics than Protestants cooperated with this Baptist preacher. Respected by employer and employee alike, Schultz upon his death in 1923 held honorary memberships in eleven national labor organizations. His message aimed at both sides of his constituency: to workers he offered sympathy and argued that Christian principles justified their requests; to employers he stressed that the improvement of factory conditions was a moral obligation.[50]

As the nineteenth century merged into the twentieth, Baptist experience with the new immigration gradually lessened the severity of the criticism denominational spokesmen had once heaped upon these people. Largely owing to the influence of such outstanding immigrant pastors as Henry C. Gleiss and Dan L. Schultz, American Baptists came to have a high regard for ethnic groups that they had once scorned because of failure to convert to Protestantism. Contrasting statements in Baptist literature at different times reveal the extent of the change in outlook. The *Baptist Home Mission Monthly*'s new awareness in 1905 that some of the Slavs were Protestants has already been cited.[51] Even so, as late as 1909 a missionary for the Home Mission Society could brand the Czechoslovaks as infidels who had little respect for the sabbath and lived only for self-gratification.[52] But in 1920 a correspondent for the *Baptist* praised the same people as "progressive, industrious, and intelligent."[53] Several years later the head of the society's foreign-speaking work described most Polish-Americans as "one of the best elements among the new immigration," substantial citizens who owned homes and took part in community affairs. What a far cry from

[50] *Ibid.*, 160; Hayne, *Old Trails and New*, 184–187; 79th Annual Report, ABHMS (1911), 52–54; 84th Annual Report, ABHMS (1916), 130–132; 85th Annual Report, ABHMS (1917), 91.

[51] See n. 38 above.

[52] D. D. Proper, "Foreign Mission Work on the Home Field," *Baptist Home Mission Monthly*, XXI (Aug., 1909), 361–362.

[53] "Czechoslovaks Blazing New Trails in America," *Baptist*, I (Feb. 7, 1920), 46–47.

Charles R. Henderson's 1888 assertion that the Poles were "ignorant, riotous, and dangerous to social peace"! [54]

The Baptist encounter with Italian-Americans, with whom they were most successful among the natives of southern and eastern Europe, graphically illustrates the evolution of their thought. Confrontation with a population strongly Catholic yielded only about 3,000 converts, but in spite of anti-Catholicism in connection with the Italian work, Baptists altered their view of the ethnic group they had once charged with flooding the country with peanut venders and organ grinders. The pattern was familiar: as small numbers of Italians became Baptists, they championed the virtues of their countrymen to American churchmen. Once more face-to-face contact with human beings proved decisive in convincing native Baptists that these aliens were not so undesirable after all. Again an outstanding immigrant pastor arose who won the approval of the upper echelons of the Baptist church, as Henry Gleiss and Dan Schultz had done, with resultant respect for the nationality that had produced him.

Italian Baptist organizations originated on a modest scale in localities where these people were found. The New York City Baptist Mission Society fostered the first congregation in 1893, and the Home Mission Society entered the scene by hiring an Italian student at Colgate University to establish a mission in Buffalo the following year. Soon Baptist churches in various cities across New York, such as Gloversville and Cortland, began to teach English to Italian immigrants in an attempt to win them. In Brooklyn the city mission society formed a foreign-speaking congregation, and in nearby New Jersey a Baptist group sponsored such institutional features as classes in civics, English, cooking, and dressmaking, along with a gymnasium and playground for children. New York City's pioneer institutional church, the Judson Memorial, opened its health center to new Americans in its neighborhood and sponsored a day nursery for

[54] Charles A. Brooks, "Evangelizing the Poles in the United States," *Missions*, XVI (Oct., 1925), 521–522. Henderson made this comment in "The New Polish Mission in the United States," 114–116.

the youngsters of working mothers. Across Pennsylvania, too, Baptists ministered to Italians at Philadelphia, Uniontown, and Scottdale.[55]

In New England a work of considerable proportions developed. The First Baptist Church of Hartford, in conjunction with the Hartford Baptist Union, opened an Italian mission in 1901. A leading Baptist businessman and banker who became interested in this operation, Charles E. Prior, discovered that these immigrants were "the most responsive and grateful people" he ever knew. His experience was typical: American Baptists could hate the organ grinders and peanut venders from afar, but not when acquainted with them through personal relationships. At Barre, Vermont, Baptists showed concern for the sons of Italy. Ariel Bellondi, the pastor who founded the church in Buffalo in 1896, two years later visited this New England town where large numbers of Italians had come to work in the quarries. Because many of these people had left the Catholic church to espouse socialism, Bellondi thought the situation propitious for evangelism, but he was soon disappointed. Some of the Italians of Barre were anarchists, some atheists, and they generally opposed all religion. As late as 1916, when the distinguished Italian-American clergyman Antonio Mangano visited this region, the foreign-born there forced him to confine his lectures to the secular aspects of Italian culture and history. Although Mangano offered classes in English and befriended the inhabitants of Barre, he reached the conclusion that preaching the gospel among them would be ineffective. Meanwhile, in Massachusetts, Boston, Lawrence, Monson, and Haverhill saw the opening of new missions for Italians.[56]

---

[55] A. S. Coats, "First Italian Baptist Church, Buffalo, N.Y.," *Baptist Home Mission Monthly*, XXII (Mar., 1900), 94–95; E. E. Chivers, "Our Baptist Italian Mission Work," *ibid.*, XXVII (May, 1905), 187–200; James M. Bruce, "A New Italian Mission," *ibid.*, XXX (Jan., 1908), 24–25; Frank H. Cooper, "How One Local Church Is Solving Its Foreign Problem," *ibid.* (May, 1908), 225; E. C. Kunkle, "The Italian Mission in Scottdale, Pa.," *ibid.* (Sept., 1908), 353–354; Chester F. Ralston, "The Local Church and the Foreigner," *ibid.* (Oct., 1908), 225; Antonio Mangano, "A Successful Mission for the Italians," *ibid.*, XXXI (July, 1909), 338–340; A. Ray Petty, "Twelve Thousand Italians in the Back Yard," *Baptist*, III (Feb. 25, 1922), 107.

[56] George M. Stone, "The Italian Mission in Hartford," *Watchman*,

Like the Baptist attempts to convert the French Canadians, efforts to win the Italians often met with Catholic opposition. Missionary pastor Angelo di Domenica claimed that an Italian daily paper in Newark, New Jersey, warned readers to shun Protestants, whom it allegedly referred to as "the plague of the human race." His brother, Vincenzo di Domenica, reported from Massachusetts that a gang of drunken Italian men had interrupted an open-air meeting with screaming and profane songs. When he asked the city for protection, the Irish Catholic marshall rejected the request and prohibited him from preaching in the streets. He fared no better in Providence, Rhode Island, where young boys stoned and insulted him. In far-off Uniontown, Pennsylvania, Reverend Hector Schisa attributed difficulty in reaching his countrymen to the great fear of hell implanted in their hearts by the Church of Rome. At Troy, New York, an Italian Baptist clergyman complained of resistance to his work by students at a local Catholic seminary.[57]

The driving force in Baptist labors among the Italians was an individual of keen understanding who refused to let himself be overcome by hostility to Catholicism. Antonio Mangano (1869–1951), who for many years directed the Italian Department of Colgate University, which he founded in 1907, verifies the validity of the generalization that every significant religious movement bears the stamp of a great personality. Born in Italy and sent to America at an early age, Mangano himself was one of the chief reasons that Baptists came to have a high regard for Italian immigrants. This ardent Baptist obtained an extensive edu-

LXXXIX (Oct. 31, 1907), 21; Charles E. Prior, "Italian Baptist Mission, Hartford, Connecticut," *ibid.*, XCI (Feb. 4, 1909), 9–11; Ariel Bellondi, "The Brothers of Columbus and Garibaldi," *ibid.*, XCV (May 22, 1913), 16–19; Bellondi, "Another Italian Mission," *Baptist Home Mission Monthly*, XX (Dec., 1898), 423–424; Bellondi, "Italian Work in Vermont," *ibid.*, XXV (Sept., 1903), 236–237; Antonio Mangano, "Italian Work in Barre, Vermont," *Missions*, VII (June, 1916), 476–477; "Italian Work at Monson, Mass.," *Baptist Home Mission Monthly*, XXVII (Apr., 1905), 141.
[57] Chivers, "Our Baptist Italian Mission Work," 197–198; Vincenzo di Domenica, "Persecution in Providence, R.I.," *Baptist Home Mission Monthly*, XXI (Jan., 1899), 24–25; Di Domenica, "Blessing and Opposition," *ibid.*, XXIV (Aug., 1902), 231; Hector Schisa, "Italians and the Gospel," *ibid.*, XXX (Mar., 1908), 109–111; "An Italian Missionary's Account of His Work," *ibid.*, XXXI (Feb., 1909), 82–83.

cation, receiving degrees from Brown and Columbia Universities, Union Theological Seminary, and Westminster Theological School in England. During his long and varied career he returned to his native land to study its language and customs; in his adopted country he rose to the presidency of the New York State Baptist Pastor's Conference.[58]

Mangano and other Italian Baptists performed the same function in American Baptist organizations as their German and Scandinavian counterparts. Constantly, over the years, foreign-speaking pastors took up the cause of their ethnic groups before the denomination, and gradually native-born churchmen accepted their arguments. Ariel Bellondi, the lesser-known pioneer in Italian evangelism, followed the earlier example in 1900 when asked if his people were politically dangerous. Evidently sensing the racial concepts so prominent in the decade just passed, Bellondi replied that Italians had loved liberty longer than Anglo-Saxons. Were not Venice and Florence republics while despots ruled England? Was not Italy the home of Mazzini and Garibaldi? Because the citizens of his homeland were generally republican in their sympathies, he averred, they would assimilate quickly into the American system of government. Gaetano Lisi, a pastor in Monson, Massachusetts, charged that writers in the United States went looking for opportunities to abuse Italians. He admitted that many of his countrymen were indeed ignorant and illiterate, but he pointed to their success in truck farming and fruit raising as indicators of physical strength and energy.[59]

Mangano, however, led the way in the campaign to elicit sympathy from Northern Baptists. Although the book that brought

[58] For brief accounts of Mangano's life, see the *Watchman-Examiner*, XXX (Jan. 15, 1942), 39, 53; XXXIX (May 17, 1951), 476; (June 7, 1951), 562; "The Pioneer Builder of Men," *Il Messaggero* (Nov., 1942), 7–8; and the typewritten manuscript in the Home Mission Society's personal files, located in the American Baptist Historical Society. On the founding of the Italian Department at Colgate University's theological seminary, see "Italian Department of Colgate Theological Seminary," *Examiner*, LXXXV (Feb. 21, 1907), 234–235; "The Italian Theological School," *Baptist Home Mission Monthly*, XXIX (Dec., 1907), 447.

[59] Ariel Bellondi, "Italian Immigration and Missions," *Baptist Home Mission Monthly*, XXIII (Feb., 1901), 40–41; Gaetano Lisi, "The Italians," *Watchman*, XCIII (Aug. 3, 1911), 19.

him national recognition, *Sons of Italy*, was not published until 1917, its author had taught the ideas it contained to students and had expressed them within the Home Mission Society for over fifteen years. More than just a polemic tract, *Sons of Italy* went beyond its essential purpose of interesting Protestants in the conversion of the Italian. Mangano described in detail the colonies of immigrants in America, telling of the low wages, wretched housing conditions, and other hardships. He portrayed the cultural shock that the farmers of Italy experienced upon arrival in the cities of the New World, and he explained their religious background. Mangano, like all Protestant Italians, criticized the Catholic church, but not in a bitter or vitriolic manner. He eschewed the emotional denunciations made by many of his co-workers and offered instead an intellectual rejection of Catholicism. Largely owing to his influence, anti-Catholic feeling never reached the heights in Baptist work among the Italians that it had in the attempt to convert the French Canadians.

The dominant feature of Mangano's writings and teachings was a predictable vindication of the "sons of Italy." The concluding chapter of the book, entitled "The Italian's Contribution to the America of Tomorrow," aimed to show that because they possessed natural good manners, politeness, and brilliance, these immigrants had much to give their adopted land. Accordingly, he urged Protestants to act with loving interest and sympathetic understanding in their overtures to the newcomers. Like the Divine Providence theorists of the 1880s, Mangano regarded America as the chosen nation that was assuming primacy in the world. But he also felt strongly that the alien who looked to her as a refuge for the oppressed could appreciate this pre-eminence better than anyone else.[60]

Mangano's guiding hand, coupled with the reasonable success Baptists enjoyed in the Italian work, brought about a major alteration in the viewpoint of native-born churchmen. In 1891, before it had made any substantial gains among them, the Home Mission Society characterized Italians as "not generally desirable acces-

---

[60] Antonio Mangano, *Sons of Italy* (New York, 1917), 195-223 and *passim*. Over 20,000 copies of this book were sold.

sions to our population, nor . . . an inviting or hopeful field for evangelical effort." Three years later the society's annual report stated that these prospective citizens were usually poor, ignorant, degraded, and suitable only for menial service, but it grudgingly admitted that they exhibited frugality and in some cases had "the knack of getting on." [61] These pronouncements were quite typical, for throughout the 1890s many Baptist writers claimed that the organ grinders and peddlers of Italy were decidedly inferior to persons from Germany and Scandinavia.[62]

In 1900, however, after a few years of noticeable achievement among these "undesirables," the Home Mission Society ceased its unfavorable comment about them and simply affirmed that they were industrious, thrifty, accessible, and potential Protestants.[63] In the first decade of the twentieth century Baptist literature shifted its perspective considerably. Compare, for example, an 1896 article in the *Home Mission Monthly* with one of 1904. The earlier commentator branded all Italians as poor, illiterate, and superstitious; the later composition claimed that Protestant churches in America had overlooked the finer aspects of their character. In 1896 multitudes of these immigrants were said to be swelling the ranks of paupers, beggars, and criminals; in 1904 the observer found cause for optimism in the second generation, which was developing into a hardy race of bright, energetic, loyal Americans under the tutelage of the public schools. To the Baptists of the earlier period, the sons of Italy should be excluded as a matter of self-preservation; by 1904 the writer could echo Ariel Bellondi's argument that the admirers of Garibaldi sought a country where they could enjoy freedom and thus would become patriotic citizens here.[64] And what had brought about this transformation? The authors of both articles were American Baptists. It is true that in 1896 the editor of the *Home Mission*

[61] 59th Annual Report, ABHMS (1891), 48; 62nd Annual Report, ABHMS (1894), 97–98.
[62] A typical example of this opinion was expressed in the *Standard*, XLV (Aug. 12, 1899), 1.
[63] 68th Annual Report, ABHMS (1900), 65–66.
[64] "And Still They Come," *Baptist Home Mission Monthly*, XVIII (June, 1896), 197; William W. Pratt, "Our Italian Mission in Passaic," *ibid.*, XXVI (Sept., 1904), 343.

Monthly was the anti-immigrant Thomas J. Morgan, while a more sympathetic individual had taken over in 1904. But this alone hardly accounts for the transition in thought. The essayist of 1896, whether Morgan or someone else, criticized the Italian from afar; the 1904 interpreter, William W. Pratt, was involved with a Baptist mission among these people in Passaic, New Jersey. Once again, experience and acquaintance with persons of the new immigration had made an American churchman more amenable to them. As in many other cases, Walter Rauschenbusch's statement proved true: one might speak disparagingly of foreigners in the abstract but would regard them as brothers upon personal confrontation.[65] Thus, in spite of the relatively small numbers of Italians (3,265 in 1920) gathered into the fold, visible accomplishments coupled with the influence of immigrant clergymen such as Mangano had a profound effect.

The impact of foreign-speaking mission work upon Protestants in general and Baptists in particular must therefore not be judged on the basis of statistical success in making converts. From this vantage point the whole operation appears as a failure, for in 1924 Protestants had only 2,985 churches and mission centers among 26 million foreign-born in the United States. Of these, only 963 operations centered their attention on the 13,800,000 persons of the "new" immigration.[66] Practically all Protestant denominations undertook this type of work in the late nineteenth and early twentieth centuries, with some more effective with one ethnic group and some with others.[67] On balance, Baptists were probably no more or less fortunate in winning immigrants to their faith than other Protestants. But the Baptist record in this area reveals how studies in the history of ideas defy statistical analysis, pointing to the meaninglessness of numbers in assessing the significance of social interaction between immigrants and Americans. In this single corner of American Protes-

[65] Walter Rauschenbusch, in *Baptist Congress Proceedings* (1888), 87.

[66] William F. McDermott, "Turning American," *Continent*, LV (Nov. 27, 1924), 1471.

[67] For a chart showing the statistics of the work among the foreign-born of the various denominations in 1889, see *Church at Home and Abroad*, V (Aug., 1889), 129.

tantism one may observe a complete about-face in attitude, from hostility toward the foreigner in the late eighties and nineties to mutual respect by the middle of the first decade of the twentieth century. Although a variety of subtle and complex factors, such as the decline in nationalism and the rise of the social gospel movement, undoubtedly entered into the making of this transformation, the personal acquaintance of Baptists and aliens from southern and eastern Europe clearly provided the major catalyst.

Experience, of course, could have led Baptists in a different direction. After all, the encounter with the French Canadians resulted in bitterness and a rise in nativism. Success was sufficient among the Germans and Scandinavians to warrant the conclusion that these groups were "acceptable," but not as many Italians, Poles, Hungarians, and the like became Baptists. That the humane view prevailed was due to a variety of elements intimately bound up in the nature of the foreign-speaking work. The pervasive influence of the Germans in the Baptist denomination stands out as crucial in determining its orientation to the new immigration. Their forcefulness sought and won the right to use their native language while receiving financial aid from the Home Mission Society and at the same time maintaining an independent polity. This policy helped to lessen the cultural shock that many immigrants must have felt upon arrival in a strange land, where the security given an individual by hearing words of comfort in his own tongue cannot be overestimated. Moreover, German Baptists set the example of defending their nationality to Americans, who accepted these arguments in part because they *did* begin to believe them, in part because they *had* to believe them in order to woo the newcomers. In the breaking down of hostility toward the southeastern Europeans, the German Baptists also played a direct role. Not only did they initiate missions among them, but such leaders as Henry C. Gleiss and Dan L. Schultz understood what it was like to be a stranger. Gleiss's comprehension of the function of the environment in urban and immigrant problems was a most proper answer to the negative results of John Wallace. Schultz's personal work among the miners of Pennsylvania, and his concern for the plight of the workingman, put into practice the ideas of a more famous German Baptist, Walter Rauschenbusch.

The failure to induce large numbers of new Americans to join the Baptist ranks is probably as much a result of the strength of the Roman Catholic hierarchy as of the decentralized Baptist polity. As early as 1925 a student of the Catholic church pointed out that the vitality and vigor of this faith in America arose in large part out of immigration.[68] Thus, from the Protestant point of view, the apprehensions of the nineties had some basis in fact. Nevertheless, Baptists began to realize in the early years of the twentieth century that tirades against the Roman Catholic church accomplished nothing but a deep alienation from the Protestant gospel. This accounts for the lesser animosity to Catholicism in the Italian work, even though many of the immigrant pastors had strong feelings. Here individuals made a profound difference. When the educated and sensitive Antonio Mangano sensed resentment against a religious message in Barre, he restricted his talks to secular topics and befriended his countrymen there as best he could. Thirty years earlier, when missionary James Williams met with resistance among French Canadians, he had complained to the Home Mission Society repeatedly and continued to push the "gospel wagon" deep into French-speaking communities.

As the Baptist confrontation with the peoples of southern and eastern Europe brought about a metamorphosis in their outlook, the intellectual and social functions they had to fulfill were closely tied to one another. Their dream of a perfect Christian society based upon acceptance of the Baptist message, while it led them to advocate immigration restriction for a season, also gave rise to a solicitude for the welfare of every human being. As the nineteenth century ended, this concern soon led to an interest in the external conditions of the immigrants' surroundings, which in turn helped to bring about divisions among Prot-

[68] Gerald Shaughnessy, *Has the Immigrant Kept the Faith?* (New York, 1925), 222.

estants. It remains to be seen whether the expansion of liberalism in religion in the form of the social gospel would foster further development of the charitable view of foreigners initiated by the social experience of the Baptists with limited numbers of aliens.

5

Liberals, Conservatives, and the New
Immigration: 1900–1914

The world of Protestantism has never been a unified one, and
it was not so at the dawn of the twentieth century. Ever since
Charles Darwin published his *Origin of Species* in 1859, theo-
logians had been forced to grapple with the religious implications
of the latest scientific information. New studies of the Bible
from Germany and Great Britain caused churchmen to rethink
the traditional doctrine of biblical inspiration. The issues of
evolution versus the Genesis story of creation; textual criticism
versus the inerrancy of the Scriptures; and a transcendent gospel
demanding personal conversion and individual salvation versus
the "theology of the Kingdom," which sought to establish heaven
on earth through the improvement of society—these issues presently divided Protestants along lines that have been referred to
as "liberal" and "conservative." Whether they took the form of
"evangelical liberalism," which attempted to restate the basic
Christian doctrines in more intelligible and convincing terms, or
"scientific modernism," which taught that science was the ultimate judge of truth in matters of religion, the changes in theology that prepared the way for such a secular interpretation of
Christianity as the social gospel created major divisions in the
Protestant realm. "Conservatives" arose to challenge the tide of
liberalism, vigorously defending the inerrancy and authority of
the Bible and insisting upon the necessity of a vital conversion
experience. While the real cleavage did not reach a breaking

point until conservatism became "fundamentalism" in the 1920s, this debate noticeably affected the Protestant clergy in the decisive years before and after 1900.[1] How would these developments affect the growth of a favorable view of the new immigration? Would the "conservatives" continue the invidious distinctions and advocacy of restriction that many Baptists had espoused in the 1890s, while "liberals" took up the cause of the immigrant? Or would the lines between conservative and liberal become less clear as both spoke out on social issues like immigration?

In the nation the conditions that gave rise to the social gospel had produced a decade of strife and unrest in the 1890s. Although McKinley's election to the presidency in 1900 appeared to indicate that the forces of unrest had been silenced and that an era of peace and prosperity was beginning, the fissures that ran through American society were not suddenly removed by the solidarity achieved during the Spanish-American War. The trend toward industrial combination, with its monopolistic tendencies that threatened the free enterprise of small businessmen, reached a new zenith with the formation of United States Steel in 1901. Great investment banking firms like that of J. P. Morgan and Company controlled an ever-increasing share of the country's wealth. To challenge this corporate power, a strong, nationally organized labor movement arose that clashed with management in a series of incidents and strikes. Many of these confrontations took place in cities, as a dwindling rural population watched with alarm the growth of the metropolis and its attendant evils. Here, in the very "storm centers" of American culture, Protestants encountered hordes of alien immigrants not of their faith. These circumstances, according to a leading historian of this period, seriously endangered internal unity again. On the threshold of the twentieth century two major forces propelled American society in different directions. The concentration of material resources and the concomitant rise of the corporation and finance

[1] For a discussion of the differences between conservatives and liberals at this time, see Winthrop S. Hudson, *Religion in America* (New York, 1965), 263–284. The origins and background of the fundamentalist movement are outlined in Ernest R. Sandeen, *The Roots of Fundamentalism* (Chicago, 1970).

capitalism were creating a stratified social order. At the same time new intellectual and moral creeds, originating in part out of Protestant traditions, called for a return to a more equalitarian life.[2]

This situation provided the impetus for a wave of reform generally known as the "progressive movement." In politics the progressives demanded, in varying degrees, the remaking of government into an agency for the improvement of human existence. A sense of guilt over the improper accumulation of riches led them to advocate the public control of private property in order to save the capitalist system from self-destruction. With guilt came a compulsion to make restitution. Things had to be set right, and progressives doggedly held to the efficacy of legislation to remove social injustice. Humanitarian leaders sought to bring aid and comfort to the impoverished workers and immigrants of city slums. Yankee Protestant values, now turned into an intense moralism, seemed to be the ideal for setting up the Kingdom of Heaven on earth through "applied Christianity."

Within the conscience of progressivism, unhappily, a certain degree of self-righteousness sustained a modicum of Anglo-Saxon racism that had been brought to life by the "scientific intellectuals" in the 1890s. Theodore Roosevelt and his friend Henry Cabot Lodge agreed with William Allen White that "we are separated by two oceans from the inferior races and by an instinctive race revulsion to cross breeding that marks the American wherever he is found." [3] Because of these beliefs, many urban progressives were anti-immigrant and made the closing of the gates one of the chief items on the agenda of reform. John Higham has asserted that, on balance, "the reformers of the early twentieth century welcomed the newcomers, appreciated their Old World customs, and rejected the prejudice which would shortly bring about immigration restriction." Oscar Handlin, on the other hand, feels that "the progressive program to destroy the

[2] George E. Mowry, *The Era of Theodore Roosevelt and the Birth of Modern America 1900–1912* (New York, 1958), 15, 37.
[3] *Ibid.*, 93.

immigrant-based political machine created," in the words of a commentator on the historical debate, "a wall of misunderstanding" between aliens and native-born Americans.[4] George Mowry, in an attempt to reconcile these opposite interpretations, notes that although the reformers' response to the large urban ghettos was Christian and humanitarian through the social settlement movement, "the attitude of the progressive toward race, religion, and color, and his attending view of the great city, was to . . . keep alive and possibly nourish a strain of bigotry that was to bear bitter fruit for the United States after the First World War."[5]

Never purely political in character, progressivism had roots in distinctly religious principles and thus affected many of the churches. The social gospel gradually captured large segments of the Protestant denominations after the turn of the century. New concepts in theology now asserted that "sin," or evil, was sociological in nature: it had originated in men's actions toward one another in suspicion and ignorance and thus could best be suppressed by the action of decent individuals who concerned themselves with the problems of society.[6] If this were true, a change in the environment would aid in the transformation of man, not vice versa, as the older generation of churchmen had thought. At last the dream of the Divine Providence theorists of the 1880s might come to fruition in the formation of a perfect civilization. Outwardly, the major American religion was in a position to lead the way to the fulfillment of this goal, for the interval spanning the turn of the century comprised what one observer has described as the "halcyon years" of Protestantism in the United States. Vast congregations filled the churches and expensive edifices were built, as Protestants participated in a wide variety of humanitarian endeavors from social settlements to boys' clubs. The clergy enjoyed esteem and regular publicity

[4] The summary statements of the debate between Higham and Handlin on this issue are from Arthur Mann, ed., *The Progressive Era* (New York, 1963), 48, 53. See Higham, *Strangers in the Land*, and Oscar Handlin, *The Uprooted* (New York, 1951), from which Mann has excerpted short selections.
[5] Mowry, *Era of Theodore Roosevelt*, 93–94.
[6] *Ibid.*, 26.

through the daily newspapers, which printed the sermons of such luminaries as Phillips Brooks, Russell H. Conwell, and Washington Gladden.[7] Walter Rauschenbusch, the Baptist of German heritage who had most eloquently defined the implications of the Kingdom of God on earth for twenty years, now received sudden recognition and respect throughout the nation.[8]

Rauschenbusch and a few other Baptists had become involved in shaping the outlines of the new social gospel as early as 1892. That year he founded a small organization known as the Brotherhood of the Kingdom. This group, which included Leighton Williams of New York and Samuel Zane Batten of Philadelphia, held summer meetings annually for over twenty years to discuss the problems of the day in the light of the "Kingdom of God." These conferences dealt with such topics as monopolies, the labor question, social work, and the single tax. In 1907 Rauschenbusch wrote *Christianity and the Social Crisis*, which established him as the leader of the social gospel movement in the United States. While Rauschenbusch set forth ideas in books and teaching, Batten became increasingly active in Baptist organizations. The year 1907 also saw the formation of the Northern Baptist Convention. At last Baptists had a central unifying agency, and at its initial meeting the NBC established a committee to investigate what the churches were doing in the area of social service. Two years later, under Batten's direction, the American Baptist Publication Society began to issue a series of pamphlets on the relation of religion to the family, to the community, to industry, and to politics. By 1913 Batten headed an official Department of Social Service of the convention, which continued to print literature on the social gospel, indicating its widespread acceptance in the denomination.[9]

For Baptists, the road to the crusade for social justice was an

[7] Winthrop S. Hudson, *American Protestantism* (Chicago, 1961), 124–125.

[8] Among Rauschenbusch's published works are *Christianity and the Social Crisis* (1907), *Prayers of the Social Awakening* (1910), *Christianizing the Social Order* (1912), *The Social Principles of Jesus* (1916), and *A Theology for the Social Gospel* (1917).

[9] Hopkins, *Rise of the Social Gospel in American Protestantism*, 131–134, 293–296. See also Walter Rauschenbusch, *Christianity and the Social Crisis* (New York, 1907).

especially tortuous one. Long committted to the nineteenth-century doctrine that each individual had the primary respon-sibility for his own fate, nevertheless the Baptists' concern for the development of a perfect Christian civilization, held by "conservatives" and "liberals" alike, presaged the theology of the Kingdom and all its ramifications. In the years from 1900 to 1914 these two themes came into a conflict that foreshadowed the later fundamentalist controversy of the 1920s. The nature of the debate at this time was not as sharply delineated by shades of belief as it was to become. Social issues now assumed priority with the Baptists just as they did with the entire nation, and a "conservative" doctrinal position did not necessarily imply a like attitude in regard to contemporary problems. Neither did a "liberal" stand mean that its advocates followed through con-sistently on all questions. In the case of immigration, presently characterized by the Home Mission Society as the supreme challenge facing the country, "progressive" theology often went hand in hand with remnants of the old nativism, while more circumspect denominational forces, such as the religious press, rose to champion the strangers they had once denounced. Old ways vied with the new, often in a confused fashion, as spiritual leaders groped their way into the twentieth century. Progres-sivism, the social gospel, the experience in mission work among new Americans—all now converged to bring about a gradual acceptance of the immigrant and his ways in some quarters of the denomination, while others retained the conviction that the "old" immigration was vastly superior to the "new." By exam-ining the individuals who played key roles in the leadership of the Baptists at this time, one can find a paradoxical verification of both John Higham's claim that the progressive mind rejected nativist prejudice and George Mowry's contention that certain progressive attitudes laid the basis for the fear of the stranger that followed World War I.

Urbanization was to be a critical factor in the coming age, and "the cry of the city" was what first sparked awareness among many Protestants. From 1900 to 1914 articles on the problems of the metropolis began to appear in the major Baptist periodicals with greater and greater frequency. In 1903 the Chicago *Stan-*

dard published a series concerned with the large middle class of the area, both foreign and American, that neither the social settlements nor the churches had reached. The young John R. Slater, shortly to begin a long and distinguished teaching career at the University of Rochester, drew up a plan for the more efficient evangelization of Chicago by Baptists. In New York, Robert Stuart MacArthur, for over forty years pastor of the large and conservative Calvary Baptist Church, called upon his congregation to transform their community into the heavenly city of the apostle John's vision—"glorified, clean, luminous, and joyful." And in Boston, Tremont Temple's George C. Lorimer realized that before foreign urbanites could even give thought to the claims of Christianity, their surroundings must be improved. A few gospel missions among new Americans were insufficient: they needed more food and better wages, and less vice and crime.[10]

As they discussed urban issues, Baptists began to converse with men outside the denomination who shared their solicitude for the fate of Protestantism in the light of what was happening. In 1905 Amory H. Bradford, a Congregational minister, told readers of the *Standard* that the transfiguration of the American metropolis would come about only if Christians would put themselves at the services of humanity. Preaching was not the only means for advancing the Kingdom; clubs and gymnasiums that drew homeless men out of the saloons also performed the work of Christ. In emotional terms he berated the "modern Shylocks" operating sweatshops at the expense of those living in cellars and attics, the "sleek, slimy, serpentine politicians," and the respectable sitting in comfortable houses unconcerned about it all. Because of his moral indignation, Bradford clearly revealed the conflict between the progressive's dislike of the city and his simultaneous anxiety for its welfare:

> Where are bred revolutions? . . . Where is the most terrible poverty? . . . Where rises the bitter cry of the unemployed? . . .

---

[10] "Chicago as a Field for Religious Work," *Standard*, L (Feb. 7, 1903), 4–11; Robert Stuart MacArthur, "The Problem of the City," *Examiner*, LXXXI (Feb. 5, 1903), 168–170; George C. Lorimer, "The Religious Problem of the City," *ibid.* (Apr. 23, 1903), 520–521.

The modern city is the standing menace of civilization—yet without the city there can be no civilization. It is the strategic point in the contest against wickedness. If that be taken for righteousness the salvation of the world will be easy; if that be lost the redemption of humanity may be deemed impossible.[11]

Bradford exhorted church members to follow the lead of the social settlement workers, attempting to ease the suffering of millions of people. Only if they did so could Protestantism hold these strategic centers, for as he pointed out, "Those who are hungry for bread do not care much about heaven or hell." [12]

Josiah Strong, the venerable Congregationalist who first sounded the alarm in 1885, was now welcomed as a writer for *Missions*, the successor to the *Baptist Home Mission Monthly*. In familiar tones he warned of the tendencies of urban areas to outstrip the countryside, to foster burgeoning slums with their attendant vice, to come under the control of unscrupulous men, and to spawn radical ideas. Strong, for many years a Divine Providence theorist, characterized the city as the heart of God's laboratory where the application of his teachings alone could lessen the dangers of the situation. Charles Stelzle, rising to prominence as the head of Presbyterian missions among immigrants, expressed similar feelings to his Baptist friends. In articles written for most of the Baptist periodicals, Stelzle foretold a revival of Protestantism that would deal fearlessly with the exploitation of little children, helpless women, and downtrodden men. Such a spiritual renaissance, demanding the salvation of men's bodies as well as their souls, would destroy forever the notion that Christian businessmen might engage in unethical practices simply because their unchristian competitors made great profit in so doing. In a word, organized religion must at last insist that the community be Christianized, and Stelzle called upon all Protestants to cooperate in the evangelization of America's "storm centers." [13]

[11] Amory H. Bradford, "The Cry of the City," *Standard*, LIII (Nov. 18, 1905), 9.
[12] *Ibid.*
[13] Josiah Strong, "The World Influence of the City," *Missions*, I (May, 1910), 317–320; Charles Stelzle, "The Churches in a Unified Program of Advance," *Standard*, LX (Nov. 23, 1912), 10.

While Baptists thus considered the pleas of clergymen outside the denomination, a number of "liberals" within were turning increasing attention to the metropolis. Although the Northern Baptist Convention esteemed Walter Rauschenbusch highly, other Baptists showed suspicion of his anticapitalist predisposition. Because of this, the religious sage of Rochester probably had a greater following in the nation at large than in his own fold. Handicapped by deafness, Rauschenbusch did not seem as influential in many of the national Baptist meetings as the popularity of his books would lead one to believe. It remained for friends and admirers, such as Shailer Mathews (1863–1941) of the University of Chicago and Samuel Zane Batten (1859–1925) of the Brotherhood of the Kingdom, to carry the prophet's message into the councils of Baptist officialdom. Mathews, an exponent of the so-called scientific modernism, advocated with Stelzle a more extensive interdenominational cooperation in city missions and led Chicago Baptists along the road to the social gospel.[14]

Batten presently became a commanding influence in Northern Baptist ranks. A friend of Rauschenbusch since the early 1890s, this zealous clergyman reveals many of the ambiguities of the progressive Protestant mind. While calling upon Christians to rectify conditions in urban immigrant communities and arguing for the environmentalist interpretation of their plight, Batten nevertheless branded the peoples of southern and eastern Europe as clearly inferior. Because he believed in the Divine Providence concept of immigration characteristic of the eighties, and possibly because of his respect for Rauschenbusch, he would not agree with the third plenipotentiary of the Brotherhood of the Kingdom, Leighton Williams, that foreigners should be shut out. Solicitous for the physical and spiritual welfare of the newcomer, he yet adopted a policy of Americanization after World War I that was closer to "100 percent Americanism" than anyone else in the denomination was willing to go.

14 Shailer Mathews, "Is Protestantism to Lose the Great Cities?" *Missions*, I (May, 1910), 321–325; Mathews, "Business Methods in Home Missions," *Standard*, LVII (Jan. 1, 1910), 5. The standard biography of Rauschenbusch is Dores R. Sharpe, *Walter Rauschenbusch* (New York, 1942).

Born in New Jersey in 1859, Batten obtained his education at Bucknell University and Crozer Theological Seminary. After serving several pastorates in New Jersey, New York, and Pennsylvania, he accepted a call to the First Baptist Church of Lincoln, Nebraska, in 1905. A charter member of the Brotherhood of the Kingdom since 1892, Batten soon after the turn of the century began to write for the Baptist journals and make his presence felt in the various annual conferences. One of his first causes was prohibition, for which he campaigned as president of the Nebraska Anti-Saloon League from 1903 to 1908. In 1908 Batten spearheaded the drive in the Northern Baptist Convention for the formation of the Social Service Committee. Except for a brief term as chairman of the Social Science Department at Des Moines College from 1910 to 1912, he devoted the latter part of his life to leading this work.[15]

Significantly, Batten's first major address to the Home Mission Society in 1903 expressed his opinions on "The New Problems of Immigration." More than any other Baptist spokesman, he perpetuated the national-origins myth among his colleagues and thus revealed that old attitudes could persist along with new ones in a single individual. In a manner that might well have caused Granville Abbott to rise from his grave and applaud, Batten proceeded to argue from the assumption that "the great and enduring nation must be the homogeneous nation. . . . The nation that breaks apart into classes and fragments cannot endure." Only now the nonhomogeneous element was not the Chinese; it came from southern and eastern Europe. One by one the Baptist leader set forth the ideas that the Dillingham Commission would make official four years later. Up to 1865 most immigrants came from Great Britain, Ireland, Germany, and Scandinavia— "people who are more or less allied [with us] in blood, in language, in customs and religion." But over the past quarter-

15 Unfortunately, there is no biography of Batten. For biographical information, see the *Nebraska Baptist Annual* (1925), 21; *Pennsylvania Baptist Annual* (1925), 137, 142; *New York Baptist Annual* (1926), 83; *Alphabetic Biographical Catalog, Crozer Theological Seminary 1855–1933* (Chester, Pa., 1933), 35; *Your College Friends: Alumni Directory of Bucknell University 1846–1940* (Lewisburg, Pa., 1940), 9; and the *Baptist*, VI (Sept. 12, 1925), 947.

century the ratio of "allied races from Protestant and enlightened Europe" had steadily fallen, while "the proportion of
alien races from Catholic and illiterate Europe" had rapidly increased. The "old" immigration came from such worthy motives
as religious and political freedom; the "new" were "malcontents
and n'er-do-wells" whose purpose in migrating was to grow
rich without hard work. The earlier influx was largely sponta-
neous; the latter was artificially induced and consisted mainly of
unskilled laborers at best.[16]

When Batten broke down his analysis according to nationalities, the only differentiation he made among southern and
eastern European ethnic groups was in the choice of unfavorable
adjectives. The Italians were "destitute of vital religion," the
Bohemians were "irreligious and infidel," the Poles had "little
appreciation of civilization." The friend of Rauschenbusch even
found many of the German "clannish," although he admitted
that most of them were industrious and energetic skilled workers
or farmers. The Scandinavians he declared desirable because they
were more "mouldable" than other foreigners. Unlike Henry
L. Morehouse, who equated the Irish with the French Canadians,
Batten easily waived the question of creed to assert that the inhabitants of the Emerald Isle made good American citizens
because they readily adopted the ways of their new land. Not so
with the benighted of eastern Europe, who refused to lose their
ethnic identities and assimilate. Showing no sign of liberality on
any aspect of the problem, the Protestant liberal told the Home
Mission Society that he had heard enough praise of "our cosmopolitan cities and our cosmopolitan customs." If America
must choose, he preferred the Puritan life and sabbath to the
Parisian mode with its continental Sunday. Batten combined the
variants of late nineteenth-century Anglo-Saxonism in a single
stroke: God had sent the strangers here to be Christianized so
they might take light to the whole world, yet the presence of a
large class who had little sympathy with Protestantism or democratic institutions threatened this dream. Refusing to commit

[16] Samuel Zane Batten, "The New Problems of Immigration," *Baptist Home
Mission Monthly*, XXV (July, 1903), 175–178.

himself to immigration restriction in 1903, the Baptist leader urged his colleagues to begin to convert *and* Americanize the unfit aliens.[17]

Although as a social gospeler he believed that corporations and businessmen constituted as great a menace to society as the dangerous classes of workingmen and foreigners, Batten nevertheless retained his special dislike of the immigrant for many years. He later conceded that if given the whole "Gospel of the Kingdom" and treated justly, recent additions to America might become her most valuable citizens. Thus he insisted that only an undying passion for justice and brotherhood on the part of the churches would win the stranger who failed to respond to an "individualistic, self-seeking gospel" set forth in a few poorly equipped mission stations. Organized religion, to Batten, ought to show a "hot hatred for evil," which he equated with the status quo. His whole philosophy—"If things are turned wrong side up, Christianity is here to turn them upside down"—did not, however, keep him from promulgating the national-origins myth in 1903 or from demanding a very chauvinistic Americanization program in 1920, which called on the foreigner to repudiate virtually his entire native culture.[18] In all of this Batten revealed not only that the progressive mind could dislike both "the sin

[17] *Ibid.*, 178–185. For views nearly identical to those of Batten, see Thomas J. Villers, "Immigration a Providential Opportunity for Evangelization," *Baptist Home Mission Monthly*, XXII (Aug., 1900), 225–231, and T. F. Chambers, "The Evangelization of New York State," *Examiner*, LXXIX (Mar. 7, 1901), 2–4.

[18] Batten, "New Problems of Immigration," 178–185. See also the following by him: "The Dangerous Classes in America," *Standard*, LIII (May 12, 1906), 9–10; "The Literature of the Kingdom," *Missions*, I (Nov., 1910), 731–732; "What Will the Churches Do about It?" *Standard*, LVIII (Apr. 22, 1911), 1, 10. The latter article, in which Batten expressed his anger at the facts made public in a report of the Chicago Vice Commission, is typical of his philosophy. For his role in the Americanization campaign, see the report of Samuel Zane Batten *et al.* in the Northern Baptist Convention *Minutes* (1920), 242–245. While Batten's position on immigration may appear to undermine the argument that experience with aliens tended to liberalize Baptist views, this is not the case. Batten was always an overseer; he did not work directly with immigrants as did the missionaries whose reports are discussed in Chapter 4. Moreover, the example of Batten sustains the earlier argument that persons of immigrant background like Henry C. Gleiss and Dan L. Schultz could understand foreigners better than native-born churchmen like John Wallace and Batten himself. See Chapter 4.

and the sinner" but that the distinctions often made between advocates of the "old" and the "new" theology, between "conservative" and "liberal" Protestants, were more blurred at this time than has sometimes been assumed. Did not Granville Abbott, who would have shuddered to be called a "liberal," lay the groundwork for Batten's plea for homogeneity in the discussion of the Chinese question in 1882? Had not the conservatives in the Baptist ranks whom Batten flayed for moral insensitivity early accepted and disseminated theories of racial inferiority in the 1880s and 1890s? [19]

The Baptist who played the major role in the denomination's transition from a hostile attitude toward the stranger to a cordial one was a man who had no formal theological training and concerned himself with religious journalism and practical applications of social gospel principles. Howard B. Grose (1851–1939) was a product of the old generation, yet a harbinger of the new. The son of a Baptist minister who pastored small-town churches in rural New York, Grose received B.A. and M.A. degrees from the University of Rochester in the days of President Martin Brewer Anderson. He became a correspondent for the *Chicago Tribune* in 1876, but in 1879 he moved into the world of Baptist periodicals with an appointment to the editorial staff of the *Examiner*. Pastorates in Poughkeepsie, Yonkers, and Pittsburgh interrupted his writing career from 1883 to 1890, and in the latter year he became president of the State University of South Dakota. After four years at the University of Chicago as registrar and assistant professor of modern history, Grose became associate editor of the *Watchman* in 1896. Thus exposed to both "conservative" and "liberal" elements among fellow Baptists, he brought a varied combination of experiences to the editorship of the *Baptist Home Mission Monthly* in 1904. Always ecumen-

[19] Batten's contemporaries of a more conservative bent than he also expounded theories of the inferiority of people from southern and eastern Europe. Thomas J. Villers, who in 1920 was to address the Conference on the Fundamentals on "Fidelity to Our Baptist Heritage," in 1900 cited "bad ancestry" and "degraded home life" as proof of the bad blood of the Poles. In the same article he charged that the large increase in immigration from Slavic nations was lowering the average intelligence and morality of the influx (Villers, "Immigration a Providential Opportunity for Evangelization," 225–231).

ically inclined, Grose became an official representative of the Northern Baptist Convention at the first meeting of the Federal Council of Churches in 1908, and for many years he served with Samuel Zane Batten on the council's Social Service Commission. As time went on, his writings embraced an increasingly interdenominational outlook.[20]

As soon as he assumed control of the *Monthly*, its pages gave top priority to the new immigration and its implications for Protestants. The February, 1904, issue portrayed the challenges the influx offered to religious forces and called upon Baptists to step up mission work on home soil. Successive articles and editorials reviewed recent discussions of this topic as well as current proposals, such as an international agency to regulate immigration and plans for the distribution of incoming aliens on agricultural land in the West. An illustrated series in 1908 deplored conditions in the steerage of the great ships that brought Europeans to America. A reporter for the *Monthly* spent a day at Ellis Island and related in detail the procedure for entrance into the United States. The Baptist observers had special praise for Robert Watchorn, the Commissioner of Immigration, for his sensitive handling of individual cases of hardship.[21]

In 1905 Grose began a major reassessment of the traditional Protestant view of the strangers from southern and eastern Europe. Speaking of the need for a new outlook, the editor of the *Monthly* bluntly asked his readers if they would accept an immigrant family in their church or would prefer to keep them at a distance in a separate mission. If Christians earnestly wished to

[20] *The University of Rochester General Catalogue 1850–1928* (Rochester, N.Y., 1928), 66. See also *Missions*, XXIV (Jan., 1933), 38. Grose served as the editor of *Missions*, which he founded in 1910 as a periodical designed to combine articles on home and foreign missions among Baptists.

[21] "A Challenge to American Protestantism and Patriotism," *Baptist Home Mission Monthly*, XXVI (Feb., 1904), 35; "Entering the New World," *ibid.*, 40–43; "A Suggested Remedy" (editorial), *ibid.*, XXVIII (Mar., 1906), 93; "Irrigation and Immigration" (editorial), *ibid.*; "From an Immigrant's Log Book: Scenes in the Steerage," *ibid.*, XXX (Jan., 1908), 15–21; (Feb., 1908), 48–54; (Mar., 1908), 96–104; "Concerning Immigration" (editorial), *ibid.* (Feb., 1908), 45–46; "A Model Gate-Keeper: Robert Watchorn, the Commissioner of Immigration at Ellis Island," *ibid.* (Mar., 1908), 91–92; "A Day at Ellis Island," *ibid.*, 93–95.

evangelize and assimilate the foreigner, he asserted, they would have to put themselves in his place and treat him in a respectful manner. The common references to the newcomer as a "problem," "menace," or "peril" would no longer do: the patronizing spirit that such terms reflected merely brought about alienation. The time had come to forget the dangers posed by immigrants and to disregard their alleged ignorance, superstitions, and low ideals. Emphasis must henceforth be placed on the providential aspects of the influx; Baptists must now realize that "the brother man for whom Christ died" threatened society only if left isolated and neglected by Protestant Americans. Where Samuel Zane Batten saw pronounced racial variations among the earth's peoples, Howard B. Grose looked "beneath all the superficial distinctions of race and class and culture and refinement" to the essential oneness of mankind, which was "to be appraised not by its accidental differences, but in the light of the incarnation which forever dignifies human nature." This approach, cognizant of the "unfailing love of God" to all men, said the Baptist editor, would now have to replace the "present attitude of aloofness" in order to take up the responsibility thrust upon Protestants by God's children recently transplanted to the New World. Personal acquaintance with the strangers, not scorn from afar, would make Christians aware of their ideas, hopes, and dreams.[22]

Grose was not content to speak to fellow Baptists alone. In 1906 he wrote two books designed to provide information about the new immigrants and to promote missionary work among them. *The Incoming Millions* and *Aliens or Americans?* were to be used in home mission study groups of the various denominations.[23] In his descriptions of European ethnic groups Grose showed a remarkable degree of sympathy and objectivity. One year before the Dillingham Commission came to its conclusions about the general differences in characteristics between southeastern and northwestern Europeans, this Baptist author knew

[22] Editorials: "Two Pertinent Questions," *Baptist Home Mission Monthly*, XXVII (May, 1905), 167; "A Question of Attitude," *ibid.*, 168; "Among the Foreigners," *ibid.* (Oct., 1905), 361.
[23] Howard B. Grose, *The Incoming Millions* (New York, 1906) and *Aliens or Americans?* (New York, 1906).

that each nationality must be considered separately. He admitted a relatively high illiteracy rate among the Italians, for example, but used facts to dispel the notion that Italy furnished more paupers than other countries. His sources came from some of the best contemporary observers: Graham Taylor, of Chicago, and Peter Roberts, who wrote of the Slavic immigrants in *The Anthracite Coal Communities*.[24] Very much aware of the continuing debate over immigration restriction, Grose affirmed the unquestioned right of Congress to set policies that were necessary to safeguard American institutions and liberties. Judicious in his factual account of the arguments over the literacy test, he appeared to approve of legislation to keep out the "appalling numbers" of delinquent or physically defective aliens. But any considerable suspension of immigration, he averred, was neither realistic nor desirable at that time.[25]

Influenced not only by Taylor and Roberts but also by the work of Jane Addams, Grose most clearly revealed his social gospel orientation in his discussion of "The Foreign Peril of the City." The title of this chapter of *Aliens or Americans?* proved misleading, for the "perils" came from Americans, not from foreigners. A complete environmentalist, he made his chief center of attack the circumstances in which immigrants lived. Both books called attention to the pathos and heartbreak of life in a tenement—the absence of light and fresh air for children, the unsanitary conditions, the neighborhood saloons—all allowed to exist because of civic corruption and the indifference of men who failed to respond to their consciences. Was it any wonder, placed in such a setting, that the strangers wished to cling to their own customs by forming colonies practically impervious to American influences? Differing with Samuel Zane Batten on the nature of the new immigration, Grose agreed with him that "every Christian ought to know the wrongs of our civilization, in order that he may help right them."[26]

For Grose, the answer lay not only in attempts at conversion

---

[24] Grose, *The Incoming Millions*, 61–65, 73–76.
[25] Grose, *Aliens or Americans?*, 87–121.
[26] *Ibid.*, 196–197.

but in creating a clamor for social reform so loud that politicians would have to listen to the aroused Christian populace. To women, he portrayed Jane Addams as most worthy of emulation. He called for the elimination of overcrowding in housing facilities, laws to prevent food adulteration, and the abolition of sweatshops and child labor. The latter were particularly responsible for the high crime rate among second-generation Americans, he affirmed. The causes of poverty were also to be found more in the environment than in the individual. The widespread unemployment among southern and eastern Europeans, he pointed out, often stemmed from a lack of job opportunities and from illness of the breadwinner brought about by a lack of sanitation. If Protestants were to protect the religious and political institutions that the immigrant allegedly menaced, they must begin to show concern for the surroundings that made him behave the way he did.[27]

None of this was new or unique in 1906, even to Baptists. Walter Rauschenbusch, Leighton Williams, and Samuel Zane Batten had preached the same ideas for over fifteen years, but they couched their arguments in a rather elaborate "theology of the Kingdom" whose implications the average church member was slow to grasp. Rauschenbusch's teachings received only a passing nod in some corners of the denomination. Batten realized that the immigrant was not entirely accountable for his plight and called upon Christians to set things right, but he fully accepted the racial distinctions first enunciated by persons far more conservative than himself. Leighton Williams, in his desire to "hold up the candle of a right civilization here," had no compunctions about closing the doors to those who might blow out the light. But Grose, in like manner influenced by the social gospel, remained more consistent in its application.

At the same time that he called for the betterment of the environment, he did not condemn the "self-seeking individualistic gospel," as Batten had, but had confidence that home mission efforts would turn aliens into Americans. In his call to Protes-

---

[27] Grose, *The Incoming Millions*, 84–95, 108, 111–112; *Aliens or Americans?*, 202–230.

tants to rectify injustices in society, Grose placed himself in the framework of the most progressive element of the Baptists. Yet he clearly believed in an individual and transcendent message, as indicated by his exhortations to Christians to personally befriend as many of the incoming millions as possible, in order to "win them to Christ." Untrained in theology and uninterested in the subtleties of its differences, the editor of the *Home Mission Monthly* bridged the gap for Baptists between the nineteenth and twentieth centuries. While completely aware of the possible effects of immigration upon domestic, political, and religious life, he expressed the optimism so characteristic of the progressive era. The third generation of immigrant children, he was confident, would respond to the American influences of freedom of suffrage, educational advantages, improved industrial conditions, equality before the law, and the protection of property. Already fifty-five when his very readable books were published in 1906, Grose continued to exercise influence among both old and young contingents of Baptists for over twenty years after that time.[28]

While the *Home Mission Monthly* and its editor proceeded with the attack upon the traditional attitude of suspicion and deprecation of the foreigner, other Baptists were doing likewise. Further articles by contributors to the *Monthly* heralded the virtues of such once-disparaged groups as the Italians, pointing to the benefits they easily absorbed from American schooling and their excellent potential for citizenship.[29] In 1904, the year Grose launched his campaign, the Home Mission Society's superintendent in the Upper Mississippi Valley did not accept the contention that the alleged change in the character of the alien influx would necessarily endanger American civilization. Agreeing with Grose that much would depend upon the treatment the newcomers received in their adopted land, Owen A. Williams felt that a rapidly developing nation still needed "hewers of wood and drawers of water." The countries formerly supplying the

[28] Grose, *Aliens or Americans?*, 262, 269ff. See also pp. 231–257.
[29] Samuel H. Lee, "Italian Characteristics," *Baptist Home Mission Monthly*, XXVII (May, 1905), 183–185. For other views similar to this, see Kate H. Claghorn, "Our Italian Immigrants," *ibid.*, 177–182.

United States with workmen could barely meet the present demand, he claimed. In spite of his position of supervising mission
endeavors to primarily Germans and Scandinavians, Williams
assured the readers of the Chicago *Standard* that Russians and
Italians, too, would make important contributions to the nobler
development of the republic. In Boston the *Watchman* concurred
that the so-called low-grade immigration from southern and eastern Europe consisted of persons possessing almost infinite ca-
pacities for achievement.[30]

Indeed, the historically conservative *Watchman*, which had
supported the literacy test in the late 1890s, now became the
champion of the hapless foreigner. Four years before Grose became editor of the *Monthly*, the Boston paper noted the harm
caused by clergymen who spoke ill of those not born in America,
adding that the spirit of human brotherhood was supposed to
govern Christian teachings. In order to eradicate racial hatred and
produce a cosmopolitan outlook, it argued, children should be
told about the excellences of other peoples and about their gifts
to humanity. No race or nationality could claim the United
States as its exclusive domain, asserted an editorial five years later
in 1905. Repudiating Samuel Zane Batten's doctrinaire insistence
upon national homogeneity, the *Watchman* envisaged a diverse
culture with limited blending. In rejecting the concept of the
melting pot, the Boston periodical claimed that relatively little
mixing would take place because the Anglo-Saxon element itself
showed reluctance to intermarry with other strains. But this did
not necessitate disunion and conflict, as Baptists from Granville
Abbott to Samuel Batten had argued. The various ethnic groups
could cooperate on the broad grounds of equality before the law
and justice in its administration. If only Protestants were willing
to wait patiently, recognizing the existing strength of racial and
religious feeling, the principles of the Constitution and of the
Christian church would unify the different components within a
few generations. By that time the public school would have thor-

[30] Owen A. Williams, "The Stranger within the Gates," *Standard*, LI (Aug.
6, 1904), 6–7; "The Immigration Returns," *Watchman*, LXXXV (July 30,
1903), 6.

oughly imbued the children of immigrants with patriotism, and the Protestant gospel would have elevated the newcomers and won their loyalty.[31]

Basking in the sunshine of such optimism, the *Watchman* reversed its earlier position on immigration restriction. The paper that had once pleaded for Lodge's literacy test in the late 1890s condemned it by 1903. Such a device, it declared, did not adequately determine ability to adjust to American institutions. Based on the false assumption that educational attainments made a people sensible and virtuous, the argument continued, the requirement of literacy had nothing to do with a person's ultimate competency for citizenship. The *Watchman* now contended that those who endorsed the Lodge bill probably suffered from some form of "Know-Nothingism." Harsh and repressive measures, whether they attempted to shut out the stranger or to keep him from naturalization and officeholding, ran counter to Divine Providence and would result in a disastrous reaction in the nation.[32]

Nevertheless, the *Watchman*'s assertion that suspicion and criticism of foreigners stemmed from the self-conceit and ignorance of uncultivated and half-civilized men fell upon deaf ears in some Baptist quarters. The Cincinnati *Journal and Messenger*, still clinging to its belief that only the closing of the gates would save America, claimed that the country had presently reached the point where all immigration would be harmful because it tended to give alien ideas pre-eminence over time-honored American principles. The midwestern paper censured all measures that would stop short of keeping out the bulk of such "undesirable races" as the Italians, Hungarians, and Russians: therefore, a plan like that of Henry Cabot Lodge was worth hundreds of half-way proposals. Neither schemes for the distribution of recent arrivals

31 Editorials: "Attitude toward Foreigners," *Watchman*, LXXXI (Sept. 6, 1900), 7; "Our Prejudices against Foreigners," *ibid.*, LXXXIII (Dec. 12, 1901), 8–9; LXXXVII (June 22, 1905), 8; XCI (Mar. 18, 1909), 5; "The Immigration Problem," *ibid.*, LXXXIX (Jan. 3, 1907), 6; "New Turn in the Immigration Question," *ibid.* (May 2, 1907), 5; "Dealing Wisely with Aliens," *ibid.*, XCV (July 3, 1913), 7–8.

32 Editorials: "How to Test Immigrants," *Watchman*, LXXXV (Dec. 3, 1903), 6; "Dealing Wisely with Aliens," 7–8.

on western farmlands nor a fixed equal annual quota from each country would accomplish the goal of excluding the "dregs" of southern and eastern Europe. The Cincinnati journal, unlike the *Watchman*, had no faith in the children of aliens, whom it regarded as more dangerous than the newcomers themselves.[33] On the restriction issue the *Journal and Messenger* was not alone among Baptists in the first decade of the twentieth century. Even the *Examiner*, no longer intensely nativist, asked, "Why not stop this flood of undesirable immigration before it is too late?"[34]

The pronouncements of the *Journal and Messenger* were more than just tinged with racism, especially in regard to Orientals. The editors maintained, as had Granville Abbott twenty years before, that the permanent introduction of Asians in America might crowd native-born citizens out of the Pacific Coast area. To them, the "yellow peril" was real; therefore, "men of so different races as Anglo-Saxon and Japanese had better dwell in different countries." Certain friends of the Chinese unwisely demanded the impartial application of restriction to all nations: this was inadequate, not because one ethnic group was superior but because the inhabitants of various corners of the earth were often unlike one another. The *Journal and Messenger* completely separated the political question of discriminatory criteria and the religious duty of Baptists to carry the gospel throughout the globe. Even the Oriental residents of the newly acquired territory of Hawaii, it claimed, should be barred from entry into the United States.[35]

The old guard of the Baptist denomination, obviously yet very much alive, did not content itself with continuing its commands to shut off the flow of aliens. Shortly after the turn of the century the *Journal and Messenger* felt that an attack upon the new

[33] Editorials: *Journal and Messenger*, LXIX (Jan. 25, 1900), 1; (Aug. 30, 1900), 1; LXXI (Apr. 17, 1902), 1; LXXII (Nov. 19, 1903), 5; LXXIII (Jan. 7, 1904), 4; LXXIV (Feb. 16, 1905), 3; (Mar. 16, 1905), 4; LXXV (Feb. 22, 1906), 4.

[34] Editorials: "Why Not Stop It?" *Examiner*, LXXX (June 12, 1902), 3–4; "The Peril of Immigration," *ibid.*, LXXXI (July 30, 1903), 957.

[35] Editorials: *Journal and Messenger*, LXXIII (Apr. 28, 1904), 3–4; (May 12, 1904), 1; LXXV (Dec. 20, 1906), 4; LXXVI (July 18, 1907), 3; (Aug. 22, 1907), 3; LXXVII (Nov. 26, 1908), 3.

attitudes toward the immigrant was in order. Jane Addams received considerable disapproval for her claim that Americans should adapt themselves to the newcomers instead of vice versa. This position was "as dangerous as dynamite," for its acceptance would mean surrender to European culture, said the paper. Grudgingly acknowledging that Miss Addams had done much good in social settlement work, the *Journal and Messenger* nevertheless denounced her for an outlook that endangered the preservation of American ideals when confronted with those of Europe.[36]

Howard B. Grose and his kind were the next objects of the assault. While not mentioning the editor of the *Home Mission Monthly* by name, the *Journal and Messenger* undoubtedly had him in mind when it commented in 1908 on the recent spate of books designed to create sympathy for the alien. Such writings, the editors charged, while naturally appealing to Christian people with their stories of human privation, usually overlooked important issues involving immigration that affected the welfare of the United States and the progress of Christianity. Compassion for the stranger and appreciation of his hardships might carry over unconsciously into the dangerous imperative that he should be permitted to come here. As a warning against this fallacy of reasoning, the *Journal and Messenger* reiterated the argument that "there is no reason why our sympathy with the suffering, and our interest in mission work should blind our eyes to the necessity of the restriction of immigration at the earliest possible moment." Until it ceased publication in 1920, this conservative periodical continued to oppose virtually all innovation taking place in the Baptist denomination.[37]

In spite of the consistency of the *Journal and Messenger*, how-

[36] Editorial: *Journal and Messenger*, LXXIV (Jan. 5, 1905), 3.
[37] Editorial: *Journal and Messenger*, LXXVII (June 18, 1908), 4. Grover P. Osborne (1848–1932) wrote the editorials for this paper from 1888 to 1920, which undoubtedly accounts for the consistency of its position. The co-editor, George W. Lasher (1831–1920), was known as "the old lion of orthodoxy." See *Journal and Messenger*, LXXXIX (Mar. 18, 1920), 3–4; *Baptist*, I (Mar. 13, 1920), 248–249. Lasher published the paper from 1875 until it ceased publication in 1920.

ever, the changing Baptist viewpoint on two matters closely related to immigration further reveals that the lines between "conservatism" and "liberalism" were often blurred at this time. Old
attitudes now vied with new in regard to the nativist themes of
anti-radicalism and anti-Catholicism. The fatal shooting of President William McKinley by an anarchist at the Pan American
Exposition in Buffalo in 1901 threatened to do more than elevate
Mark Hanna's "damned cowboy" to the White House. Suddenly
the ancient fears of the foreign revolutionary, in limbo for several
years, came alive. Dr. Madison C. Peters, pastor of a Baptist
church in Brooklyn, wrote that as long as the "hungry hordes of
ignorant and lawless Europe" poured into America, not one in
twenty of whom would become a good citizen, the nation's material advancement would be impeded and its presidents placed
in danger of assassination. In an article for the *Standard* Reverend
E. B. Woods dredged up the hoary argument that anarchism was
not indigenous to the New World but was a wholly foreign
plant brought to its shores and nourished among the isolated
masses of aliens in the United States. Woods suggested that no
community should tolerate sinister radicals, from whom even the
freedom of speech should be withdrawn.[38]

Yet in 1901 such sentiments were not to gain the widespread
currency they had had among Baptists in 1886. James M. Coon
of Englewood, Illinois, who wrote Sunday school lessons for
the denomination for many years, issued a rebuttal to E. B.
Woods in the same number of the *Standard* in which the latter
commented on McKinley's death. While the anarchist should be
made to feel the strong arm of the law, Coon said, Americans
ought to look within their own society rather than abroad for
the conditions that produced such rebels. Christians were not doing enough, he claimed, to correct the abuses that caused human
misery. Because the middle and poorer classes failed in many
ways to receive the benefits of modern civilization, segments of
the population became hostile to the social order. Until Christian

[38] Madison C. Peters, "Stamping Out Anarchism," *Examiner*, LXXIX (Sept.
19, 1901), 9; E. B. Woods, "The Anarchist," *Standard*, XLIX (Sept. 21, 1901), 6.

businessmen, to cite one example, gave up the practice of hiring children to work for a pittance, the resentment of the dispossessed would not abate.[39]

Several years later Melbourne P. Boynton, a Chicago Baptist who would one day join the fundamentalists, pointed to the folly of repressive measures against anarchists. Rather than recommending the passage of harsh new laws, Boynton urged that public officials provide compulsory lecture courses for recent arrivals designed to acquaint them with the institutions, ideals, and opportunities of their adopted land. He advocated wider powers for park commissions so they could sponsor picnics and outings for foreign city dwellers, and he called upon all Protestant churches to cooperate more intelligently in their efforts to win the stranger. City mission societies of the several denominations ought to divide up the work among various nationalities, he said, and splendidly equipped institutional churches should be built. Boynton, who addressed the famous Conference on the Fundamentals held in Chicago a few years later, proved that a theological conservative could be quite liberal toward immigrants. His faith was quite naive, for he firmly maintained that "no hand is strong enough to cure anarchy, but the warm heart can."[40] In Boston, Francis H. Rowley agreed with Coon and Boynton that the blame for the deepening of class lines in America lay not with the socialist or the radical but in the unchecked power of successful and ostentatious wealth. He, too, placed responsibility on church members, whom he advised to apply Christian principles in all commercial and business relations, and to avoid indifference to poverty and distress.[41]

Even the Baptists' traditional antipathy to Catholicism showed signs of mellowing under the aegis of the new modes of thought. To be sure, much anti-Catholic feeling lay underneath the sur-

[39] James M. Coon, "How to Treat the Anarchist," *Standard*, XLIX (Sept. 21, 1901), 10–11.
[40] Melbourne P. Boynton, "The Cure of Anarchy," *Standard*, LV (Mar. 21, 1908), 7. See his article "The Churches and Sound Doctrines," *Watchman-Examiner*, X (June 22, 1922), 779–781, for an example of his theological views.
[41] Francis H. Rowley, "The Problem of the Immigrant," *Watchman*, XC (Mar. 26, 1908), 9–11.

face of Baptist expressions of opinion in the early twentieth century. Every year at the Home Mission Society's national meetings
James N. Williams, leader of the now declining evangelistic
endeavors among French Canadians, took the rostrum to present
the usual stories of horrible Roman Catholic deeds inflicted upon
Baptist missionaries. Here and there a clergyman mourned the
passing of the "old" New England, whose character was only a
memory living in historic sites, endowed institutions, and a few
venerable families. Articles appearing in such papers as the *Journal and Messenger* trotted out the alleged antagonism of Rome
to the public school system, the free press, the government, and
all aspects of human progress in general.[42]

A fresh spirit finding many champions in persons of conservative inclination presently arose to challenge the age-old abhor-
rence of the Vatican and its adherents. Lemuel C. Barnes (1854–
1938), then pastor of an institutional church in Pittsburgh and
later an organizer of the Federal Council of Churches, drove the
first chink into the Baptist anti-Catholic armor in 1901. Although
an ecumenicist, Barnes was thoroughly evangelical in outlook.
He had been active in bringing the famous revival team of
Dwight L. Moody and Ira B. Sankey to Pittsburgh in 1885, and
as late as 1920 he confessed that the early instillation of missionary ideals "held me steady" amid "the storms of intellectual questioning of everything in my theological course." Educated at
Kalamazoo College and Newton Seminary in the 1870s, his career as a respected Protestant leader lasted well into the 1930s.[43]

[42] 68th Annual Report, ABHMS (1900), 125–131; Orville Coats, "The New
New England," *Baptist Home Mission Monthly*, XXVII (Apr., 1905), 139–
141; A. B. Whitney, "Roman Catholic Hindrance to American Progress,"
Journal and Messenger, LXXII (May 28, 1903), 3. For other examples of anti-
Catholicism at this time, see James N. Williams, "Some Reasons Why We
Should Evangelize the French Canadians in This Country," *Baptist Home Mis-
sion Monthly*, XXIII (June, 1901), 169–173; Alexander Blackburn, "A Marvelous
Work in Massachusetts," *ibid.*, XXVII (June, 1905), 236ff.; "The Catholic
Point of View," *ibid.*, XXVIII (Nov., 1906), 395–396; L. A. Freeman, "Gospel
Work among the Foreign Born," *Watchman*, LXXXV (July 16, 1903), 23.
[43] Lemuel C. Barnes, "Count Your Blessings," Feb. 16, 1920, 1 (typewritten
MS, in American Baptist Historical Society). For biographical information on
Barnes, consult the typewritten biographical sketch in the Home Mission So-
ciety's files, and the *New York State Baptist Annual* (1938), 64.

In 1901 Barnes attempted to define the responsibilities of Baptists toward Roman Catholics. The first step, he said, was to distinguish between "good" and "bad" Catholics and to rate the church and its people by their ideals and best attainments rather than by their vices. To "bad," or lapsed, laymen, Baptists had the obligation to proclaim the same message of salvation that they would to anyone who was "lost." But for the faithful, Baptists also had good news—the doctrines of individual liberty before God unlimited by ecclesiastical hierarchy, and of direct communication with him without the mediation of priests or sacraments. Although this statement might make Barnes appear as intolerant as the haters of "Romanism" of a previous day, his whole attitude was different. He called attention to the beliefs that Catholics and Protestants held in common, and he spoke of the debt Christianity owed to the monks who had preserved learning and piety in the Middle Ages and to the missionaries who had carried the faith throughout Europe and England. Whatever disagreements remained between Baptists and Catholics, he averred, ought to be discussed in an honest and considerate manner among "Christian brethren." For Barnes, the era of propagating truth with the sword of bitterness and rancor had passed. His reference to Roman Catholics as "our Christian brethren" was just short of revolutionary in light of the feelings of the preceding decade.[44]

Barnes did not stand alone in his opinions, even though he may have been in a minority. The *Watchman*, ultimately to become the voice of Baptist fundamentalism after its merger with the *Examiner*, noted in 1903 the obstacles to effective mission work among Catholic immigrants, adding that in spite of their superstitions and corruptions, destructive criticism gained nothing. If Baptists destroyed an individual's belief in Catholicism, often nothing took its place. Aware that recent converts to Protestantism usually felt intensely hostile toward the church they had just left, the *Watchman* nevertheless cautioned that any clergyman who emphasized anti-Catholicism aroused insuperable preju-

[44] Lemuel C. Barnes, "Our Mission to Roman Catholics," *Watchman*, LXXXIII (July 18, 1901), 13–15.

dices and thus reduced his chances for success. The duty of Baptists, it asserted, was to build up rather than tear down, and to preach Christ rather than to fight Rome.[45] Several years later the *Watchman* reprinted a speech by the president of the Massachusetts Baptist Mission Society, who had declared the Protestant goal of turning Catholics away from their church an improper approach. Instead, John M. Lyon had asserted that Baptists ought to attempt the reform of that religion. Secretary Henry L. Morehouse of the Baptist Home Mission Society answered Lyon with the traditional argument that Protestants must continue to convert Catholics from an ecclesiastical system opposed to the spirit of republican institutions and the gospel.[46]

Significantly, the *Watchman*'s comment on this debate revealed the conservative motivation for suddenly abandoning anti-Catholicism. Although Morehouse spoke for most Baptists, the paper stated, the time had come to stress the real Christian elements of the Roman Catholic church. These were the days of denial of the supernatural and personal actions of God in the affairs of men, its editorial columns exclaimed. While many repudiated the infallible authority of the Bible and the deity of Christ, the church proclaimed "essential" (not yet "fundamental") truths with a bold firmness and unswerving loyalty unequaled by any other Christian body. Had not the popes repeatedly insisted that deviations from these tenets constituted "errors"? While the doctrine of papal supremacy, the intercession of priests between man and God, and the church's interference in affairs of the state prevented active fellowship between evangelical Protestants and Catholics, a new respect was in order. Christians of orthodox mind now had to decide whether their attitudes would be more influenced by the papacy or by shared beliefs in the Bible, the reality of miracles, and Jesus Christ as God.[47]

While these developments were taking place, Baptists of a

[45] Editorial: "The Foreigners of Connecticut," *Watchman*, LXXXV (Oct. 22, 1903), 12–13.
[46] Editorial: "Are Roman Catholics Christians?" *Watchman*, LXXXIX (Nov. 14, 1907), 7.
[47] *Ibid.*

more liberal persuasion continued the criticism of Catholicism begun by an earlier generation. Samuel Zane Batten, for all his sympathy for the poor and desire to right the wrongs of society, used the older pejorative term "Romanism" when referring to Catholics. The first item in Batten's interpretation of America's destiny required that she be a Protestant nation, and much of the fault he found with immigration, when not based on racial criteria, stemmed from a conviction that millions of aliens from Catholic countries knew nothing of democratic institutions. Again and again he called attention to the problems posed by the presence of a large class in the United States that was "anti-Protestant in religion." [48] Even Howard B. Grose, who rejected most of Batten's antipathy to and fear of foreigners, could not keep from deploring the effects of a parochial school system largely sustained by immigration. The chief defender of the newcomers from southern and eastern Europe himself made quite clear his insistence that Catholic immigrants must be weaned away from their church because he felt that "the foundation principles of Protestant Americanism and Roman Catholicism are irreconcilable." [49]

Nevertheless, by 1914 Northern Baptists as a whole had come a long way from the nativism of the 1890s. Perhaps nothing illustrates this fact so vividly as the contrast between the Baptist response to the great strike of foreign workers at Lawrence, Massachusetts, in 1912 and their reaction to the Haymarket riot in 1886. The earlier incident had brought condemnation of the accused anarchists and denunciation of radicalism by such Chicago Baptists as Eri B. Hulbert.[50] The walkout in the textile mills at Lawrence and the subsequent invitation to IWW leaders to organize the affair called forth criticism of capital and labor

[48] Batten, "New Problems of Immigration," 180, 181, 183.
[49] Grose, *The Incoming Millions*, 99. Some Baptists at this time questioned even the necessity of converting the Catholic, asserting that Protestantism should rather focus its efforts on the unchurched. The beneficial environment of Protestant America, ran this argument, would change Catholicism in due time. See, for example, W. E. Darrow, "Our Attitude toward Roman Catholicism," *Standard*, LIX (Mar. 9, 1912), 9.
[50] Eri B. Hulbert, "Our Peril and Our Defense," *Standard*, XXXIV (June 23, 1887), 2.

alike, with clergymen on both sides.[51] But the Baptist pastor in Lawrence, Elisha M. Lake (1864–1937), did not equivocate. His distrust of the IWW as "subversive of popular government" did not keep him from stating categorically that the desires of work-ingmen to better themselves and give their children a chance to succeed were normal and right. Because employees were power-less as individuals, he argued, they needed a union to face the employers in a position of solidarity. Lake blamed the mill opera-tors of Lawrence, whose goals of large dividends caused them to place workers in a "grind" from top to bottom. In the spirit of Rauschenbusch and of the progressive era at its zenith, the Baptist minister asserted that only state and national action could deal adequately with such situations as had arisen in his city. "Let the government turn on the flood light of investigation," he exclaimed, "and begin direct legislation for the many instead of the privileged few." [52]

What a far cry from the hysteria that swept the Baptists of Chicago and elsewhere in 1886! This time no voice of a promi-nent Baptist seminary professor characterized the dregs of Eu-rope as "the people who misrule our cities, who foment our strikes, who range themselves as lazzaroni, hoodlums, boycotters, Mollie Maguires; who appeal to bludgeons, the torch, dynamite, social and political revolution." [53] In the place of Hulbert's tirade came an equally forceful utterance that condemned a "wicked, merciless and competitive" industrial system "at the bottom of the whole problem." The same intense moralism that censured everything foreign and non-Protestant in 1886 had now turned

[51] Donald B. Cole, *Immigrant City: Lawrence, Massachusetts, 1845–1921* (Chapel Hill, N.C., 1963), 3–5.

[52] Elisha M. Lake, "On the Battle Line of Industrialism: The Situation in Lawrence, Mass.," *Standard*, LX (Nov. 2, 1912), 7; Lake, "Causes of the Industrial Unrest in Lawrence: A Second and Explanatory Article," *ibid.* (Dec. 21, 1912), 6–7. Other Baptists felt that some sort of federal intervention was desirable in Lawrence, but not all were as sympathetic toward the strikers as Lake. See Frederick B. Gruel, "The Strike at Lawrence, Mass.," *Watchman*, XCIV (Feb. 22, 1912), 9–10, and editorials in the same issue of the *Watchman*, p. 6. For a Baptist reaction similar to that of Lake, in this case involving the labor situation at Fall River, see Arthur C. Baldwin, "Practical Problems in an Industrial Center," *Standard*, LIX (June 1, 1912), 16–17.

[53] Hulbert, "Our Peril and Our Defense."

into opprobrium against one of the American institutions which was said to bring misery to the stranger: the unbridled capitalist economy![54] In the nation the Lawrence strike gave strength to the cause of immigration restriction as the Haymarket affair had done in the previous generation.[55] But now many Baptists would not follow. The critics of Granville Abbot in 1882, the minority speakers at the Baptist Congress in 1888, and such individuals as Howard B. Grose and Walter Rauschenbusch had not wrought in vain. While significant numbers of Baptists consistently believed that some limitation of the influx was desirable, neither restrictionism nor nativism would ever again become the obsession they had been in the 1890s.

The years from 1900 to 1914 also witnessed a change in attitude toward the immigrant in other Protestant denominations, most evident in the Presbyterian church. Up to about 1904 spokesmen for that faith branded the new immigration as an evil and a menace, worried that America was becoming a dumping ground for the ignorant and degenerate of Europe, declared such groups as the Italians and Poles undesirable, and supported restrictive measures like the literacy test.[56] By 1913, however, Presbyterian correspondents and editors of religious newspapers claimed that all people were one underneath the superficial ethnic differences and held that the immigrants from southern and eastern Europe were full of promise, a glorious opportunity for the Christian church.[57] Representatives of Congregationalism in 1908 issued a qualified endorsement of a better control and sifting of the stream of incoming foreign life, but on the eve of World War I they reproved references to the newcomers as the "scum

[54] Lake, "Causes of the Industrial Unrest in Lawrence," 6–7.

[55] Cole, *Immigrant City*, 9–11.

[56] Editorials: "The Immigration Evil," *Christian Work*, LXIX (Nov. 15, 1900), 697; "Immigration Restriction," *ibid.*, LXXIV (Apr. 25, 1903), 589; "The Growing Immigration Evil," *ibid.*, LXXV (July 18, 1903), 79; "The Invasion of Aliens," *ibid.* (Nov. 14, 1903), 654; "Pass the Lodge Bill," *ibid.* (Dec. 26, 1903), 890; "Anarchists Excluded," *ibid.*, LXXVI (May 28, 1904), 735; "The Cry Is Still They Come," *ibid.*, LXXVII (Sept. 17, 1904), 381.

[57] Albert J. Nock, "Foreigners and Folks," *Christian Work and Evangelist*, XCIV (Apr. 19, 1913), 505–506; S. L. Testa, "What to Do with the Immigrant," *ibid.*, XCV (Nov. 22, 1913), 670; "On Making Americans" (editorial), *ibid.* (Nov. 29, 1913), 689–690.

of Europe" and expressed confidence with Presbyterians that the American melting pot would produce a nation of remarkable homogeneity.[58] In 1906 one Methodist writer proclaimed immigration a peril that endangered the welfare and stability of the republic, yet two years later another censured this frame of mind and characterized immigration as a providential movement for the more rapid spread of the Redeemer's Kingdom.[59] The Episcopal church did not exactly follow the pattern, for within this period its major denominational paper alternated between demands for "wise and just" limitation of "unassimilable" immigration and such statements as "Every able-bodied immigrant not of the criminal class that comes is an addition to the wealth of the country." [60] The reasons for the shift in outlook in these various corners of Protestantism were probably similar to those that affected Baptists, including the influence of foreign-speaking clergymen.

Clearly, the winds of change blew with uneven force and consistency upon Northern Baptists in this transitional time. Outstanding "conservatives" like Robert Stuart MacArthur of New York, along with those more inclined toward the social gospel like George C. Lorimer of Boston, both called for the renewal and regeneration of American cities, now widely regarded as "the storm centers of civilization." [61] Denominational "progressives," such as Samuel Zane Batten, preached a "hot hatred"

[58] "The Alien Spirit" (editorial), *Independent*, LXIV (Jan. 23, 1908), 216–217; "Immigration Facts and Problems," *Congregationalist*, XCIII (Jan. 18, 1908), 76; Harold McConaughy, "A New Approach to the Immigrant," *ibid.*, XCVI (Mar. 4, 1911), 276–278; "Race or Language" (editorial), *Independent*, LXXIX (Aug. 31, 1914), 294–295; "The Assimilation of Immigrants" (editorial), *ibid.*, LXXVIII (Apr. 20, 1914), 120. See also "On Making Americans," 689–690.

[59] Albert Erdman, "Thoughts for Thanksgiving Day," *Christian Advocate*, LXXXI (Dec. 13, 1906), 18–19; A. J. Loeppert, "Future of Foreign-Speaking Churches in America," *ibid.*, LXXXIII (May 28, 1908), 12–13. Loeppert was a German Methodist.

[60] Editorials: "Immigration," *Churchman*, XCVI (Aug. 17, 1907), 229; "The Dangers of Unrestricted Immigration," *ibid.*, CIX (June 6, 1914), 726–727; "Immigration as a Moral Issue," *ibid.*, CX (July 4, 1914), 12. In this case the favorable pronouncements came earlier than the suggestions for restriction.

[61] Lorimer indicated his sympathy with the social gospel especially in his book *Christianity and the Social State* (Philadelphia, 1898).

against the social evils of the day that spilled over into an acceptance of the idea that certain foreigners were inferior to others.
Equally committed to the social gospel but led in a slightly different direction by it, Howard B. Grose set out to convince Protestants that while they must win the newcomers from southern and
eastern Europe to their faith, at the same time the strangers must
be regarded as human beings of equal worth who could be trans-
formed from aliens into Americans. To this the very circumspect Lemuel C. Barnes added that not even the Catholic religion
precluded the consideration of the immigrants as "Christian
brethren." The Boston *Watchman*, soon to be a voice of fundamentalism, followed in the train of Barnes and Grose, while the
most conservative Baptist publication of all, the *Journal and
Messenger*, kept up its nativist propaganda!

The social gospel created a milieu in which a new receptivity
toward persons of the Old World would be possible, but this
did not follow inevitably from its premises. When combined
with an ardent moralism, as in the case of Samuel Zane Batten,
the new theology could lead to all the anomalies of the progressive mind, one of which was a concern for the immigrant as the
victim of his environment along with severe criticism of non-
Protestant nationalities. Not only Batten, but Leighton Williams
and Charles R. Henderson, allowed themselves to be swept up in
this type of thinking, which demonstrates that little positive
correlation in fact existed between one's involvement in the
social gospel and his participation in the increasingly liberal
attitude toward eastern Europeans.

Only when social Christianity kept its concern for the spiritual and material welfare of the individual in balance did its general outlook help to bring about a pro-immigrant disposition.
Howard B. Grose provides the best example of this equilibrium.
Not a trained theologian, he could at once speak of "winning
the alien to Christ and improving his external surroundings,"
without making any pronouncements on "an individualistic, self-
seeking gospel" as did Batten. Experience with the newcomers,
the influence of foreign-speaking pastors, the ethos of the new
theology coupled with the humanitarian features implicit in the

old—these factors had brought the Baptists to the edge of the modern age in 1914. A shot fired half-way around the world in a small Balkan village would shortly determine whether their recently modified *Weltanschauung* could withstand the shock of a conflict with the traditional sources of immigration, or whether they, like many Americans, would return to nativism upon involvement in World War I.

In the year 1914 progressivism was at high tide. Political life, many Americans believed, might be made over through legislation. Reformers within and without the churches clearly identified the objects of their attacks, from city machines to sweatshop operators. Except for a four-month war with Spain in 1898, followed by a two-year campaign to suppress the Filipino rebels, the generation that lived from 1865 to 1914 had known the ways of peace. Even after the assassination at Sarajevo, many citizens of the United States regarded the prospect of a resurgence of "Europe's wars and Europe's woes" with traditional indifference. When the shooting began in late summer, however, few could avoid sympathizing with one side or the other, in spite of Woodrow Wilson's plea for complete neutrality. Persons of German or Irish extraction held high hopes for the Central Powers, as did certain progressives who regarded Germany as the reformer's model social state. By and large, nevertheless, the fellow feeling of Americans went out to the nation that had founded and fostered their own civilization. John Bull, often resented in the nineteenth century and threatened by Grover Cleveland over the Venezuelan boundary dispute as recently as 1895, now was cast in the role of a stricken brother under assault by a repressive military machine.

After 1914 things would never be the same, either in the world or in the United States. When some German-Americans appeared to have a higher regard for the Fatherland than for their adopted homeland, the whole concept of the melting pot came into question. Where did the loyalties of the many aliens in this country really lie? Had the customary assumption that Americanization would take place automatically under the light of beneficent institutions proved true in practice? Was it time to close the gates at last if assimilation had failed? Was democracy in danger, not only from hostile forces without but also from the "hyphenates" within?

These queries, sporadic and isolated for generations, suddenly became loud and insistent along with the drums of war. How would the Northern Baptists, recently emphasizing the idealistic aspects of their faith, seek to answer them? Would their nativism, relatively dormant since 1900, come to life again along with the anti-foreign phobias of other Americans? Or would their new credo of respect for the immigrant withstand the storm now breaking upon Christian civilization? Would their long-held belief in the sufficiency of the Protestant gospel to Americanize the newcomer remain viable in the midst of a national loss of confidence? If Baptists joined the drive for "Americanization" arising out of the nation's involvement in the conflict, what direction would they take—the road of compulsion and restriction or the highway of gentle persuasion and humanitarian sentiment? The evidence suggests that while World War I fostered a fear of the immigrant in certain quarters, the forces that had led the Baptists to a humane view of the immigrants now resisted the secular culture to defend the foreigner in three areas—in Americanization work, in new types of evangelism, and in the debate over the National Origins Act.

In the years immediately preceding the outbreak of World War I, Baptists were vigorously putting into practice the concern for the city and the immigrant they had shown when discussing the social gospel in the first decade of the century. More and more articles appeared in the Baptist papers outlining ways to improve life in the slums, with praise for such individuals as Jacob Riis. Prescriptions for amelioration ranged all the way from health education for foreign-speaking families to legal con-

demnation of all buildings unsuitable for habitation and subsequent erection of structures according to specific standards.[1]
City mission societies presently assumed much of the responsibility among new Americans, and Superintendent Charles Hatch
Sears of the New York City Baptist organization went before the
Northern Baptist Convention annually to ask for funds for
downtown churches whose native-born memberships were
rapidly departing for the suburbs, leaving no financial base for
evangelizing the community.

While a student at Union Theological Seminary in 1901, Sears
became a special worker in Edward Judson's institutional church,
the Judson Memorial. In 1906 he acquainted readers of the
Home Mission Monthly with the extensive depletion of urban
congregations because of perpetual migration from the center
of the metropolis to its outskirts. To Sears, churches in this situation should not close their doors but ought to continue their
ministry through new methods, such as street preaching, services
in Bowery hotels, and clubs with gymnasiums and other facilities.
Even if everyone did not convert, the Protestant presence would
influence the ideas of immigrants and thus partially Americanize
them, he claimed. This tireless Baptist added ten departments to
the Church Extension Society in New York, which he headed,
and wrote several books advocating an all-out effort for "the
redemption of the city." Not only in Manhattan but in Chicago,
Cleveland, and Detroit, aggressive urban Baptist clergymen carried their message to the stranger in churches that would have
become deserted without their zeal.[2]

[1] See, for example, "Charity and the Americans of Tomorrow: Conditions
in City Slums and Methods of Improving Them," *Standard*, LVII (July 30,
1910), 3, 10; "Tenement Life in a Great City," *Missions*, VI (Feb., 1915), 97–
100; Henry Clay Vedder, "The Gospel and the Slum," *Examiner*, XCI (Feb. 6,
1913), 171–173.

[2] Charles H. Sears, "City Mission Ideals," *Baptist Home Mission Monthly*,
XXVIII (Aug., 1906), 301–306; Sears, "An Animated Church," *Examiner*,
LXXXVI (Apr. 30, 1908), 500–501. See also "City Mission Ideals," *ibid.*,
LXXXIV (June 14, 1906), 746–749; "The Institutional Church," *Watchman*,
XCI (Sept. 16, 1909), 6; and the report of the Committee on City Mission
Problems, Northern Baptist Convention *Minutes* (1909), 121–125. Other relevant
books include Charles H. Sears, *The Redemption of the City* (Philadelphia,
1911); Sears, *The Crowded Ways* (New York, 1929); Sears, *City Man* (New
York, 1936); and Edward Judson, *The Institutional Church* (New York,
1899).

In the Home Mission Society a leader of remarkable forcefulness came from his position as executive secretary of missionary
work of the Cleveland Baptist Association to take charge of
denominational attempts to attract the foreign-born. Charles
Alvin Brooks (1871–1931) attributed his interest in the immigrant to the writings of Howard B. Grose. His experience in
the polyglot center of Cleveland from 1907 to 1914 well fitted
him for the post of superintendent of city missions and foreign-
speaking work for the Home Mission Society, which he assumed
in the latter year. In 1913 Brooks had visited Europe to investigate the movement of peoples to the United States, and he
brought to his new job an understanding and tolerance that
won him widespread respect both within and without the Baptist
fold. Described at the time of his death as an "evangelical" who
had positive convictions, he received praise for his educational
activities and for bringing men and women "into fellowship with
the Savior." That he bridged the gap between "fundamentalist"
and "liberal" throughout the 1920s is evidenced by the presence
of Harry Emerson Fosdick at his funeral and by the eulogy of
the *Watchman-Examiner*.[3]

From the start, Brooks pursued his obligation to the Home
Mission Society with enthusiasm. In a single year he traveled
20,000 miles, holding conferences on the immigrant and the city
with Baptist leaders in major urban areas. He attended the meetings of city mission societies, of state conventions, and of the
various foreign-speaking Baptist conferences. In 1916 he edited
and published a manual of methods for Protestant missionaries
to new Americans. This book included selections on the teaching
of English, the proper approach to immigrant children, and the
use of religious literature, with such notable contributors as
Samuel Zane Batten and Howard B. Grose. Brooks's volume,
together with a new work by Lemuel C. and Mary Clark Barnes
and the older books of Grose, served as handbooks for the many
church workers who now interested themselves in the welfare of
the stranger. In addition to his writings and duties for the Home

---

[3] Biographical information is available in the *Illinois Baptist Annual* (1931),
44; *Missions*, XXI (May, 1930), 281; XXII (Mar., 1931), 145–148; *Watchman-
Examiner*, XIX (Jan. 22, 1931), 105; and the *Baptist*, XII (Jan. 31, 1931),
145–146.

Mission Society, Brooks acted as chairman of the Committee on
Foreign-Speaking Bodies of the Northern Baptist Convention
and also participated in the Committee on Immigrant Work of
the interdenominational Home Missions Council. More than any
other individual, this energetic and humane clergyman helped
to steer his denomination away from the bigotry and prejudice
that overtook many Americans when the storm clouds broke.[4]

For the United States the skies did not darken visibly until
1916. But in the previous year the first instances of sabotage by
agents operating from the German embassy in Washington became known. Coupled with the sympathy of the powerful
German-American Alliance toward the Central Powers, these
incidents brought down the wrath of large numbers of Anglo-
Saxons upon the heads of the "hyphenates." The preparedness
movement shortly aggravated anti-Germanism, and before long
nativism would again flow at high tide.[5] In its path were hundreds of innocent victims, among them some 30,000 German-
Americans who called themselves Baptists. As early as 1914 a
German Baptist minister in Wisconsin defended the course of
his native country in the war on the ground that Germany had
to meet with military force the enemies which surrounded her.
The following year George A. Schulte, superintendent of German work for the Home Mission Society, told that organization
that while German Baptists were trustworthy Americans, they
felt a natural empathy with their brethren in Europe. Therefore,
they raised $14,000 to assist those suffering because of the fight-
ing in Germany, Austria, and Russia. In 1916 Schulte publicly
breathed a sigh of relief that the United States had not entered
the open and bloody conflict and added that the mission of German Baptists here was peace coupled with fidelity to Christ and
to their adopted land. Sympathy for the stricken Fatherland, he

[4] Charles A. Brooks, ed., *The Church and the Foreigner* (New York,
1916); 84th Annual Report, ABHMS (1916), 26–27; 85th Annual Report,
ABHMS (1917), 52; Mary Clark Barnes and Lemuel C. Barnes, *The New
America* (New York, 1913). Brooks later wrote a very brief history of Baptist home mission efforts among immigrants, *Through the Second Gate* (New
York, 1922).
[5] Higham, *Strangers in the Land*, 197ff.

affirmed, did not imply that German-Americans were disloyal to the United States.[6]

Before the delayed decision of Woodrow Wilson to commit his nation to the Allied cause, German-speaking Protestants expressed their friendliness to the Central Powers in the religious press. Careful not to specifically endorse the German military leaders, these papers generally claimed that the unlawful acts of Germany were in response to illegalities perpetrated by Great Britain. Like the secular German-American publications, religious ones demanded an embargo on contraband, especially ammunition. German pastors and laymen held various opinions on the war, some moderate and some extreme. After April, 1917, the Postage and Espionage Act forced many German Protestant periodicals to become totally silent on the struggle, while the persuasive influences of "100 percent Americanism" compelled others to profess absolute allegiance to the United States. Some journals even confessed that Germany's treatment of Russia and Roumania had shattered their illusions about the Fatherland. Ultimately, the European conflagration dealt a blow to missions among the Germans in America, for state legislation prohibiting the use of German in church services in certain areas of the West placed the older generation out of reach.[7]

Most of the Northern Baptist press and official organizations made little comment on the war throughout its duration. The *Watchman-Examiner* explained at the outset that because the international scene dominated secular newspapers, the strife would receive scant attention in its columns. Fear of antagonizing German Baptists was obviously a motive for this discreet silence, for in 1915 the *Watchman-Examiner* begged its readers not to let racism creep into Baptist churches and affect their spiritual life. Accordingly, it published only a few articles calling on aliens to escape the odium of disloyalty by renouncing

[6] Christian Dippel, "A German View of the War," *Standard*, LXII (Oct. 3, 1914), 6–7; Albert J. Ramaker, "The German-Speaking Churches of America during the War and After," *ibid.*, LVI (Mar. 22, 1919), 725–726; 83rd Annual Report, ABHMS (1914), 73–74; 84th Annual Report, ABHMS (1916), 90–92.

[7] Ramaker, "German-Speaking Churches of America during the War and After," 725–726.

their ties to Germany and by making clear their sympathies with America. Again attempting to soothe the German-speaking members of the denomination, the *Watchman-Examiner* claimed that the fidelity of nine-tenths of the persons of German origin here was unquestionable.[8]

In reality, other Protestant groups led the way in efforts to assuage the nation's new-found fear of German-Americans. The religious papers of the Congregational church especially took pains to affirm the patriotism of these citizens, many of whom had been in America a long time and had first come in order to escape the same type of militarism that presently controlled Germany. A 1917 editorial in the *Independent* asserted that hostilities between Germany and the United States did not justify mistreatment of individuals of German heritage in America, a country whose sense of decency and self-respect ought to prevent the abuse of aliens. The *Congregationalist* also expressed disapproval of "petty persecution," adding that German-Americans should declare themselves decisively for their adopted land in order to remove suspicion. This statement was carefully balanced by another that the nation should let these people go on about their business unmolested throughout the conflict.[9] Two Presbyterian journals agreed with these sentiments, one maintaining that German-Americans, while in no way responsible for the war, could not rightfully be expected to cry out against the Kaiser with the same hot indignation of native-born Americans. The *Continent* criticized the current intolerance of the German language, claiming that the mother tongue provided the best vehicle for the conveyance of American ideals to immigrants.[10] In Boston a Methodist spokesman proclaimed at the

[8] Editorials: "The War and Our Attitude," *Watchman-Examiner*, III (Jan. 14, 1915), 38; "We Want No War among Ourselves," *ibid.*, V (Mar. 29, 1917), 391.

[9] George A. Plimpton, "Americans and German Americans: Their Mutual Obligations," *Independent*, LXXXIX (Feb. 26, 1917), 346; "The Alien within Our Gates" (editorial), *Independent*, XC (Apr. 2, 1917), 99; "The Germans in America" (editorial), *Congregationalist*, CII (Apr. 12, 1917), 467; "Fair Dealing with German-Americans" (editorial), *ibid.* (Aug. 9, 1917), 168.

[10] Editorials: "The German-American," *Christian Work*, CII (Mar. 31, 1917), 393–394; "Don't Revile Foreign Speech," *Continent*, L (May 29, 1919), 676.

height of the struggle that Christians must learn to appreciate the history of different nationalities, their noble traits, their achievements in art and literature, and their latent possibilities.[11] Some of the deepest Protestant apprehensions of German-Americans at this time came in fact from a Baptist source. The Cincinnati *Journal and Messenger*, representing many churchmen of conservative persuasion although completely out of tune with denominational leadership, published many editorials relating to the wartime position of those of German ancestry in the United States. Outwardly, the *Journal and Messenger* concurred with the *Watchman-Examiner* that nearly all of these citizens were as loyal to the government as anyone and would fight for America if necessary. But the Cincinnati paper's editors saw danger in recent arrivals from Germany yet unnaturalized, and they approved President Wilson's order that such persons could not live within one-half mile of a factory engaged in defense contracts. Throughout the months following the congressional declaration of war, the *Journal and Messenger* supported various proposals to restrict the movements of foreigners in America, such as the federal plan to remove enemy aliens from coastal areas and the suggestion to bar Germans, Austrians, Bulgarians, and Turks from working in munitions plants or on docks and piers. For German spies and those "guilty of treason," the paper advocated immediate death. Its columns repeatedly accused the German-American Alliance of destroying Americanism and asserted that the German-language newspapers were a great danger to the nation. The United States, in the words of the *Journal and Messenger*, wanted no immigrants unwilling to drop the hyphen and accept all genuine American principles immediately.[12] The chief attention of the Cincinnati *Journal and Messenger* during the war centered upon the teaching of German in the public schools. The editors quickly joined the widespread agita-

[11] "How Unchristian Is Race Prejudice," *Zion's Herald*, XCV (Aug. 8, 1917), 1000.
[12] Editorials: *Journal and Messenger*, LXXXVI (Apr. 5, 1917), 3–4; (Apr. 12, 1917), 20; (June 14, 1917), 4; (Aug. 9, 1917), 4; (Nov. 8, 1917), 20; (Nov. 22, 1917), 19; LXXXVII (Mar. 14, 1918), 20.

tion for the discontinuation of elementary-level classes in this language, even questioning its use in the secondary grades. The textbooks used to instruct pupils in German, ran the argument, were filled with militaristic propaganda and history falsified to favor Germany. Even if linguistic manuals contained only selections from German literature, they were still wholly un-American. The *Journal and Messenger* rejoiced that every week a city school system somewhere jettisoned German, and it demanded the boycott and investigation of publishers and authors of pro-German works.[13] Attacks of this severity upon German-Americans, however, were not frequent either among Baptists or in other major Protestant denominations.

The behavior of the *Journal and Messenger* was not particularly surprising in the light of that paper's forty-year campaign to close the gates to virtually all aliens. From 1912 to 1916 its columns continually pressed for the adoption of the literacy test and the exclusion of Asians. When the device originally proposed by Henry Cabot Lodge passed Congress over Wilson's veto in 1917, the Baptist editors in Cincinnati could at last feel satisfied that this measure would help preserve the purity and homogeneity of the American people. The next step, they said, ought to involve the fixing of a quota for each foreign country. While most of the Baptist papers that had endorsed the literacy test in the 1890s now either ignored or condemned it as unfair, the *Journal and Messenger* not only approved of the new law but recommended the indefinite suspension of immigration from Germany, Austria, Turkey, and Bulgaria. "Desirable" additions from selected nations should hence forth be the rule: "Our doors should never again be wide open to the world."[14]

The legislation of 1917 had few immediate effects, for the war had largely cut off the migration of peoples from the Old World. But the presence of an unassimilated mass of persons al-

[13] Editorials: *Journal and Messenger,* LXXXV (Aug. 31, 1916), 3; (Nov. 16, 1916), 4; LXXXVI (Apr. 26, 1917), 3; (May 31, 1917), 3; (Dec. 6, 1917), 4; LXXXVII (Jan. 31, 1918), 3.
[14] Editorials: *Journal and Messenger,* LXXXI (May 16, 1912), 6; LXXXIII (Feb. 5, 1914), 3; (Sept. 24, 1914), 3; LXXXIV (Jan. 7, 1915), 4; LXXXV (Jan. 27, 1916), 4; LXXXVI (Feb. 8, 1917), 4, 21; LXXXIX (Jan. 30, 1919), 3.

ready in the United States suddenly became alarming. For many years Americans had accepted the idea of the melting pot, in which all ethnic groups in this country would be blended more or less automatically into a high type of manhood. Implicit in the positive variants of Anglo-Saxonism and Divine Providence in the 1880s, the concept of the amalgam refined by the solvent of Protestant Christianity still lived among Baptists during the progressive era. In 1913 Lemuel C. Barnes, co-author of *The New America*, spoke of the manifold "fresh ore" daily pouring into the American melting pot that might well produce a people of the uppermost mettle the world had ever known. The same year the *Watchman* asserted that the purpose of God in sending immigrants to the New World became clearer and clearer. As Baptists worked among them, the paper claimed, they could not help feeling the bond of Christian brotherhood that transcended all national and racial differences. All great civilizations resulted from fusion, argued the *Watchman*, and the constant infiltration of the spirit of Christ into the American crucible would transform men and women into individuals who would become the salt of the new America.[15]

For several generations the effectiveness of the refining process had been more or less taken for granted by both religious and secular spokesmen in the United States. The German Baptists had steadily maintained, and their American counterparts believed, that the gospel alone would make the stranger into a loyal citizen so thoroughly that forced "Americanization" programs were not necessary. By the time of World War I, however, such patriotic organizations as the Daughters of the American Revolution and the Societies of Colonial Dames had begun to print literature and sponsor classes in civics for the teaching of "Americanism" to immigrants. In 1907 the YMCA began instruction for new Americans, and the North American Civic League, founded in Boston in 1908, advised recent arrivals on job opportunities, housing, and transportation. With the coming of the war, the various state and local Americanization agencies gradu-

[15] Lemuel C. Barnes, in 78th Annual Report, ABHMS (1910), 60; "The New American" (editorial), *Watchman*, XCV (May 22, 1913), 7.

ally moved toward "100 percent Americanism," which in practice demanded conformity and renunciation of former attitudes,
beliefs, and ways of living.[16]

After the United States joined the Allied cause, thousands of
groups suddenly awakened to the ubiquity of large numbers of
"unassimilated" immigrants. Schools, churches, business organizations—all began to show concern. Now the spirit of the
Americanization crusade shifted from one of cosmopolitanism
and sympathy to an atmosphere of fear and nationalism. Articles
appeared that questioned the value of foreign-language newspapers. Teachers in New York City handed out loyalty-pledge
cards to second-generation pupils in the hope that their parents
would sign them. In Iowa the governor banned all speech other
than English in schools, church services, and conversations in
public or over the telephone. The Revenue Act of 1918 imposed
a double income tax on "nonresident" aliens, and many private
industries adopted a policy of promoting only those who were
citizens or in the process of taking out naturalization papers.
Even Frances Kellor, who had begun her work in the Americanization movement as a humanitarian reformer, urged the suppression of unrest and disloyalty and the remaking of minority
cultures.[17]

At the same time a more liberal spirit was afoot, drawing upon
the tradition of the social settlements and the doctrine of "immigrant gifts." According to this outlook, foreign nationalities
would enrich the character of their adopted land with cultural
contributions. During the war clergymen, educators, and intellectuals propagated this view. Some organizations operated
within this frame of reference, sponsoring affairs at which new
Americans were encouraged to present the folklore and dances
of their homelands. With the decline of national unity after the
end of hostilities, however, the Americanization campaign again
became chauvinistic. The "Big Red Scare" of 1919, following
in the wake of the Communist revolution in Russia, fostered a

[16] Higham, *Strangers in the Land*, 234–245. A monographic study is Edward
G. Hartmann, *The Movement to Americanize the Immigrant* (New York,
1948).
[17] Higham, *Strangers in the Land*, 245–249.

reversion to repressive tactics. The American Legion, founded that year, pressured Congress to require all residents of the United States to learn English. State laws authorized night-school language classes for immigrants, and Oregon required the foreign press to print literal translations of everything published. Subsiding in 1920 and 1921, this final phase of the Americanization crusade failed in many of its coercive goals and turned to an intense restrictionism that culminated in the National Origins Act of 1924.[18]

Baptists and other Protestants, long active in attempts to convert the immigrant to their religion, now faced a choice. Would they agree with many fellow citizens that "Americanism" must be forced upon the many residents of the nation who did not yet speak English and thus mingle freely with the native-born? Or would the Protestant denominations accept a sort of cultural pluralism, within the understandable limits of their faith, and repudiate "100 percentism"? Baptist history for thirty years previous had shown tendencies that could have led them either to the nationalist Americanization of fear or to the more cosmopolitan Americanization of love.[19] The 1890s had laid the basis for one, the social gospel and the early twentieth century for the other. In making their fateful decision, many Northern Baptists, as well as significant numbers of other Protestants, differed more from the rest of the country than at any time in a generation. Under the direction of its supervisor of work among the foreign-born, Charles A. Brooks, the American Baptist Home Mission Society and its female counterpart steadfastly rejected nativism and "100 percent Americanism" in favor of what they proceeded to define as "Christian Americanization." Various Protestants, notably the Presbyterians, followed the Baptist example of a cosmopolitan approach to the problems of assimilation.

In 1918 Brooks reported to the Home Mission Society that the war had made a previously indifferent populace aware of the potential dangers of a mass of foreigners unadjusted to

18 *Ibid.*, 250–263.
19 The distinction between the two variants of the Americanization movement is Higham's (*ibid.*, 237, 251).

American ways and unevangelized by the churches. Because their Americanization was so important, the society appropriated $5,000 to initiate a campaign and formed a special committee of representatives from national, state, and local Baptist organizations. When describing these steps to the Northern Baptist Convention, Brooks stated that his program had the objective of the "complete assimilation of people of foreign antecedents into the life of America." Shortly thereafter he made it clear to the denomination that his plans would not succumb to the prevailing anti-immigrant sentiment. In an article for *Missions* late in that year, Brooks charged that popular demands for drastic and radical elimination of every vestige of "foreignism" had wrought much harm. What a shock it must be to new Americans, he emphasized, to have been neglected by their adopted countrymen for so long and now to be treated with rudeness and intolerance. Many immigrants would have willingly gone to fight for the United States, he noted. To Charles Brooks, the wholesale endeavor of certain government authorities to restrict the German language, even in the churches, was "embarrassing." [20]

In 1919, while many Americans were turning to anti-Bolshevism and compulsory Americanization, Brooks published a slender volume for use by all Protestants in home mission study courses. Intended to set the tone of Christian Americanization, this book provided the guiding influence in the efforts of the major denominations, including Baptists, to implement its ideals. Brooks pleaded in his introduction for the recognition of migration as one of the most potent factors in the development of the human race, and reiterated the missionary destiny of the United States espoused by his predecessors in the 1880s. If Christians took the proper approach, he said, "we shall be able to think of all races with which we are dealing as the children of God." Admitting that the great European conflagration had destroyed the false optimism of the melting-pot theory, which assumed instantane-

[20] 86th Annual Report, ABHMS (1918), 29–34; Northern Baptist Convention *Minutes* (1918), 126; Charles A. Brooks, "Missions to the People of Foreign Speech, as Affected by the War," *Missions*, IX (Nov., 1918), 820–823.

ous and automatic assimilation upon breathing American air, Brooks raised the question of whether sudden interest in the stranger arose out of love or fear.[21]

Brooks's general definition of Americanization was couched in rather ambiguous terms. He spoke of the extension of American ideals and the English language to every community until no foreign colonies remained untouched. Constantly insisting that to be effective, the process must act on immigrant and indigenous resident alike, the Baptist minister addressed himself to both. For those transplanted to the New World, a desirable adjustment involved appreciation of this country's outlook and unreserved acceptance of the rights and duties of citizenship. For native Americans, it meant cultivating respect for the newcomers and for their ability to contribute to domestic life, along with a genuine practice of democracy in personal relationships with the stranger. Thus placing himself outside the intense nationalism of the time, Brooks emphasized that one did not become a "good" citizen merely by learning English and adopting new habits. The essence of Americanization, he held, issued from a slow, indirect, and often unconscious spiritual process. In short, the foreigner would no longer assimilate automatically, but action must be at a gradual pace that did not alienate the immigrants. This became clearer when Brooks stated emphatically what "Christian Americanization" was not. It did not demand the disowning of anything in an ancestral heritage consistent with the spirit of the United States. Because it did not foster the hatred or contempt of other nations, it was not a war issue. Most important, said Brooks, Americanization ought not to embrace nativism, which to him amounted to race pride degenerated into race prejudice. Brooks understood the meaning of the term "nativism" well and was one of the few Baptists ever to use it. For him, this essentially primitive instinct was unworthy of modern civilization and was especially incompatible with the American value system. Such anti-foreign feelings, he affirmed, selfishly excluded all people not born in America from its privileges.[22]

21 Charles A. Brooks, *Christian Americanization* (New York, 1919), 2–8.
22 *Ibid.,* 8–12.

Because of these cosmopolitan tendencies, Brooks renounced resort to fiat or force in Americanization programs. Probably through his influence, the Northern Baptist Convention disapproved of the current propaganda designed to compel all foreigners to become citizens after a reasonable length of residence. Baptists rejected demands that immigrants give up newspapers and activities in their own language in favor of English. Such proposals, said the Northern Baptist Convention in 1920, were ostensibly "100 percent" patriotic but in reality were un-American because they required arbitrary compulsion. Brooks himself called attention to the fact that some of the world's most creative philosophers and artists wrote in non-English syllables, and he insisted that every newcomer have the privilege of praying, singing, and speaking in familiar tones. While he argued that English must be taught to the stranger so he could understand his obligations to society, Brooks unequivocally condemned the action of western governors in prohibiting the use of German. How could America, he asked, thus violate her cherished liberties to enforce a worthless artificial unity? Would not a better way be found in Christian women entering immigrant homes as friends to give instruction in English on a voluntary basis? [23]

As a part of his argument, Brooks attacked the racial implications of the recently passed literacy test. Rejecting the idea that one race assimilated more easily than another, he maintained that the ability to adjust to a new culture was an individual rather than an ethnic matter. To him, as to Howard B. Grose, the American environment often provided the greatest obstacle to assimilation. The hostile attitudes toward the foreign-born, the social isolation, the exploitation of new arrivals—all slowed down the transformation of the alien. Government policy, he said, had concerned itself too much with restriction and not enough with the problems of a stranger attempting to find his way in an unfamiliar land. Brooks concluded his handbook with a chapter on the proper role of the churches in achieving national unity through Americanization. He called for local volunteers to show love toward prospective citizens in a manner free from

23 *Ibid.*, 42–68.

patronage or condescension. Both English-speaking and foreign-speaking congregations should participate, he claimed. The
former might sponsor classes in the American language; the
latter might begin a bilingual ministry. Public welfare, Brooks
held, was a legitimate field of Christian service: "Only a spiri-
tually dead church could be indifferent to the social issues of the
present fateful era." Above all, Christians everywhere ought to
stand ready to help individuals who were in any kind of need.[24]

The entire approach of Charles A. Brooks to Americanization
work was called into question by Samuel Zane Batten at the 1920
meeting of the Northern Baptist Convention. Appointed to head
the newly formed Department of Immigration and Americanization, Batten issued a severe statement that again hinted at an
unfavorable comparison between the "old" and the "new" immigrations. Did not the latter perpetuate unfavorable characteristics through their own press and in their closely knit "colonies"? Baptists, said Batten's committee, had the responsibility
of enlisting the support of the newcomers for ideas of democracy, social equality, Puritan morality, law and order, and the
economic welfare of all. In spite of these admirable aims, however, Batten called for the ultimate end of foreign-speaking
congregations. The use of alien tongues in the churches, stated
the 1920 report, acted against Americanization efforts. The social gospel leader, who in 1903 had criticized immigrants from
southern and eastern Europe, still retained a measure of anti-
foreign bias as late as 1920.[25]

When the debate between Brooks and Batten found its way
into other Protestant denominations, advocates appeared on both
sides. Methodist spokesmen came closest to following the position of Batten. During the war the Methodist Home Board set
up a Bureau of Americanization, which offered advice to clergymen working in polyglot neighborhoods and sent out representatives to acquaint the laity with the difficulties of assimilation. At
the outset a new policy encouraged foreign believers to come

24 *Ibid.*, 64–65, 75–100, 133–156.
25 Samuel Zane Batten *et al.*, in Northern Baptist Convention *Minutes*
(1920), 242–255.

into American congregations rather than remain in separate parishes. Soon Methodist churchmen proclaimed that the maintenance of non-English annual conferences was un-American, requesting their elimination. "We must have an end of the hyphen," exclaimed *Zion's Herald* in 1919. "We want no more groups that place a descriptive name before the word American." [26] In general, Methodists seemed to approve of the secular program of Americanization that was sweeping the country. The *Christian Advocate* worried that a preoccupied public had allowed immigrants to cherish and cultivate divisive institutions, customs, and tendencies that should have been left in Europe or eradicated here, adding that the Americanization movement would result in a more homogeneous people.[27] *Zion's Herald* praised President Wilson's proposal to teach English to those unfamiliar with it, claiming that "if the country is to be united against all foes from within and without, there must be a thorough Americanization of all classes." [28] Here and there individual Methodists pleaded for an appreciation of the good qualities of aliens and for a spirit of "interracial tolerance" in activities designed to help them adjust to their adopted land.[29]

Presbyterians, by contrast, largely chose Brooks's path to Americanization. In 1921 a writer for the *Continent* deplored "panicky programs" that were born of anxiety begotten of superficial signs. Showing great faith in the unconscious assimilation of the melting pot, he eschewed popular methods of coercing the newcomer.[30] An earlier editorial in the same period-

[26] "Eliminate the Non-English Conferences," *Zion's Herald*, XCVII (Oct. 15, 1919), 1327; "Knocking the Hyphen out of the Church," *ibid.*, XCVI (Sept. 18, 1918), 1202; "Church Must Help, Not Hinder, Americanization," *ibid.* (Oct. 9, 1918), 1286–87.

[27] Editorial: "To Americanize New England," *Christian Advocate*, XCII (Nov. 8, 1917), 1165–66.

[28] "Americanizing the Foreign Born," *Zion's Herald*, XCVI (Aug. 28, 1918), 1091.

[29] "An Americanization Conference," *Zion's Herald*, XCIV (Jan. 26, 1916), 99–100; David D. Forsyth, "Methodism and Americanization," *ibid.*, XCVI (Oct. 30, 1918), 1391; Timothy Douglas, "Real Americanization," *ibid.*, XCVIII (Aug. 11, 1920), 1066.

[30] N. B. Barr, "Wanted—New Respect for the Foreign Born," *Continent*, LII (Feb. 24, 1921), 210–211.

ical had emphatically stated, "All forms of fear and selfishness which hysterically insist on subjecting the immigrant to suspicious repression imply a denial of the brotherhood of man which would stultify the church." Real Americanization, this observer concluded, was based on the Kingdom of God, in which every man stood on an impartial level.[31] Edward A. Steiner, the noted authority on immigration, was welcomed as a contributor to this journal, and he promptly denounced the campaign to abolish the foreign-language press at a time when it provided the only approach to American ideas for many persons. Sharing Charles Brooks's conviction that Americanization was a progressive process and a matter of contacts rather than compulsion, Steiner presented to Presbyterians his call for economic and social justice for the immigrant.[32]

In another Presbyterian paper William Pierson Merrill discussed Americanization extensively with an attitude very similar to that of Charles Brooks. He refused to accept the prevailing belief that the problem could be solved by shutting out all those not in sympathy with American ways and customs, noting that this nation existed to demonstrate that elements of the utmost diversity could be welded together. Carefully rejecting the argument that Americanization involved the suppression of the distinctive features of an alien's heritage, Merrill maintained that these characteristics ought to be encouraged to enrich the life of the United States. The customary modes of adjustment—naturalization and teaching the English language and respect for the flag—were not panaceas, he pointed out. To him, the great essentials of this work included making America all that it should be, and fostering acquaintance between Americans and the newcomers would convince the latter of this country's value and attractiveness.[33] Other contributors to the Presbyterian religious

---

[31] Editorial: "Church's Part in Americanization," *Continent*, LI (Feb. 12, 1920), 189.
[32] Edward A. Steiner, "For Both Native Born and Immigrant," *Continent*, L (May 8, 1919), 546–548ff.
[33] William Pierson Merrill, "Americanization," *Christian Work*, CX (Apr. 23, 1921), 498–500.

press revealed that these views were widespread in this denomination.[34]

Among Baptists themselves the position of Charles Brooks prevailed, in practice, over that of Samuel Batten. In two new frontiers of Baptist activity, women's work with immigrants and the establishment of community centers, the influence of the author of *Christian Americanization* was evident. Several years before he wrote, Mary Clark Barnes of New York City had organized a Fireside League in 1912 for instruction in English through Bible lessons. This small organization later grew into the Neighbor's League of America, a group of women who carried on the teaching of the American language in homes. In 1918 the Neighbor's League extended its efforts to the families of foreign-speaking soldiers and sailors in cooperation with the American Red Cross in New York.[35] By the following year the Women's American Baptist Home Mission Society had its own Christian Americanization Department, with Alice W. Brimson as secretary. Miss Brimson, who provided the guiding force along with Charles Brooks in Baptist Americanization endeavors, set forth a humanitarian policy upon assuming her task. Her familiarity with the secular aspects of the nationwide campaign convinced her that the churches had a unique contribution to offer. Their mission, she averred, was to spread only the ideals of the United States that were rooted in the teachings of Christ: brotherhood, equality of privilege, and traditional human rights. Mention of the latter was especially significant, for by 1919 few persons in the country talked about the rights of the stranger but, rather, concerned themselves with his duty to conform. To Alice Brimson, however, Christians ought to give

[34] William E. Brooks, "A Prophet of Real Americanization," *Christian Work*, CIX (Aug. 28, 1920), 255–257; Cornelius M. Steffans, "The Cultivation of Americanism," *Continent*, XLIX (Apr. 18, 1918), 430; Marc N. Goodnow, "A New Emphasis in Americanization," *ibid.*, L (July 7, 1919), 871–872; Fred H. Rindge, Jr., "Americanization—A Very Christian Task," *ibid.*, LIV (Nov. 22, 1923), 1427.
[35] *Together: Historical Sketch of the Women's American Baptist Home Mission Society* (pamphlet) (New York, 1933), 13–14; Mary Clark Barnes, "The Neighbor's League of America—How It Works," *Watchman-Examiner*, V (Aug. 23, 1917), 1095. See also *Watchman-Examiner*, VI (Apr. 25, 1918), 545, and Mary Clark Barnes, *Neighboring New Americans* (New York, 1920).

the newcomer something more than the characteristic haste and love of gain, more than a knowledge of English and of American institutions.[36]

Other Baptists also showed that Brooks's teachings were influential. Bertha W. Clark, who visited immigrant families in New York, cautioned fellow missionaries to avoid the errors made by those who were met with hostility because they lacked sensitivity to the feelings of human beings. "The attitude of foreign people toward us will never change," she wrote, "except by a change in the attitudes of us Americans." Social workers who went out "slumming" in automobiles, she warned, or those who behaved in a patronizing manner, violated the alien's desire to retain independence and self-respect. Because the public school was the institution least objectionable to them, the teaching of English should be carried on there. Moreover, instruction in language would be most successful when not based on the assumption that English was superior.[37] As another colleague of Miss Brimson and Miss Clark summed up the Baptist interpretation of Americanization, "It meets the immigrant with all that is great in our own land; and on the other hand bids him conserve the music, the art, the literature of his own country." [38] Simultaneously with the Women's American Baptist Home Mission Society's Christian Americanization work, local Baptist agencies engaged in similar activities. State conventions gently exhorted foreign-speaking churches to use English on a gradually increasing scale, and the city mission societies joined the crusade in Buffalo, Detroit, New York, Philadelphia, and Pittsburgh.[39]

The ideas of Brooks were also used in the development of so-called Christian centers, or the Baptist version of a combination settlement house and institutional church. After the war Baptists established several "community houses" in the polyglot

---

[36] Alice W. Brimson, "The What, Why and How of Christian Americanization," *Standard*, LXVII (Oct. 11, 1919), 129–130.

[37] Bertha W. Clark, "American Attitude the Essential in Americanization," *Missions*, XII (Mar., 1921), 161–164.

[38] Mary Putnam Denny, "The Genius of America," *Missions*, XII (Sept., 1921), 470.

[39] 87th Annual Report, ABHMS (1919), 89–117.

sections of Chicago, Philadelphia, New York, Buffalo, and East Hammond, Indiana. Designed to attract rather than coerce foreigners to learn about their new country, these institutions fostered education and training rather than "drives" or "campaigns." In the words of Secretary Brooks, their presentation of the gospel was launched in a practical, nonsectarian manner appealing to the common people. Accordingly, the center named for him in Indiana attempted to ameliorate its environment by circulating petitions for public reform. The East Hammond Civic and Improvement Association, under the guidance of Brooks House, explained to property owners the benefits of paved streets, sidewalks, sewers, street lights, and parks. It urged area businessmen to form a chamber of commerce and allowed various groups to hold meetings in Brooks House. In this way the Christian center extended its influence into the community it served beyond the normal features of the institutional church, such as gymnasiums, reading rooms, and nurseries. Brooks House, as did other similar Baptist organizations, offered classes for adults in English, citizenship, home economics, music, and physical education.[40]

While Baptists thus pursued new social frontiers, the question of restricting immigration loomed large in the nation in the wake of the recent conflict. Temporarily overshadowed by demands for Americanization and conformity, proposals for closing the gates again came into prominence by 1920. The issue now before the American people was no longer the desirability of restriction but the degree and method through which it should be achieved. With a gradual passing of faith in the melting pot, the ideal of a cosmopolitan nationality also disappeared. Agitation for the exclusion of foreigners presently arose from labor units, from "100 percenters," and from industrialists. As a con-

[40] Charles A. Brooks, "A Gulf Stream in the Sea of Life," *Baptist*, V (Dec. 8, 1923), 1419–20; Mary Lathrop Bishop, "The Community Center," *Missions*, X (Dec., 1919), 914–915; John M. Hestenes, "Earning the Name of Community House," *ibid.*, XIV (Sept., 1923), 460–461. Hestenes was the director of Brooks House. See also "Where My Children Are Going," *ibid.*, X (Nov., 1919), 796–798.

sequence, Congress passed the Emergency Immigration Act in 1921, which established an annual quota from each country of 3 percent of persons living here in 1910 who had come from the various nations of Europe. When this failed to keep out a sufficient number of immigrants from the southern and eastern parts of the Continent, the National Origins Act became the law of the land in 1924. Henceforth the quota system would be levied according to the composition of the American population in 1890. The long campaign of the restrictionists who differentiated among several "races" of Europeans had at last achieved victory.[41]

The postwar Baptist response to immigration restriction revealed all the ambivalences of a generation, but the reaction of denominational leadership again distinguished Northern Baptists from many other Americans. Some prominent Baptist spokesmen agreed with their fellow citizens that immigration for the most part should cease, yet others continued to rely upon the melting-pot process and steadfastly opposed discriminatory measures. The *Journal and Messenger*, as previously noted, kept up its crusade for closing the doors until it closed its own doors in 1920. Because this paper had called for restriction consistently since the 1880s, however, its position could not be said to be in any sense an outgrowth of the war.[42] This was not the case with *Missions*, whose editor, Howard B. Grose, now endorsed curtailment of the influx. In 1922 Grose upheld the recently passed Emergency Immigration Act against its critics, claiming that it was a necessary safeguard in spite of the resultant hardship and separation of families. The international struggle had shown, he said, that persons had been entering the country who were not American in purpose or sympathy. Such people often evaded military service and were ready at every opportunity to turn upon the government that had given them refuge and liberty.

41 Higham, *Strangers in the Land*, 300–331.
42 See, for example, "A Dangerous Immigration Bill" (editorial), *Journal and Messenger*, LXXXVII (June 20, 1918), 4, and LXXXVIII (Aug. 28, 1919), 3.

Because of this and the recession of 1921–22, the man who had written *The Incoming Millions* in 1906 to champion the cause of the immigrant by 1922 was calling for the enactment of "permanent, constructive legislation." [43]

Even Antonio Mangano, the leader of Italian Baptist mission work in the United States, joined the postwar drive for the restriction of immigration. Like Grose, Mangano had economic aspects in mind. The Italian-born Baptist feared that in a glutted labor market foreign workers would suffer most. The nation must realize the necessity of limiting the flow, he said, in order to remake the character of the many newcomers already here. The thrift, industry, music, and art of Europeans were not enough: all had worth, but none of these contributions guaranteed the future of the country by an "appreciation of moral values." Two considerations ought to guide federal policy, stated Mangano in 1921. The first, the interest of America herself in carrying on the experiment in democracy, logically preceded the second, the welfare of the immigrants themselves. [44]

By 1924 editor Grose of *Missions* gave his hearty approval of the National Origins Act. The melting pot, he affirmed, had become too congested to produce an assimilated and satisfactory product. Because of this, a radical departure from the traditional custom of the open door seemed justifiable. Even the quota system based upon the 1890 census pleased Grose. His insistence in 1906 that each southern and eastern European nationality must be considered separately had become tempered by 1924 with a cautious assertion that the new law would allow the entrance of those "most desirable." While he did not completely repudiate his earlier defense of immigrants, Grose concluded that the adoption of the National Origins Act would mean that "the America of our grandchildren will be a vastly better place to live in." Reflecting upon the modification of his own thought, the Baptist journalist commented, "It would seem that we have

[43] Editorials: "What Shall the United States Do about Immigration?" *Missions*, XIII (Mar., 1922), 143; "The Check on Immigration," *ibid.*, XIV (Sept., 1923), 467.

[44] Antonio Mangano, "Shall We Restrict Immigration?" *Baptist*, II (May 21, 1921), 492–493, 495.

come to see that quality is more important than quantity in this matter of immigration." [45]

But if Grose and Mangano, like many Americans, lost a measure of faith in the melting pot because of the war, some Baptists and other Protestants could still accept a qualified belief in the amalgamation process. Early in 1918 the *Watchman-Examiner* expressed confidence that by 1975 the different elements would become so Americanized that only a few stray racial habits would remain. When American citizens voted for persons with foreign names in 1975, stated the paper, they would elect high-minded Christians who would perpetuate the nation's best ideals. As late as 1919 the Home Mission Society could assent to a modified version of the melting pot. Looking forward one hundred years, its official report contemplated the election of a president who traced his ancestry through twenty nationalities and yet had been raised a Christian. In the midst of the doubt and despair gripping the rest of the country, these Baptists thus showed confidence in the long-range effects of their present missionary endeavors among new Americans. [46]

The discussion of restriction and the immigrant by other Protestant denominations, like that of the Baptists, revealed a varied response. Two Presbyterian correspondents took pains to assert the falsity of the common idea that large numbers of foreigners were responsible for Bolshevist agitation, adding that the newcomers in fact brought a great store of tradition, talents, and ideals. Another called attention to the narrow, obstructive nativists who demanded special consideration because their ancestors came here early. A fourth condemned the current indictment of the immigrant by pointing out his contributions—in the doing of America's work and in the development of an international mind through his presence. [47] An editorial in the Con-

[45] Editorial: "Restricting Immigration," *Missions*, XV (Sept., 1924), 442.
[46] "American Blood in 1975" (editorial), *Watchman-Examiner*, VI (Mar. 14, 1918), 329; 87th Annual Report, ABHMS (1919), 41.
[47] Barr, "Wanted—New Respect for the Foreign Born," 210; Cornelius M. Steffans, "The Immigrant—Menace or Opportunity?" *Continent*, LI (Jan. 15, 1920), 74; S. Parkes Cadman, "America's Duty to the Alien," *Christian Work*, CX (May 7, 1921), 551–552; Kenneth D. Miller, "What Are These Immigrants Doing to Us?" *ibid.*, CXVII (Dec. 6, 1924), 655, 658–659.

gregational *Independent* in 1924 agreed with these sentiments that the variety of strains had enriched and strengthened the American people in the past and would continue to do so, noting that the problem of where to draw the line in restriction was delicate. Churchwoman Lucia Ames Mead, however, had earlier expressed a guarded voice when she approved of legislation that would limit immigration to America's powers of assimilation, in proportion to the present Americanized citizens of foreign origin.[48]

Methodists likewise wavered over the question of what to do with the foreigner in the years following World War I. In 1916 an editorial in *Zion's Herald* affirmed that the melting pot was working steadily, and all races were welcome if they had the "American spirit." As late as 1924 a Methodist contributor to that journal set out to refute the ideas of Madison Grant, asserting that a diversity of ethnic types was essential to national greatness. Although he suggested a possible temporary suspension of the influx to allow time for assimilation, this observer insisted that any selective regulation be on the basis of character rather than race.[49] At the same time the editor of the National Methodist Press and former pastor of an Italian colony favored shutting off the flow until a new policy could be formulated. Like the restrictionists of the 1890s, Reverend H. E. Woolever believed that southern and eastern Europeans did not readily adjust to American ways and clung to allegiance to their native lands. Calling for the elimination of those incapable of "being helped," he exclaimed, "What this country needs is more producers and fewer pedlers [*sic*]."[50]

Among many Baptists cosmopolitanism still lived in the early 1920s while dying in other corners of the nation. In the spirit of "Christian Americanization" a number of Baptist leaders con-

48 "Immigration" (editorial), *Independent*, CXII (Mar. 1, 1924), 114–115; Lucia Ames Mead, "America's Immigration Problem," *Congregationalist*, CV (Sept. 2, 1920), 284–285.
49 "A Question That Will Not Down," *Zion's Herald*, XCIV (Oct. 4, 1916), 1255; John H. Whitaker, "The Overburdened Melting Pot," *ibid.*, CII (Sept. 17, 1924), 1194–96.
50 H. E. Woolever, "America—Alien or American," *Zion's Herald*, CII (Feb. 27, 1924), 261, 273.

tinued to reject "100 percent Americanism" for its requirement that foreigners despise the country of their birth and its language and literature.[51] Consequently, the Northern Baptist Convention in 1925 protested the racial overtones of the National Origins Act. The exclusion of Orientals, said its annual report, declared to the world that the white man chose to develop his civilization without regard for the yellow peoples of the earth. The quota system itself brought disapproval from Northern Baptists who refused to go along with the Howard B. Grose of the 1920s, remembering instead his ideals of 1906. At a time when the United States suffered from much propaganda designed to feed racial and religious prejudice, stated the official denominational resolution, Baptists had a particular responsibility to emphasize their Christian principles. In a brief paragraph the Northern Baptist Convention renounced the national-origins concept that some of its spiritual forefathers had helped to define in the 1890s:

> The gospel of our Lord and Savior Jesus Christ, as Baptists understand it, does not lend itself to religious persecutions, nor to invidious discriminations between races. Neither the "Nordic" nor any other group has the ear of the Almighty to the exclusion or injury of any other race. The question of race relationship must be honestly faced. . . . The Good News of the gospel is to all the people of the world.[52]

Presbyterians were delighted with this position, and one of their religious papers reprinted an address on the new law by the president of the Northern Baptist Convention, Corwin S. Shank.[53] While Methodist Woolever endorsed the National Origins Act for its Anglo-Saxon favoritism and praised the use of the 1890 census as an instrument to keep out the undesirable,

---

[51] See, for example, Charles H. Sears, in 91st Annual Report, ABHMS (1923), 113, and Carl E. Swansson, "The Golden Rule in the Treatment of Foreigners," *Missions*, XVI (Nov., 1925), 601.

[52] Northern Baptist Convention *Minutes* (1925), 166–167. See also James A. Francis, address to the Northern Baptist Convention, in *Watchman-Examiner*, XII (June 12, 1924), 742–746.

[53] Corwin S. Shank, "Race Prejudice," *Christian Work*, CXVI (June 28, 1924), 818–819.

a Congregational source agreed with Baptists and Presbyterians that the discriminatory quotas were unfair, especially to Orientals.[54]

Clearly, many Protestants were at odds with their fellow Americans by 1925, offering a challenge to the values of the secular culture. How could Baptist leadership be so plainly among those who questioned the suspicious view of the stranger? Were there not strong anti-immigrant feelings rooted in their previous forty-five-year history that not even the new humane view could completely eradicate and which World War I might have easily brought to the surface? The fact was that now an even older tradition came to the fore and predominated over nativism in Northern Baptist ranks. Shortly before America entered the war, the Home Mission Society repeated its belief of the 1880s that this country had enjoyed a providential preparation for exerting a Christian influence upon the globe. The society proclaimed in 1916 that the United States was to be *the* Christian nation, whose democracy would be the foe of despotism and whose freedom of life and faith would become increasingly attractive to the oppressed in other lands.[55] Many Americans soon lost confidence in this vision of an international mission, but not all of the Baptists. In the midst of the "tribal twenties," at a time when their own membership was breaking apart over the "fundamentalist-modernist" controversy, Northern Baptist clergymen could speak of the United States as the place where "human liberty is teaching the world the truth of freedom." From America, many churchmen were confident, "the followers of Christ imbued with his spirit will go forth . . . into other countries in all continents, to repeat there the process of individual, family, social, industrial, national, and international salvation." [56]

---

[54] H. E. Woolever, "America—Alien or American—The Educational and Religious Aspects of Immigration," *Christian Advocate*, XCIX (Jan. 10, 1924), 41–42; Woolever, "Happenings at the Nation's Capital," *ibid.* (Mar. 20, 1924), 361; "Be Fair to Japan" (editorial), *Congregationalist*, CIX (Apr. 24, 1924), 516.

[55] 84th Annual Report, ABHMS (1916), 65–68.

[56] 91st Annual Report, ABHMS (1923), 26.

Belief in Divine Providence, often questioned by those who were dismayed at conditions about them and who feared a foreign influx, yet had its day in the Baptist court. Neither the nativism of the 1890s, the demands for conformity of the world war, nor the phobias of the twenties could destroy it. Before the war Baptist modes of thought had frequently reflected prevailing opinions in secular quarters, from the Anglo-Saxonism of the 1880s and 1890s, to the restrictionism of the nineties, to the progressive movement of the early twentieth century. In the era from 1914 to 1925, however, their refusal to ostracize their German Baptist brethren, their insistence upon *Christian* Americanization based on sympathetic concern rather than coercion, and their official condemnation of the National Origins Act and its racial implications set many Northern Baptists apart from popular views. In this time of testing for the American nation and its ideals, Baptists on the whole honored their long-held precepts of religious liberty, the equality of all men before God, and the worth of each individual. In this respect the years from 1914 to 1925 constituted one of their finest hours.

7 / Conclusion

The years from 1880 to 1925, transitional for many American values and institutions, represented a cycle of denominational history for the Northern Baptists that was shaped by the rapid changes in the nation. Under the impact of the migration from farm to city, a predominantly rural culture became an urban one, bringing problems for city churches that were made more acute by the influx of non-Protestant aliens. The rising industrialism that accompanied urbanization left many persons in a state of shock and suffering that ultimately caught the attention of devout religionists. An impersonal society, coupled with rampant materialism, challenged clergy and laymen alike to find new ways to bring spiritual and material sustenance to millions who had never heard the Protestant message. What one historian has called the unifying "search for order" in this era found its way into the churches in attempts by such groups as the Baptists to centralize a heretofore disparate ecclesiastical organization and in the beginnings of the ecumenical movement. The emergence of America as a world power and its involvement in World War I moved Protestants to respond, in one way or another, to the implications of living in a shrinking world.[1]

Several dominant conclusions emerge from the history of the Northern Baptist response to immigration in this important era.

[1] For a good acccount of the changes in this period, see Robert Wiebe, *The Search for Order 1877–1920* (New York, 1967).

These may be briefly stated as follows: (1) In the case of the Baptists, the debate over the Chinese in the 1880s preceded and was directly related to later anti-immigrant sentiment. (2) Throughout the 1880s a belief that immigration was part of God's providential plan for building the most Christian nation on earth held nativistic fears in check among Baptists. A spiritual solution to human problems in the form of evangelization of all Americans was said to be the answer to any dilemmas arising out of assimilation. (3) In the 1890s some Baptists, partly under the influence of their own anti-Catholic tendencies, saw their faith in a purely spiritual approach to the immigration question shaken, and they called upon the government to keep out undesirables as hope gave way to a circumscribed yet potent nativism. (4) The belief in national origins as a basis for distinction among immigrant groups, which became widespread at this time, had a popular basis with religious roots as well as a foundation among the "scientific intellectuals." (5) As limited numbers of aliens became Baptists around the turn of the century, their influence in the denomination helped to mitigate anti-immigration views on the part of American Baptists. (6) There was little or no positive correlation between the social gospel and the rise of a pro-immigrant disposition among Baptists, for "conservatives" often defended the foreigner while "liberals" retained a belief in the invidious distinctions of the 1890s. (7) By the time of World War I the experience of the Baptists with various groups of the new immigration, coupled with the elements of religious freedom contained in their own tradition, enabled them to resist the anti-foreign sentiment that swept the country and even to oppose the National Origins Act on the ground that it discriminated according to race.

The debate over the Chinese influx in the 1880s clearly preceded and was directly related to the rise of later anti-immigrant feelings among Baptists. Throughout the discussion one finds Baptist spokesmen on both sides of the issue—in defense of the Chinese because of the hopes of successful missionary work in China, and in favor of excluding these Orientals from America because of the threat to the nation's homogeneity. Although most of the Baptist champions of the Chinese lived in the East and many of the critics held pastorates on the West Coast, proximity to the Chinese did not automatically bring about an adverse reaction. California clergymen themselves were profoundly divided over the matter, as exemplified by Granville Abbott and Oliver Gates. At any rate, while those concerned about national homogeneity may have correctly anticipated the reality of racial problems, the defenders of the Chinese in the 1880s had the larger vision of the potential Christianization of the country and the world. Their hopes flew in the face of contemporary fears and for a time challenged the values of the secular culture.

When these and other Baptists looked around at the beginning of the 1880s, like many other Americans, they possessed an almost naive optimism concerning their fate and destiny amid the tides of change. The views of the pessimists, which declared that most immigrants were indeed undesirable, could not weaken their conviction that providence would take care of mankind if God's children made known the tenets of a pure and simple gospel. Whatever problems beat down upon man and society could be most adequately resolved by a spiritual solution. In the case of immigration and any attendant evils, many Baptists in the eighties believed that the conversion of the foreigner to Protestantism would automatically insure his Americanization and enable him to get on in the contemporary environment. Upon the arrival of the decade often considered the beginning of the "new" immigration, the American Baptist Home Mission Society confidently assured itself that "when the enemy shall come in a flood, the Spirit of the Lord shall lift up a standard against him." [2] This expression reflected the hopefulness of an entire generation unconcerned with the transformations taking place in the world about them, yet for Baptists the spirit of the Lord had to act through his followers. Their early interest in the evangelization of the immigrant constituted decisive rejection of a passivism which assumed that human affairs would look after themselves.

Convinced of their unique role, Baptists felt a special respon-

[2] 49th Annual Report, ABHMS (1881), 64–65.

sibility to develop the highest and most Christian civilization on earth. At first this seemed possible because of the gathering of nations on the North American continent. Protestant Christianity was the solvent that would refine and remake all, thus creating a homogeneity of culture and values necessary to fulfill the Baptist dream. But, concurrently, signs appeared that the vision might be only a cruel mirage. The Chinese on the Pacific Coast, for the most part, did not alter their mores and morals to fit the Protestant way. Accordingly, some Baptists linked them with two other groups long regarded as incompatible with America: Catholics and foreign radicals. The Chinese problem and the social unrest of the eighties helped to turn Anglo-Saxon optimism into a succeeding decade of distrust.

With "men's hearts failing them for fear," they often give up or modify previous beliefs. In the 1890s some Northern Baptists lost faith in the efficacy of a strictly religious approach to social issues, and they called upon the state to restrict immigration. Chary of the Populists' demands to relieve current distress, they nevertheless accepted one feature of the Populist movement, the search for a bogeyman or scapegoat. But for Baptists the *bête noire* of the day was not the House of Rothschild. The man who threatened Protestant civilization did not sit in counting rooms; he walked the streets as a peddler or organ grinder. He was not a builder of a great railroad who charged discriminatory rates; he spoke in a strange tongue and on occasion stopped the trains to obtain a higher wage. He was found throwing bombs in Haymarket Square and hurling eggs at Baptist missionaries in New England. He followed the "army of priests" who paraded the avenues of the strongholds of Puritanism with rosaries and crosses. Because he refused to convert to Protestantism, he was considered "ignorant, riotous, and dangerous to social peace." And thus the religious roots of nativism blossomed into the desire for restriction based on distinctions according to national origins. Whatever else has been said regarding the basis of the national-origins concept in an elite group of "scientific intellectuals," the Baptist story clearly reveals that this idea had a popular foundation in the notion of inferiority based on religion rather than race. As this conviction became stronger in the 1890s, many Baptists not only began to request the secular authorities to help them realize their ideal, but they nearly deserted the principle of "soul liberty," or the right of an individual to determine his own fate. Not a single Baptist actually denied the right of a Catholic to worship according to his conscience, but many wished to close the gates that allowed the peoples of the earth to fulfill their hopes in America. Did not the Baptist goal of a Protestant nation and conformity to its precepts in some measure conflict with their historic commitment to spiritual independence?

And yet one must not overstate the case for Baptist nativism in the 1890s or be too harsh in judgment of it. Their Anglo-Saxonism, even at its most extreme, did not blight the attempt to "win the stranger to Christ" by approaching him personally. The voice of tradition was always present to draw limits around anti-foreign sentiment, just as it kept some Baptists from joining the American Protective Association because that organization's oath seemed inconsistent with religious freedom. Walter Rauschenbusch exemplified this restraining influence when he told the pro-restrictionist Baptist Congress in 1888 that even dynamiters and anarchists were useful because they had set men to thinking about social questions. The very core of the Baptist faith, the decentralized polity and autonomy of the local congregations, prevented the myth of national origins from gaining a permanent foothold as it did in other segments of American society. Rauschenbusch's 1888 demand that the doors be left open to all of God's children may have been ignored for a season, but he was not silenced or forced to leave the denomination. Moreover, ideas such as his helped to keep the Baptist drift toward anti-immigrant feelings in the 1890s from becoming complete and irreversible.[3]

Because of their traditional concern for the welfare of every human being, Baptists were able to control many of their inherent prejudices. As a significant number of German and Scandinavian immigrants became Baptists, they argued for con-

[3] See the *Baptist Congress Proceedings* (1888), 86–87, 93–94.

sideration on grounds of equality. The relatively few Italians, Poles, and other eastern Europeans who converted proved that an "Italian knife" was actually no worse than an "Irish shillalah." In this way the role of foreign-speaking Baptists proved decisive in bringing about a change in the attitude of American churchmen. As each group defended itself, native Baptists listened and accepted many of the arguments. Persons of the "old" immigration then took the lead in evangelistic efforts with the "new" ethnic contingents. Thus the entire missionary experience of the Baptists with these people, however limited in numbers, had special significance as the major catalyst in creating a more favorable view of the stranger and in mitigating nativist tendencies.

The arrival of the social gospel on the American religious scene helped further the developing split between "conservative" and "liberal" Protestants. Since the social gospel was generally tied to a liberal view of things, one might expect participation in it to go hand in hand with the growth of a charitable attitude toward immigrants. Such, however, was not the case: little correlation in fact existed between the social gospel and a pro-immigrant disposition. The increasingly positive regard for southern and eastern Europeans, begun by experience with them, was brought to fulfillment by more contacts and acquaintances after the turn of the century. Often "progressive" social gospel theology coexisted with remnants of the older nativism, while more conservative elements of the Baptist denomination accepted the immigrant for what he was. The most that can be said of the social gospel in this respect is that it created an atmosphere in which a liberal view of the immigrant was possible. At the same time its intense moralism frequently precluded the development of that very outlook in such leading social gospel figures as Samuel Zane Batten.

The democratic polity of the Baptists throughout this period had a twofold effect. While it made change slow at the congregational level, such a structure paradoxically allowed for innovation by Baptist leaders with a minimum of friction at the top. Thus the shift in attitude from a negative outlook to a positive view of the new immigration could take place with relatively little ill will. No heresy trials marred the Baptist image in these years, and the denomination simply would not permit argumentative individuals to disrupt its ranks.[4] The Baptist clergy generally got along well with one another because of their historical refusal to enforce creeds or confessions. Because of this, metamorphosis of ideas came about smoothly on a gradual scale.

At the same time polity that made easier the turn in new direction also constituted a hindrance in preaching to immigrants accustomed to look to their church for authority. Several explanations may account for the failure to attract many Catholics to the Baptist faith. The negative approach of the 1880s and 1890s, with its severe criticism of Catholic beliefs, undoubtedly fostered alienation. The stories of James N. Williams, leader of French Canadian missions in New England, gave ample proof of the hostility resulting on both sides when a member of a Catholic family became a Protestant. But even the institutional methods and mitigation of anti-Catholicism in the early twentieth century did not bring about mass conversions. The inefficacy of Baptist polity was only part of the difficulty. The antipathy of the Catholic hierarchy toward Protestants at a time when the church in America was still insecure also weighed heavily, as did the fact than many newcomers, uprooted from all of their Old World customs and surroundings, naturally clung to the one link they could retain with their homeland, namely the religion they had held since childhood. Persons abruptly ripped loose from their moorings often look for some authority to hold them steady during the stress, and the congregational government and libertarian tradition of the Baptists could not meet this psychological need of the stranger.

In evaluating the position of the Baptists on immigration, one must ask which viewpoints showed the closest approximation to reality. Were the fears of the pessimists that the huge influx

---

[4] This is proven by the resignation of the head of the Russian Baptist Bible Institute after he had accused some of its board of directors of heresy in 1914. For accounts of this controversy, see William Fetler, "Why I Resigned from the New York Russian Training School and Why I Am Still in the United States," *Watchman-Examiner*, V (Nov. 29, 1917), 1531–32, and Charles A. Brooks, "Mr. Fetler and the Russian Bible Institute," *ibid.*, 1532–33.

of foreigners would destroy homogeneity and result in a congeries of clashing elements correct? Or did the Divine Providence optimists, who believed that Protestant American institutions such as the freedom of worship and the public school would mould and assimilate the newcomers, more accurately assess the situation? A recent sociological investigation shows that in a sense both were right. Milton M. Gordon, in *Assimilation in American Life*, concludes that in one respect the United States is "a multiple melting pot in which acculturation of all groups beyond the first generation of immigrants has been massive and decisive." But after arguing that most Americans accept the outlines of Anglo-Saxon Protestant values, Gordon adds that "structural separation on the basis of race and religion . . . emerges [here] as the dominant sociological condition." In other words, the majority of immigrants have ultimately assented to the prevailing ideological assumptions of their adopted country, but individuals of various ethnic groups have not developed the primary relationships with one another necessary to reduce prejudice.[5] Thus Baptists from Granville Abbott to Samuel Zane Batten, who recognized the value of homogeneity, and those from Abbott's 1882 critics to Charles A. Brooks and his cosmopolitanism, all exhibited a measure of foresight!

And what of the national-origins myth? Scholars writing in the past twenty years have added many qualifications to this idea, so that a simple differentiation of peoples into "old" and "new" immigrations will not do.[6] Baptists accepted this concept temporarily in the 1890s, but the fact that they based much of their assumption of inferiority on religion rather than race made it easier for them to give up the distinctions as their anti-Catholicism subsided. While "scientific" racists like Madison Grant had a considerable following in the early twentieth century, Baptists under the guidance of Howard B. Grose's writings and their own acquaintance with southern and eastern Europeans

[5] Milton M. Gordon, *Assimilation in American Life* (New York, 1964), 234–239.
[6] Handlin, *Race and Nationality in American Life*, 93–138; Jones, *American Immigration*, 177–206; Brinley Thomas, *Migration and Economic Growth* (Cambridge, 1954), 153–154, n. 1.

learned that each nationality must be considered separately. Because of this, many of them were wary of putting persons into "types" or "categories" long before the historians became skeptical of the conclusions of the Dillingham Commission.

The fear of Baptists and other Protestants that Roman Catholics would become predominant in many areas did not prove groundless. While the papal plot to subjugate the United States never materialized, a Catholic author many years ago concluded that on the basis of the evidence, "It is due to immigration that the Catholic Church in America today stands out among her sister churches of all other nations, the equal of any, if not indeed superior to all, in loyalty, vitality, fidelity, and stability." [7] In the light of these facts, was Daniel C. Eddy's 1889 assertion that "the plans of the Vatican . . . to make this a Roman Catholic country, are inspired by immensity of immigration," so far wrong when stripped of its hostile and emotional phraseology? [8] Even the alarm over the French Canadians was not entirely unfounded from the Baptist point of view. A modern economist has discovered that while English immigrants from Canada tended to go to booming centers, the French Canadians often settled in states where the population was declining. If this is correct, then the strangers from Quebec did threaten to replace native Americans in certain parts of Massachusetts, New Hampshire, Rhode Island, and Maine. [9]

The history of the Baptist response to immigration in the late nineteenth and early twentieth centuries has several implications for the present day. Religion, it appears, may have more to offer the world in which it exists when it does not become politicized. While considering the Chinese question in the 1880s, Baptists resisted the tendency to join the political furor for exclusion because of their desire to convert the Chinese both here and in China. In this way they kept from being overwhelmed by the current wave of racial intolerance. At the same

[7] Shaughnessy, *Has the Immigrant Kept the Faith?*, 222.
[8] Daniel C. Eddy, "Immigration," *Baptist Home Mission Monthly*, XI (Sept., 1889), 247–252.
[9] Thomas, *Migration and Economic Growth*, 137.

time their dream of a Christian society through Divine Providence, even if naive, led to a challenge of the values of the secular culture, while their hope of perfection gave rise to a humane view of life. In the 1890s, by contrast, Baptists sought political solutions to the immigration problem and in so doing let prejudice have full sway. Then they acquiesced to the mores of the contemporary scene rather than altering their direction. In certain respects the social gospel recommended a political approach to current issues. As part of the progressive crusade to remake the world through legislation, this version of Christianity sometimes became secularized. The results were mixed, for often an anti-immigrant bias remained along with zeal for transforming the earth into a better place to live. Yet after World War I Baptist leaders trained in the social gospel effectively rejected the popular drive for "100 percent Americanization," insisting that such a procedure be carried out in a Christian manner. The classic example of the beneficence of a religious endeavor without political overtones is the change in attitudes brought about by Baptist mission work among immigrant groups.

None of this implies that religious sects should take no stands on public questions—only that such assumptions of position provide a more viable challenge to the secular culture when Christian ethics are given priority over political considerations. Throughout much of this period Baptists did allow ethical values to have this sort of pre-eminence in their thoughts and actions. Their reliance upon personal conversion did not in fact constitute a retreat from the problems of the day, and their slowness in adopting the social gospel actually arose out of their heritage of religious freedom and unwillingness to enforce unity upon the denomination. This characteristic, rather than weakening the church, gave it versatility and the ability to center its efforts on a variety of fronts. Neither the spiritual needs of individuals nor the more material requirements relating to the environment were neglected by Northern Baptists.

By the time of the passage of the National Origins Act in 1924, Baptist history had completed the full swing of the cycle begun forty-five years before. In the 1880s the belief in God's providential plan for a Protestant America led them to the heights of hope. During the last decade of the nineteenth century they walked the valley of despair as a nativism and anti-Catholicism reminiscent of the 1840s and 1850s reared their heads. From 1900 to 1914 they reached the summit of righteous indignation against the evils of the environment, brought to this point under the intensely moralistic light of the social gospel. On the eve of World War I Baptist clergymen and the denomination as a whole faced a choice. Either they could return to nativism, as did many Americans, or they could honor their historic respect for the right of people to shape their own destiny. Some Baptist leaders now again urged restriction of immigration, but in this instance they did so with discretion and without malice. Was it not Howard B. Grose, the defender of the new immigration, who tactfully suggested in 1922 that closing the door might be best for all concerned? Did not Antonio Mangano, a son of Italy, argue for limitation of the influx because he feared the newcomers might have difficulty finding jobs in America?

For the Northern Baptist Convention and the American Baptist Home Mission Society, however, even such a step might be unfair. The society and its ardent missionary Charles A. Brooks held that Americanization should be Christian and voluntary, esteeming the ancestral heritage of new Americans. The convention protested the discriminatory quota system of the National Origins Act and its racial implications. And thus the cycle was complete. The assertion of the Baptist role in America's international mission in 1925 was not too far removed from the Divine Providence theory of the 1880s that God had destined all the races of mankind to build a nation that would serve as an example to the world. The persistence and elaboration of this theme enabled the Baptist faith by 1925 to make many of its adherents whole and ready to repudiate the nativism and provincialism of the ensuing decade of the 1920s.

It is sometimes said that World War I destroyed the confidence of the progressive era and ushered in a wave of reaction. The conflict may have destroyed the easy optimism of faith in human perfectibility through legislation, but the Baptist credo rested upon a more solid foundation than that of many Americans. Their belief in God's providence, their solicitude for human welfare as expressed in various types of mission work among new Americans, even their zealous desire to make the country Protestant through and through—on balance, all ultimately combined admirably to enable them to accept the majority of immigrants as potential Christians and brothers who deserved fair treatment in the best of the American tradition.

Bibliography

PRIMARY SOURCES

Manuscripts

Manuscript materials available for this study include the correspondence files of the American Baptist Home Mission Society and the Samuel Zane Batten Papers, both located in the American Baptist Historical Society, Colgate-Rochester Divinity School, Rochester, N.Y. Unfortunately, most of the correspondence for the years 1880–1925 was sold by the Home Mission Society for scrap paper many years ago, and only a very few items survive. The Batten Papers, which are uncataloged and unindexed, contain material that confirms the general impression of Batten that one receives from reading printed material by and about him.

Printed Reports

The most valuable printed reports for this study are those of the American Baptist Home Mission Society, published annually for each year of the period under consideration. Owing to the cost of printing, few lengthy speeches were reprinted in these reports, and those printed are brief. Usually, each annual report contains a section on the work of the society with foreign-speaking people, which often reveals attitudes. A special volume published for the society's fiftieth anniversary in 1882 does include full-length speeches made at the 1882 meeting and is therefore especially worthy of attention. Issued under the title *Baptist Home Missions in North America* (New York: American Baptist Home Mission Society, 1883), this publication contains historical sketches of prominent Baptists and of the various phases of the Home Mission Society's work.

Also worth consulting are the reports of the American Baptist Publication Society from 1880 to 1925. This organization was responsible for printing much of the multilingual literature that was distributed to immigrants, and its annual reports contain an occasional promotional speech. Samuel Zane Batten participated for many years in the publication society, and some of his activities are given in its records.

Beginning in 1907, the minutes of the Northern Baptist Convention began to appear. In their pages is revealed the concern of the whole denomination for the evangelization of the immigrant. The accounts therein, however, are brief.

Least useful are the minutes of Baptist state conventions and local associations. The state minutes examined in detail were those of states with large urban populations: New York, Connecticut, Massachusetts, Pennsylvania, Illinois, New Jersey, Ohio, and California. Association minutes consulted included those of Chicago, New York, Pittsburgh, and Cleveland, but all are surprisingly lacking in substantial information. They are useful for verification of the names of individual clergymen involved in immigrant work. The American Baptist Historical Society in Rochester has the only complete file of state and local Baptist minutes in the United States.

A special printed report that is of great significance is the *Seventh Annual Report of the Baptist Congress for the Discussion of Current Questions* (1888). The Baptist Congress held annual meetings in which distinguished Baptists, both Northern and Southern, discussed the issues of the day. As such, the congress constituted more of a forum than the Northern Baptist Convention was ever to become. In 1888 one of the major topics was "The Limits of Immigration" (pp. 69–95), in which prominent Baptists argued back and forth concerning the wisdom of immigration restriction. In the congress's *Proceedings* the speeches are reprinted in full. The 1888 volume also contains a discussion of "Romanism" that is valuable for insight into Baptist anti-Catholic feeling at the time.

Periodicals

The bulk of the documentation of this study is from several major Baptist periodicals in existence during most of the years from 1880 to 1925. Circulation figures for the year 1892 are available for most of these from *George Batten's Directory of the Religious Press* (New York: George Batten and Co., 1892).

One of the most alert journals as far as current issues were concerned was the New York *Examiner*, a weekly publication that was the result of the merger, before 1880, of several lesser Baptist papers. Its circulation was national in scope, although primarily in the East. Circulation in 1892, 25,000.

The Boston *Watchman* was the spokesman of Baptists in New England. Somewhat more conservative than the *Examiner*, it had more articles of a strictly religious nature and fewer on current topics, yet it did show an awareness of many issues of the day. Circulation in 1892, 17,000; distribution, general.

Both of these papers had an existence quite separate from one another up to the year 1913, when they decided to merge into the *Watchman-Examiner*. By that time the paper was of a smaller size, but it still featured regular editorials and articles of general interest produced by

206 Immigrants, Baptists, and the Protestant Mind

the combined staffs of the two formerly independent papers. For many years the *Watchman-Examiner* was regarded as a major voice of Northern Baptists, especially those of conservative tendencies, as evidenced by its "fundamentalist" position during the theological debates of the 1920s. Still in existence today as a very small publication, the *Watchman-Examiner* no longer speaks for a majority of the denomination. But in the years 1880–1925 the *Examiner*, the *Watchman*, and then the two combined, all weeklies, provided a window on the Baptist world. Research in these papers is difficult because they are unindexed.

In Chicago the *Standard* was a weekly with a considerable readership. Published for some years before 1880, this paper survived until 1920. It was one of the first Baptist periodicals to give attention to the immigrant question, and it had more material on nonreligious matters than other Baptist papers. Many lengthy speeches and sermons of clergymen were reprinted in its pages, editorials were common, and so were letters from Baptist correspondents in various parts of the country. Frequent accounts of the activities of the Chicago Baptist Social Union are of value in studying the growth of a social conscience among Chicago's Baptists. Circulation in 1892, 13,500; distribution, general.

On the West Coast the *Pacific Baptist* of Portland, Ore., was the leading Baptist paper. Its files during the 1880s contained some brief items on the Chinese question, but not nearly as many as might be expected because of the heavily religious emphasis of its contents. This is the only one of the leading Baptist papers of which the American Baptist Historical Society does not have complete files, but many of the volumes not in its collection may be obtained on microfilm from the University of Washington Library in Seattle. Distribution, primarily regional in Pacific Coast states.

By far the most conservative of all the major Baptist papers outside the South was the *Journal and Messenger* of Cincinnati. Unlike the other Baptist periodicals, the *Journal and Messenger* had the same editors for most of the years from 1880 to 1920, George W. Lasher and Grover P. Osborne, which undoubtedly accounts for the consistency of its anti-immigrant position and intense nativism. While the other Baptist papers changed their editorships and ownerships several times in these years, as well as their views on the immigration question, Lasher and Osborne doggedly maintained that restriction was the only solution up to the demise of their paper in 1920. For the *Journal and Messenger* immigration became an obsession, as is proven by the frequency of editorials concerning issues relating to it, while in the other Baptist periodicals immigration was only one of many current problems with which they were concerned. Circulation in 1892, 11,700; distribution, central western states.

All of the above periodicals were strictly independent of official denominational control, for there was no comprehensive national Baptist organization until the formation of the Northern Baptist Convention in 1907. But the American Baptist Home Mission Society had been of a national character ever since its founding in 1832. In 1878 the society decided to publish an official monthly periodical, under the editorship of its corresponding secretary, that would be called the *Baptist Home Mission Monthly.* This is the most useful of all Baptist periodicals for this study, for it both furnished factual information on work with immigrants and revealed attitudes as well. In the 1880s Henry L. Morehouse served as editor, while Thomas J. Morgan held that position from 1894 to 1902. During the years 1904–1909 the *Monthly* devoted much attention to the immigration question while under the able editorship of Howard B. Grose, whose attitudes were both humane and sympathetic. Circulation in 1892, 12,000; distribution, general.

Late in 1909 Grose decided to merge the *Baptist Home Mission Monthly* with the Baptist Foreign Missionary Society's official paper, creating a new periodical called *Missions.* Grose continued as editor of this publication for many years, and the sections of it devoted to home mission activities now replaced the information previously given in the *Home Mission Monthly.* While still valuable for the study of home mission activities, *Missions* did not give as full accounts as did the earlier periodical.

For information on the work of the Women's American Baptist Home Mission Society, consult its official monthly publication, *Tidings.* The accounts contained in it are very brief.

The year 1920 saw the old independent Baptist papers in considerable difficulty. Publication costs had risen constantly, and in spite of reductions in size the weeklies were in financial trouble. Sentiment grew in the Northern Baptist Convention for a single official Baptist weekly paper, and with the folding of the *Standard* and the *Journal and Messenger,* the *Baptist* was launched upon a short-lived career. From the beginning this paper reflected the spirit of change and increasing liberalism that was abroad in the Northern Baptist Convention. Many of the editors of the old papers, such as George W. Lasher, were now dead, and a new generation of clergymen was arising to do battle over theological issues in the 1920s. The files of the *Baptist* from 1920 to 1925 do not reveal much about the immigration question or the debates that led up to the passage of the National Origins Act. The fundamentalist-modernist controversy now held the center of the stage here and in the *Watchman-Examiner.* The *Baptist* ceased publication in the 1930s, a victim of the depression.

The journals of other denominations throw light on their activities during this period. For Presbyterians, see the *Christian Work and Evangelist,* the *Continent, Church at Home and Abroad,* and the *Presbyterian Quarterly Review.* Methodist publications include the *Christian Advocate* and *Zion's Herald.* For Congregationalists, see the *Independent* and the *Congregationalist.* The leading Episcopal periodical at this time was the *Churchman.*

Books

Abbott, Edith. *Immigration: Select Documents and Case Records.* Chicago: University of Chicago Press, 1924.
A source book, covering the span from 1751 to 1924. Case histories paint a clear picture of immigrant problems.

Abbott, Grace. *The Immigrant and the Community.* New York: Century Co., 1917.
The director of the Immigrants' Protective League of Chicago shows how both the immigrant and the community suffered materially from the American failure to plan for his protection and adjustment to American life.

Balch, Emily G. *Our Slavic Fellow Citizens.* New York: Charities Publication Committee, 1910.
Miss Balch, who spent considerable time with the Slavic communities of Europe and America gathering data for this book, discusses conditions on both continents. Her book was read and used by such Baptist writers on the new immigration as Howard B. Grose.

Barnes, Lemuel C. *Elemental Forces in Home Missions.* New York: Fleming H. Revell Co., 1912.
A leader of Baptists and an early participant in the Federal Council of Churches sets forth his thesis that migrations to the United States were providential and a part of God's plan for American international pre-eminence.

Barnes, Mary Clark. *Neighboring New Americans.* New York: Fleming H. Revell Co., 1920.
Describes ways in which Christian women might be good neighbors to new Americans, including recommendations on the teaching of English.

———, and Lemuel C. Barnes. *The New America: A Study in Immigration.* New York: Fleming H. Revell Co., 1913.
A study book for Protestants interested in home missions. In its descriptions of the new immigration it represents the twentieth-century attitude of Baptists who were becoming more sympathetic to the immigrant.

Brooks, Charles A. *Christian Americanization: A Task for the Churches.* New York: Council of Women for Home Missions and Missionary Education Movement of the United States and Canada, 1919.
A slender volume that sets forth the Baptist attitude in the Americanization movement which followed World War I. Reveals a liberal and humane view of the newcomers and repudiates methods of coercion in Americanization. It clearly separated Northern Baptists from the "100 percenters."

———, ed. *The Church and the Foreigner.* New York: N.p., 1916.
A brief work of a promotional nature.

———. *Through the Second Gate.* New York: American Baptist Home Mission Society, 1922.

Describes briefly the work of Baptists among the various nationalities of immigrants. Contains very little interpretative material.

Brown, T. Edwin. *Studies in Modern Socialism and Labor Problems.* New York: D. Appleton, 1886.
One of the first books by a Baptist with a social gospel orientation.

Daniels, John. *America via the Neighborhood.* New York: Harper and Brothers, 1920.
Examines several foreign-speaking communities in the United States and explores the role of the social settlement, the church, the school, and other neighborhood agencies in Americanization.

Davis, Philip H., ed. *Immigration and Americanization.* New York: Ginn, 1920.
A book of readings with such contributors as Henry Cabot Lodge, Prescott F. Hall, Edward A. Steiner, and E. A. Ross.

Grose, Howard B. *Aliens or Americans?* New York: Young People's Missionary Movement, 1906.
A landmark in setting forth the new and sympathetic Baptist attitude toward immigrants shortly after the turn of the century. Issues a call to the churches for intensified home mission work among new Americans.

———. *The Incoming Millions.* New York: Fleming H. Revell Co., 1906.
With *Aliens or Americans?*, this book marked a change in Baptist attitudes toward the new immigration. Contains a special appeal to Christian women to take an interest in the newcomers.

Gulick, Sidney L. *The American Japanese Problem.* New York: Charles Scribner's Sons, 1914.
Suggests that the maximum annual immigration quota from each country be based on a fixed percentage of those from each land already here and naturalized, the proposal that found its way into the National Origins Act of 1924.

Hall, Prescott F. *Immigration and Its Effects upon the United States.* New York: Henry Holt, 1906.
The leader of the famous Immigration Restriction League describes the evil effects—racial, economic, social, and political—of immigration and discusses proposed remedies for solving the problem.

Hayne, Coe. *Old Trails and New: True Life Stories of Baptist Home Mission Fields.* Philadelphia: Judson Press, 1920.
Recounts the activities of a number of Baptist workers among the foreign-born. Hayne also wrote articles on Dan L. Schultz, the Baptist "Labor Evangelist."

Jenks, Jeremiah W., and W. Jett Lauck. *The Immigration Problem: A Study of American Immigration Conditions and Needs.* New York: Funk and Wagnalls, 1911.
A comprehensive study of immigration problems drawn from material gathered by the investigation of the U.S. Immigration Commission in 1910. Supports the theory of different characteristics between northwestern and southeastern Europeans, accepted for many years but now questioned by modern historical research.

Judson, Edward. *The Institutional Church.* New York: Lentilhon and Co., 1899.
A brief volume designed as a handbook for pastors of the institutional church; gives detailed instructions for clergymen and outlines the church's role in society.

Kellor, Frances. *Immigration and the Future.* New York: George H. Doran Co., 1920.
Discusses racial relations in America during World War I and looks toward the future prospects of immigration into this country as it would affect business and the domestic economy.

Lorimer, George C. *Christianity and the Social State.* Philadelphia: American Baptist Publication Society, 1898.
The pastor of Boston's Tremont Temple sets forth his reflections upon the relation of religion to the problems of modern society.

———. *Studies in Social Life.* Chicago: Bedford, Clarke, and Co., 1886.
One of the first statements of social gospel principles by a Baptist. Lorimer has been neglected by scholars but is worthy of attention.

Louthan, Henry, ed. *The American Baptist Pulpit at the Beginning of the Twentieth Century.* Williamsburg, Va.: Published by the editor, 1903.
A collection of sermons by such leading Baptist clergymen as A. C. Dixon, Lathan A. Crandall, Russell H. Conwell, and Augustus H. Strong. Valuable for the biographical sketches included.

Mangano, Antonio. *Religious Work among Italians in America.* New York: American Baptist Home Mission Society, 1917.
A brief survey of Protestant mission work among Italians by the Baptist leader of such activities in his own denomination.

———. *Sons of Italy.* New York: Missionary Education Movement of the United States and Canada, 1917.
A sensitive work that sold over 20,000 copies. Sets out to win sympathy for Italians by describing them and their life in America.

———. *Training Men for Foreign Work in America.* N.p., n.d.
A short tract designed to enlist mission workers among Italian immigrants.

Moxom, Philip S. *The Industrial Revolution.* Boston: N.p., 1886.
A short pamphlet that set forth ideas of social Christianity in the year of the Haymarket riot.

Rauschenbusch, Walter. *Christianity and the Social Crisis.* New York: Macmillan, 1907.

———. *Christianizing the Social Order.* New York: Macmillan, 1912.

———. *Prayers of the Social Awakening.* Boston: Pilgrim Press, 1910.

———. *The Social Principles of Jesus.* New York: Association Press, 1916.

———. *A Theology for the Social Gospel.* New York: Macmillan, 1917.
Rauschenbusch's various books, notably *Christianity and the Social Crisis,* established him as one of the major social gospel leaders in the United States.

Roberts, Peter. *The New Immigration.* New York: Macmillan, 1912.

Describes with great sympathy the industrial efficiency, social life, and relation to native Americans of newcomers to this land. Roberts's books were read by Baptists who became interested in the new immigration.

Sears, Charles H. *City Man.* New York: Harper and Brothers, 1936.
A discussion of the role of religion in the city, by a Baptist who was active in urban mission work for many years.

————. *The Crowded Ways.* New York: Council of Women for Home Missions and Missionary Education Movement, 1929.
Another volume designed to point readers to the responsibilities of Christians in the betterment of urban life.

————. *The Redemption of the City.* Philadelphia: Griffith and Rowland Press, 1911.
Sears's first book discusses the ways in which municipal governments, charitable agencies, and the churches could help solve the problems of modern American cities. The churches, he argues, were the primary agencies for social redemption of the foreign-speaking population.

Steiner, Edward A. *The Immigrant Tide: Its Ebb and Flow.* New York: Fleming H. Revell Co., 1909.
Describes with keen understanding human interest stories about immigrants.

————. *On the Trail of the Immigrant.* New York: Fleming H. Revell Co., 1906.
A narrative that tells of the various ethnic groups and some of their experiences in their adopted land. Steiner's books were read by such Baptists as Howard B. Grose.

Together: Historical Sketch of the Women's American Baptist Home Mission Society. New York: Women's American Baptist Home Mission Society, 1933.
A short pamphlet that is useful for its discussion of the role of Baptist women in the "Christian Americanization" movement.

Warne, Frank Julian. *The Immigrant Invasion.* New York: Dodd, Mead, 1913.
Examines contemporary proposals, such as the literacy test, and asserts that the basis for a national immigration policy ought to rest on America's ability to assimilate the newcomers economically.

SECONDARY SOURCES

Aaron, Daniel. *America in Crisis.* New York: Alfred A. Knopf, 1952.
Contains Richard Hofstadter's important essay "Manifest Destiny and the Philippines."

Abel, Theodore. *Protestant Home Missions to Catholic Immigrants.* New York: Institute of Social and Religious Research, 1933.
A very brief volume designed to acquaint readers with the general nature of mission efforts among foreign-speaking Catholics in the United States.

Abell, Aaron I. *The Urban Impact on American Protestantism, 1865–1900.* Cambridge, Mass.: Harvard University Press, 1943.
Invaluable for understanding the growth of Protestantism's social conscience in the post–Civil War era. Covers humanitarian work such as that of the Salvation Army, the churches' response to labor, and the rise of the institutional church.
Abrams, Ray H. *Preachers Present Arms: A Study of Wartime Attitudes and Activities of the Clergy in the United States, 1914–1918.* New York: Round Table Press, 1933.
Gives background material on the American Revolution, the Civil War, and the Spanish-American War. Discusses the pacifist movements and pro-war sentiment among the clergy from 1914 to 1918.
Allen, Robert A., Jr. "The Presbyterian Response to Immigration: The Changing Nature of Presbyterianism, 1870–1914." MS seminar paper, University of Rochester, 1964. Private possession of the author.
A short paper containing valuable information on Charles Stelzle, who headed Presbyterian mission work among immigrants in the early years of the twentieth century.
Alphabetic Biographical Catalog, Crozer Theological Seminary 1855–1933. Chester, Pa.: Crozer Theological Seminary, 1933.
Because many Baptist clergymen studied at Crozer, this volume is useful for biographical information.
Alumni Directory of the University of Chicago 1861–1910. Chicago: University of Chicago Press, 1910.
Contains information on graduates of the University of Chicago, which was founded by Baptists.
Anderson, Charles H. *White Protestant Americans: From National Origins to Religious Group.* Englewood Cliffs, N.J.: Prentice-Hall, 1970.
A study of white Protestant Americans that deals in part with their ethnic origins and discusses the past and present status of Protestantism in American life.
Backlund, J. O. *Swedish Baptists in America.* Chicago: Baptist Conference Press, 1933.
A short history of Swedish Baptists in the United States, including their missionary enterprises, literary efforts, educational activities, and charitable institutions.
Billington, Ray A. *The Protestant Crusade, 1800–1860: A Study of the Origins of American Nativism.* New York: Macmillan, 1938.
Stresses mainly the anti-Catholic aspects of anti-foreign sentiment in the United States in the first half of the nineteenth century.
Burns, Edward McNall. *The American Idea of Mission.* New Brunswick, N.J.: Rutgers University Press, 1957.
Explains at length the different connotations attached to the concept of "mission" at various times in American history from colonial days through the twentieth century, including its religious interpretations.
Calvert, John B. *Men Who Have Meant Much to Me: Addresses and Essays.* New York: Fleming H. Revell Co., 1918.

Contains biographical information on some of the Baptist leaders of the early twentieth century.

Carstenson, M. C., et al. *Seventy-five Years of Danish Baptist Missionary Work in America.* Philadelphia: Danish Baptist General Conference of America, 1931.
An "official" history of the Danish Baptists in America. Discusses in detail the various local churches, especially in Wisconsin, Minnesota, and the northern plains states.

Cathcart, William, ed. *The Baptist Encyclopedia.* Philadelphia: Louis H. Everts, 1881.
A large volume containing biographical sketches of Baptist clergymen and prominent laymen who were alive when it was published; much of the information on authors of articles cited in the present work is available nowhere else.

Cole, Donald B. *Immigrant City: Lawrence, Massachusetts, 1854–1921.* Chapel Hill: University of North Carolina Press, 1963.
A fine study that explains the background of the famous Lawrence textile strike of 1912, with attention to the immigrants' constant search for security in America. Thoroughly documented and written with a sensitivity to historical trends.

The Colgate-Rochester Divinity School General Catalogue 1819–1930. Rochester: Baptist Education Society of the State of New York, 1930.
Contains helpful biographical material on the graduates of the old Rochester Theological Seminary and the Colgate-Rochester Divinity School. Especially useful for data on German-American Baptist clergymen.

Coolidge, Mary Roberts. *Chinese Immigration.* New York: Henry Holt, 1909.
With emphasis on California, this work traces the development of anti-Chinese politics and restrictions, giving attention to the problem of the competition of Chinese labor.

David, Henry. *The History of the Haymarket Affair.* New York: Farrar and Rinehart, 1936.
The standard monograph on the Chicago Haymarket riot of 1886.

Ellis, John Tracy. *American Catholicism.* Chicago: University of Chicago Press, 1955.
A short volume in the Chicago History of American Civilization Series. Portrays the historical role of the Catholic church in the United States at a glance.

Ernst, Robert. *Immigrant Life in New York City 1825–1863.* Port Washington, N.Y.: Ira J. Friedman, 1949. Reissued 1963.
A detailed study of immigrants in New York that makes use of manuscript census schedules to ascertain the occupational status of immigrants.

Fine, Sidney. *Laissez Faire and the General-Welfare State.* Ann Arbor: University of Michigan Press, 1955.
Contains a chapter on the social gospel that shows how its premises and beliefs attack the concept of laissez-faire.

Garis, Roy L. *Immigration Restriction.* New York: Macmillan, 1927.

A comprehensive work on the regulation of immigration into the United States from early times to the 1920s, but poorly written and has very little interpretative analysis.

Gausted, Edwin Scott. *A Religious History of America.* New York: Harper and Row, 1966.
A modern history of religion in the United States, replete with quotations from original sources.

Goodykoontz, Colin B. *Home Missions on the American Frontier.* Caldwell, Idaho: Caxton Printers, 1939.
Originally a dissertation under the direction of Frederick Jackson Turner, this book discusses the work of Protestants from the East in new settlements on the western frontier in the nineteenth century. Its main emphasis is on Congregationalists and Presbyterians, but also gives brief accounts of other denominations such as the Baptists.

Gordon, Milton M. *Assimilation in American Life: The Role of Race, Religion, and National Origins.* New York: Oxford University Press, 1964.
A brilliantly written sociological study that explores different theories of assimilation, such as Anglo-Saxon conformity, the melting pot, and cultural pluralism. Most newcomers, Gordon concludes, have adopted the dominant Anglo-Saxon values, even though assimilation in terms of primary relationships has been very slow.

Handlin, Oscar. *Immigration as a Factor in American History.* Englewood Cliffs, N.J.: Prentice-Hall, 1959.
Brief analysis of the importance of immigration in shaping U.S. history.

———. *Race and Nationality in American Life.* Boston: Little, Brown, 1948.
Restudying the facts of the Dillingham Commission of 1907, Handlin arrives at different conclusions regarding the invidious comparison between the "old" and the "new" immigrations. A landmark in modifying the national-origins myth.

———. *The Uprooted.* New York: Grosset and Dunlap, 1951.
With great sensitivity and lucidity of style, this work portrays the feelings of immigrants as they were transplanted from the Old World to the New.

Hansen, Marcus Lee. *The Atlantic Migration, 1607–1860.* Cambridge, Mass.: Harvard University Press, 1940.
A classic study by a famous expert on immigration.

———. *The Immigrant in American History.* Cambridge, Mass.: Harvard University Press, 1940.
A series of essays that explore such topics as the relation of immigration to expansion, to democracy, to American Puritanism, and to American culture. Emphasis is on the nineteenth century.

Hartmann, Edward G. *The Movement to Americanize the Immigrant.* New York: Columbia University Press, 1948.
An examination of the Americanization campaign in the years during and after World War I. Discusses the work of both private and governmental agencies.

Higham, John. *Strangers in the Land: Patterns of American Nativism 1860–1925.* New Brunswick, N.J.: Rutgers University Press, 1955. The best study to date of anti-foreignism in America. While perceptive and sensitive to trends in the nativist movement, Higham does not develop fully the relation of religion to nativism.

Historical Catalogue of Brown University 1764–1894. Providence, R.I.: P. S. Remington and Co., 1895. An old volume containing biographical sketches of a number of prominent Baptists who graduated from Brown before 1895.

Hopkins, Charles H. *The Rise of the Social Gospel in American Protestantism, 1865–1915.* New Haven, Conn.: Yale University Press, 1940. The standard work on the social gospel movement in America. Covers all denominations, but has relatively little information on the Baptists.

Hudson, Winthrop S. *American Protestantism.* Chicago: University of Chicago Press, 1961. A concise and up-to-date history of the impact and scope of Protestantism in America from colonial times to the present.

———. *Religion in America.* New York: Charles Scribner's Sons, 1965. A modern history written with a nondenominational approach. Discusses urbanization as it affected the churches as well as the rise of fundamentalism in the early twentieth century. Protestant groups are emphasized throughout.

Hutchinson, E. P. *Immigrants and Their Children 1850–1950.* New York: John Wiley and Sons, 1956. A monograph prepared for the Bureau of the Census. With the use of its statistics, it examines the occupational status of immigrants of the first and second generations.

Jones, Maldwyn Allen. *American Immigration.* Chicago: University of Chicago Press, 1960. A synthesis of the findings of modern scholarship that includes the recent interpretation of the "old" versus "new" theory of immigration, which was accepted by historians and the American public for many years.

Jordan, Philip D. "The Response of the Methodist Episcopal Church to Immigration, 1865–1908." MS seminar paper, University of Rochester, 1963. Private possession of the author. Points to trends in the Methodist reaction to immigration which indicate that further research on this topic would be useful.

Kinzer, Donald L. *An Episode in Anti-Catholicism: The American Protective Association.* Seattle: University of Washington Press, 1964. Explores in detail the history of the extremist anti-Catholic movement of the 1890s. Although Kinzer uses modern historical methods, more work needs to be done on the relation of Protestant groups to the APA.

Lindberg, John S. *The Background of Swedish Immigration to the United States.* Minneapolis: University of Minnesota Press, 1930. Examines the reasons that Swedes came to America.

Mann, Arthur, ed. *The Progressive Era: Liberal Renaissance or Liberal Failure?* New York: Holt, Rinehart and Winston, 1963.

The editor of this book of readings has neatly summarized the debate between John Higham and Oscar Handlin regarding the attitude of the "progressives" toward the immigrant.

May, Henry F. *Protestant Churches and Industrial America.* New York: Harper and Brothers, 1949. Reprinted by Octagon Books, 1963.
Discusses the conservatism prevalent in American churches at mid-nineteenth century, and looks at the sources of change that took place in theology and church life in the last quarter of the century. Included in his treatment of the response of Protestantism to industrialization and urbanization is a full discussion of social Christianity.

Mowry, George E. *The Era of Theodore Roosevelt and the Birth of Modern America 1900–1912.* New York: Harper and Brothers, 1958.
A volume in the New American Nation Series. Contains chapters on the intellectual and social backgrounds of progressivism as well as a perceptive discussion of the political aspects of the movement.

Myers, Gustavus. *History of Bigotry in the United States.* New York: Random House, 1943.
The standard reference work for the subject of prejudice in America. Deals at length with such topics as nativism, witchcraft, Know-Nothingism, the APA, the Ku Klux Klan, and anti-Semitism.

Newman, Albert H. *A Century of Baptist Achievement.* Philadelphia: American Baptist Publication Society, 1901.
A history of Baptist activity in all the nations of the world, with emphasis on America and England.

———. *A History of Baptist Churches in the United States.* New York: Charles Scribner's Sons, 1915.
Chronicles Baptist history from the time of Roger Williams to the eve of World War I. Contains a special section on Southern Baptists and gives attention to such splinter sects as the Seventh-Day Baptists and Free-Will Baptists.

Niebuhr, H. Richard. *Christ and Culture.* New York: Harper and Row, 1951.
Examines the relationship of Christianity to the culture of which it is a part.

Olson, Adolf. *A Centenary History.* Chicago: Baptist Conference Press, 1952.
An account of Swedish Baptists in America, well documented and comprehensive in scope.

Ramaker, Albert J. *The German Baptists in North America.* Cleveland: German Baptist Publication Society, 1924.
A short history of German Baptists, by a professor long active in the German Department of Rochester Theological Seminary.

Rochester Theological Seminary General Catalogue, 1850–1920. Rochester, N.Y.: E. R. Andrews Printing Co., 1920.
Of use for biographical data on well-known Baptists.

Sandeen, Ernest R. *The Roots of Fundamentalism: British and American Millenarianism 1800–1930.* Chicago: University of Chicago Press, 1970.
Attempts to prove that fundamentalism, generally regarded as a

twentieth-century phenomenon, in fact had its origins deep in the nineteenth century.

Sandmeyer, Elmer C. *The Anti-Chinese Movement in California.* Urbana: University of Illinois Press, 1939.
Traces the anti-Chinese sentiment in California during the latter part of the nineteenth century. Well documented, and invaluable for an understanding of the Chinese question.

Saveth, Edward N. *American Historians and European Immigrants, 1875–1925.* New York: Columbia University Press, 1948.
Included in this study of the reaction of many prominent historians to immigration are useful discussions of Anglo-Saxon race theories and the concepts of the frontier and of the urban melting pot.

Seager, Robert, II. "Some Denominational Reactions to the Chinese in California, 1856–1892." *Pacific Historical Review,* XXVIII (1959), 49–66.
Useful for its survey of Protestant reactions to the Chinese, but unfortunately the Baptists are largely omitted in the analysis.

Seward, George F. *Chinese Immigration.* New York: Charles Scribner's Sons, 1881.
Seward, former U.S. minister to China, felt that the Chinese should be allowed to come to America because of the great service they rendered on the Pacific Coast, and he believed that most of the common objections to these people were unwarranted. His book discusses the many material results of Chinese labor in California.

Shannon, James. *Catholic Colonization on the Western Frontier.* New Haven, Conn.: Yale University Press, 1957.
A study of the religious settlements founded by Bishop John Ireland of St. Paul, Minnesota, in the western counties of that state. Written with keen awareness of the techniques of modern historical scholarship.

Sharpe, Dores R. *Walter Rauschenbusch.* New York: Macmillan, 1942.
The standard biography of Rauschenbusch by an individual who was well acquainted with him. Very laudatory of its subject and hence lacks critical analysis.

Shaughnessy, Gerald. *Has the Immigrant Kept the Faith?* New York: Macmillan, 1925.
An older work designed to show that, on balance, the American Catholic church has been successful in holding the allegiance of its foreign-born members, and that much of its strength and growth was due to immigration.

Smith, Elmer W., ed. *Colgate University General Catalogue.* Hamilton, N.Y.: Colgate University, 1937.
Contains biographical information on the graduates of Colgate University and its affiliated seminary, which merged with Rochester Theological Seminary in 1927 to become the Colgate-Rochester Divinity School. Inclusive dates are 1822–1937.

Smith, H. Shelton, Robert T. Handy, and Lefferts A. Loetscher. *American Christianity: An Historical Interpretation with Representative*

Documents. Vol. I, 1607–1820; vol. II, 1820–1960. New York: Charles
Scribner's Sons, 1963.
Well-prepared volumes covering such topics as Puritanism, the Great
Awakening, religion on the frontier, and modern theology and ecu-
menicism. The documents are drawn from both Catholic and Protes-
tant sources, and each one is introduced by an explanatory section.
Starr, Edward C. *A Baptist Bibliography: Being a Register of Printed
Material by and about Baptists; Including Works Written against the
Baptists.* 16 vols. Philadelphia: Judson Press; Chester, Pa., and Roches-
ter, N.Y.: American Baptist Historical Society, 1947–71.
A carefully compiled list of Baptist source materials, by the curator
of the American Baptist Historical Society. It is presently complete
through the letter "N."
Stephenson, George M. *A History of American Immigration, 1820–1924.*
New York: Ginn, 1926.
A general survey dealing with immigration as a factor in American
political development. Also discusses the European background and
anti-immigrant sentiment in the United States.
————. *The Religious Aspects of Swedish Immigration: A Study of
Immigrant Churches.* Minneapolis: University of Minnesota Press,
1932.
A fine study of the role of religion in a single ethnic group. Includes
material on religious efforts among Swedish immigrants by all denomi-
nations, with a section on the impact of American Baptists upon
Sweden.
Stevens, Daniel G. *The First Hundred Years of the American Baptist
Publication Society.* Philadelphia: American Baptist Publication Soci-
ety, 1925.
The "official" history of the Baptist organization responsible for
printing much of the literature of the denomination, including books
and tracts in foreign languages.
Stewart, Walter S. *Later Baptist Missionaries and Pioneers.* 2 vols. Phila-
delphia: Judson Press, 1928–29.
A series of sketches of Baptist missionaries that is valuable for its ac-
count of James N. Williams, who headed Baptist mission efforts
among the French Canadians of New England for many years.
Stiansen, P. *History of the Norwegian Baptists in America.* Wheaton, Ill.:
Norwegian Baptist Conference of America, 1939.
Emphasizes Wisconsin and Minnesota. Crowded with endless names
and facts, and has no analysis whatsoever.
Sweet, William Warren. *The Story of Religion in America.* New York:
Harper and Brothers, 1930.
Devoting half of its emphasis to the colonial period, this volume then
carries the story of the various Protestant denominations through the
age of big business.
Thernstrom, Stephan. *Poverty and Progress: Social Mobility in a Nine-
teenth Century City.* Cambridge, Mass.: Harvard University Press,
1964.

Thernstrom's examination of occupational mobility in Newburyport, Mass., from 1850 to 1880 convinced him that immigrants there did move up the social ladder slowly in this period, even though mobility was limited. His study combines the methodology of sociology and history.

Thomas, Brinley. *Migration and Economic Growth: A Study of Great Britain and the Atlantic Economy.* Cambridge: Cambridge University Press, 1954.
A study of the economic aspects of migration from Great Britain to the United States. Deals with the social status of immigrants in America, the origin and economic impact of restriction, and the relation between immigration and investment.

Torbet, Robert G. *A History of the Baptists.* Philadelphia: Judson Press, 1950. Reissued, Valley Forge, Pa., 1963.
The most recent history of Baptists in America from colonial times to the present, written by a Baptist. Includes a section on British and European Baptists.

Tyler, Poyntz, ed. *Immigration and the United States.* New York: H. W. Wilson Co., 1956.
A collection of scholarly and journalistic articles that presents divergent viewpoints on such topics as "100 percent Americanism," the international implications of U.S. immigration policy, and the McCarran-Walter Act of 1952.

The University of Rochester General Catalogue 1850–1928. Rochester, N.Y.: University of Rochester, 1928.
Contains short biographical sketches of all graduates of the University of Rochester in these years, many of whom were prominent Baptists.

Vedder, Henry Clay. *The Baptists.* New York: Baker and Taylor Co., 1902.
A very brief history designed to acquaint the layman and church member with the nature of the denomination.

———. *A Short History of Baptist Missions.* Philadelphia: Judson Press, 1927.
An account of Baptist mission efforts throughout the world, containing a short sketch of the work with immigrants in the United States. Vedder ultimately became one of his denomination's most liberal clergymen.

West, Herbert Faulkner, ed. *The Autobiography of Robert Watchorn.* Oklahoma City: Robert Watchorn Charities, Ltd., 1959.
Watchorn, who was Commissioner of Immigration in New York for many years, ended many abuses and improved procedures for the registration of immigrants at Ellis Island. He received high praise for his work from such Baptists as Howard B. Grose.

Wheelock, Lewis F. "Urban Protestant Reactions to the Haymarket Affair, 1886–1893." Unpublished Ph.D. dissertation, University of Iowa, 1956.
A close look at the way in which urban American clergymen responded to the events at Haymarket Square and their aftermath.

White, Charles L. *A Century of Faith*. Philadelphia: Judson Press, 1932. The "official" history of the activities of the American Baptist Home Mission Society from its origin in 1832 to 1932. Written by a Baptist who was long active in home mission work, this factual account contains some interpretation and also notes trends.

Wiebe, Robert. *The Search for Order 1877–1920*. New York: Hill and Wang, 1967.
The progressive movement, Wiebe feels, represented the triumph of a new bureaucratic-minded middle class and revealed the culmination of the underlying search for order, unity, and stability in this period in American history.

Wittke, Carl. *German Americans and the World War*. Columbus, Ohio: State Archaeological and Historical Society, 1936.
By studying the German-language press of Ohio, which had the largest number of these papers before the war, Wittke generalizes about the reaction of German immigrants in the whole country to the international conflict.

———. *We Who Built America*. Englewood Cliffs, N.J.: Prentice-Hall, 1939.
A comprehensive history of immigration from the colonial period to the twentieth century. Includes a discussion of nativism, especially as it related to the "new" immigration.

Your College Friends: Alumni Directory of Bucknell University 1846–1940. Lewisburg, Pa.: N.p., 1940.
Contains very brief biographical data on graduates of Bucknell, many of whom were Baptists.

Index

Chinese merchants: leaders of Chinese in U.S., 13-14; expected to Christianize and Americanize China, 18-19
Chinese morals: criticized, 14
Chinese prostitutes, 14
"Christian Americanization," 175-183, 188-189. *See also* Americanization
Christian centers, 183-184
Christianity and the Social Crisis, 135
Church Edifice Department, 5
Church trial: at Chico, Calif., 33-34
City mission societies, 98, 154
Civilization: American, ideal concept of, 9; western, struggles with eastern civilization, 15
Clark, Bertha W., 183
Cleveland, Grover, 77, 91, 164
Colgate University: Italian Department, 123
Communism: feared by Martin B. Anderson, 11; and immigrants, 55, 107; and Haymarket riot, 58, 61. *See also* Anarchists; Radicalism; Socialism
Communist revolution, 174-175, 187
Community centers. *See* Christian centers
Congregationalists: missions to Chinese in America, 15, 34*n;* divided over Chinese immigration, 19-20; on immigration restriction, 94-95, 187-188; on anarchists and socialists, 95; on urban problems, 137-138; on the new immigration, 160-161; and German-Americans in World War I, 170; on the National Origins Act, 190
Conversion: necessary for baptism, 3; of freedmen, 5; of Chinese in America, 15, 25; effected by American institutions, 42; answer to all immigration problems, 53, 58; necessary for immigrants, 97; insisted on by conservatives, 131; and social problems, 146-147, 201
Conwell, Russell H., 135
Coolies, 14, 31
Coon, James M., 153-154
Cultural pluralism, 25, 175
Czechoslovak Baptist Union, 112
Czechoslovaks, 120. *See also* Bohemians

Danes: home mission work among, 105, 106
Darwin, Charles, 131
Darwinism, 1-2
Daughters of the American Revolution, 173
Delano, H. A., 82
Democracy: in Baptist churches, 3-4, 89. *See also* Polity
Denison, A. A., 22-23
Der Sendbote des Evangelium, 99
Dillingham Commission: declares new immigration undesirable, 39; prelude to, 83; and national-origins concept, 140, 145, 200
Domenica, Angelo di, 123
Domenica, Vincenzo di, 123
Dowling, George T., 57, 58, 62
Duboc, A. M., 22
Dunkards, 99

Eastern Orthodox Church, 40, 113
East German Conference, 100
East Hammond Civic and Improvement Association, 184
Eddy, Daniel C., 68-69, 200
Edgren, John A., 106
Ellis Island: Baptist mission work, 110-111. *See also* Castle Garden, N.Y.
Emergency Immigration Act of 1921, 185
Environmentalism: rejected, 115-116; and social gospel, 134; endorsed, 139, 146-147, 178
Episcopalians: and Chinese, 15, 19; on new immigration, 161
"Evangelical liberalism," 131

Federal Council of Churches, 144, 155
Fetler, William, 113
Finns: Swedish Baptists minister to, 105
Fleishmann, Konrad, 99
Foreign missions: in China, 15, 22
Fosdick, Harry Emerson, 167
Fox, Norman, 67
Freedmen: missionary work among, 5, 97
French Canadians: mission work among in New England, 71-75, 155, 198; inferiority of claimed, 87, 88;